A History of
POOLE
and Neighbourhood

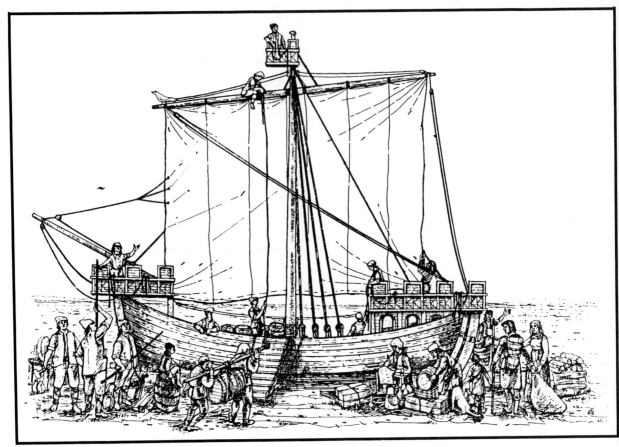

Early 14th-century Poole ship, based on the La Pole seal.

A History of
POOLE
and Neighbourhood

Cecil N. Cullingford

Phillimore

1988
Published by
PHILLIMORE & CO. LTD.
Shopwyke Hall, Chichester, Sussex

ISBN 0 85033 666 X

Printed and bound in Great Britain by
RICHARD CLAY LTD.
Chichester, Sussex

Dedicated to the Memory of
Sir Peter Thompson, John Hutchins,
John Sydenham, Harry Peace Smith,
Herbert Spencer Carter and Bernard C. Short,
historians of the Borough and County
of the Town of Poole,
and of Ralph Sharpe,
whose line drawings did so much to promote appreciation
of the buildings of Poole and its neighbourhood

Contents

List of Illustrations

Frontispiece: Early 14th-century Poole ship

Illustration   Acknowledgements

The author is grateful to the following for giving their permission to reproduce illustrations: Bodleian Library, Oxford, 59; Borough of Poole Museum Service and the Poole Historical Trust, 24, 37, 41, 67, 68, 69, 71, 87, 88, 102, 103, 104, 105, 109, 111, 118, 121, 129, 131, 134, 135, 139, 144 and 149; Mrs. B. Butler, 48 and 49; the Vicar and Churchwardens of Canford Magna, 14, 15, 16; the Headmaster of Canford School, 145; Dorset Record Office, 21, 45, 63, 84 and 96; John Hammick, 94 and 95; the Vicar-designate and Churchwardens of Hampreston and Stapehill, 63; Andrew Hawkes, 36, 97, 117, 119, 122, 123, 124, 128, 130, 137, 140, 143 and 148; H. F. V. Johnstone, 72 and 73; A. J. Miller, 98; Poole Borough Archives, 65; Royal Commission on the Historical Monuments of England, 9, 35, 38 and 55; the Rector and Churchwardens of St James's, Poole, 74, 106 and 107; K. A. P. Smith, 23, 44 and 54 (reproduced from the history by his father, H. P. Smith); D. W. Robin Whicker, 132; Allen White, 19; Wiltshire Library and Museum Service, 64; the Rector and Churchwardens of Wimborne Minster, 12 and 60.

Grateful thanks are due also to those people who actually produced illustrations for this book: Rodney Fry who drew maps 8, 81 and 150, and also produced the predigree charts; Julien Lightfoot for drawing no. 66; David Prior for taking photographs 12, 21, 28, 43, 45, 47, 75, 84, 93, 138 and 141, and for improving on much of the other photographic material; the late Ralph Sharpe for drawing nos. 1, 2, 10, 17, 20, 27, 28, 53, 58, 62, 76, 91, 110, 114 and 116; Frank Turland for drawing the frontispiece and nos. 3, 4, 5, 6, 11, 22, 25, 26, 30, 34, 39, 40, 50, 78, 101, 112, 125, 136 and 146.

The author is also grateful to the following for producing artwork which has been reproduced as tailpieces to various chapters: the late Ralph Sharpe (pages 37, 55 and 199); and Frank Turland (pages 75 and 145). The tailpiece on page 93 has been reproduced by kind permission of Alan J. Miller.

The following photographs were taken by the author who holds the copyright: 7, 13, 14, 15, 16, 18, 31, 32, 33, 42, 46, 49, 52, 56, 60, 61, 67, 68, 70, 74, 77, 79, 80, 82, 85, 86, 89, 90, 99, 100, 106, 107, 108, 113, 115, 120, 126, 127, 133, 142, 145 and 147.

Preface and Acknowledgements

Forty years ago Harry Peace Smith published the first volume of what he intended should be a history of Poole from the earliest times. At the time of his premature death in 1952 he had carried the story down to the reign of Charles II, but sadly he left behind no notes covering the next three centuries. In writing this history from the earliest times to the present day, it has been my aim to include recent important work in the field of archaeology and also to survey the extraordinary development of Poole during the past 40 years. Moreover, since Poole is now part of a vast conurbation with a population approaching 440,000, extending from Upton to Highcliffe, I have included examples of developments and personalities associated with villages and towns within a 12-mile radius of the old town of Poole. In fact there has been a very close connection between Poole and this area forming its neighbourhood. Thus, events in Wareham in the 12th century did much to stimulate the rise of Poole, whilst in the 18th century Poole's Newfoundland trade drew precisely upon this neighbourhood to provide its labour force and its essential goods, just as the wild heathland extending from Poole harbour to Christchurch was England's prime smuggling area.

Because I have cast my net wider, I have been obliged to omit much material which I had collected. I can but hope that I have managed to achieve a balanced treatment. I have tried to preserve as much human interest as possible and to let the people of Poole and its neighbourhood speak for themselves – even in archaic English. Because of limitations of space it has not been possible to give as many detailed references to sources as I would wish, but it is to be hoped that general readers, and especially young readers still at school, will be encouraged by the many quotations which I have included to seek out the sources from which these come and to learn more in this fascinating field of local history.

I could not have completed this book without the help of many people, and first and foremost I want to thank my wife for her help in typing and for her forbearance in the postponement of many other projects. I also owe a special debt of gratitude for the encouragement and generous help which I have received from Ian Andrews, Poole's Town Clerk; John Hillier, his predecessor; Derek Beamish, local historian; Harry Johnstone, for so many years Poole's Reference Librarian; Graham Smith, Curator of Museums – all leading members of the Poole Historical Trust, whose publications have done so much to stimulate interest in local history. I am especially grateful to Norman Field, for so many years my colleague at Poole Grammar School, and to Keith Jarvis and Ian Horsey for their help in the archaeological field. I also much appreciate the encouragement which I have received from Keith Smith, who has allowed me to use some illustrations contained in the history written by his father, H. P. Smith, and from Tim Sharpe, who has so readily given permission for the use of many fine sketches drawn by his father, Ralph Sharpe, for my earlier book, *A History of Dorset*. Much of the success achieved by a book nowadays depends on its illustrations and so I would especially like to thank Frank Turland for the skill and artistry displayed in his line drawings and for the readiness with which he often executed assignments at very short notice; John Goodman for his technical skills in providing such good prints from photographs supplied by the Poole Museum Service; Andrew Hawkes for generously lending many pictures from his fine collection of Poole postcards; John Hammick for his generous help in obtaining photographs of Merley House; and David Prior for giving

xiii

up so much time to photograph documents for me and for printing improved versions of many of the photographs which I and others provided.

Among the many other people who have provided information, answered queries or facilitated my researches and photography are the following: Hugh Jaques (County Archivist) and his staff at the Dorset Record Office; R. N. R. Peers (Curator of the Dorset County Museum) and his staff; Alan J. Miller; the Poole Harbour Commissioners; the staff of the Dorset County Libraries, especially the Poole Reference Library; Robert F. Bailey; Councillor Herbert C. R. Ballam; Malcolm R. Bowditch; John Bugler; Brenda Butler and the late Richard Butler; Frank Chamberlain; Councillor Peter J. Coles; Alan Cook of Upton Country Park; Alfred J. A. Cooksey; Philip E. Cutler; Rev. Walter Dickinson; Elizabeth Edwards; John Edwards; the Editor of the *Evening Echo*, Bournemouth; Peter Fielden; Brian J. Galpin; Roger Guttridge; Martin D. P. Hammond; Dr. Lesley E. Haskins; Leslie Hayward; Jack Hicks; James C. Holland; Jude James; John le Carré; Eric Lewis; Julien Lightfoot; Malcolm Lowe; Ivy Manuel; Biddy Matthews; Anne Norbury; Royal Marines, Poole; Rev. Christopher J. Smith; David N. Smith (Estate Warden, Kingston Lacy); Judy Smith; Andrew Spree; Ken Standing; Stanley A. H. Swain; John Travers; Howard Webber (Administrator, Kingston Lacy House); Robin Whicker; Col. Peter F. White; and Frank Whitehead.

Chapter One

The Prehistoric and Roman Prelude

The great Domesday Survey of 1086 made no mention of Poole, although Canford was featured as a very large manor, the boundaries of which roughly coincided with those of the modern borough of Poole. It is unlikely that Poole existed as a town until the late 12th century and then it would have been a very small port developing out of a fishing hamlet. Nevertheless, from the prehistoric, Roman and Saxon periods of our national history when there was no identifiable town or community of Poole, there survived – within, say, a twelve-mile radius of the peninsula on which the town of Poole grew up – ample evidence of the main stages of human development and cultural change during the many centuries before there was a Poole.

When the earliest groups of men moved into what is now south-east Dorset, Britain was not an island, and a continuous line of chalk hills stretched to the south of Poole across from the Purbeck Hills to what is now the Isle of Wight, whilst the rivers Frome, Stour and Avon, like the Test and Itchen, were tributaries of a great Solent river flowing eastwards and linking up with a greater river flowing westwards into the Atlantic across a great plain which after a process of sinking and flooding was to become the English Channel.

1. Paleolithic hand-axe from Corfe Mullen.

During the immensely long Paleolithic (Old Stone) Age down to say 10,000 to 8,000 B.C. our district around Poole would have been tundra during the Ice Age, but during the eight or more warmer periods which alternated with the glaciations small nomadic groups of men would have been moving about south-east Dorset, hunting animals and birds and gathering roots, wild fruits and nuts, and for that purpose using roughly chipped but skilfully fashioned tools such as multi-purpose pear-shaped hand-axes, as well as scrapers and borers made from flint found in abundance in the neighbouring chalklands. The Dorset-Hampshire border has yielded the biggest concentration of flint hand-axes to be found anywhere in Britain. Some of these may have been washed down the Stour valley from more distant locations, but the alluvial soils near this concentration of river may well have been rich in food and game which attracted Paleolithic man. Some fine examples of their implements found in this area are to be seen in the museums of Poole and Bournemouth.

During the so-called Mesolithic (Middle Stone) Age from 10,000-8,000 B.C. to about 4,000 B.C. the glaciers finally retreated northwards, the climate became warmer, and the melting of the ice led to massive flooding. This, together perhaps with some sinking of the land, resulted about 6,000 B.C. in Britain and Dorset being cut off from the European continent by sea. Examination of pollen in the soil of the Poole Basin indicates the spread of pine and birch trees and later of elms and oaks. Mesolithic men may well have tried to alter their environment by setting fire to areas of woodland, for there is evidence of the spread of fire-resistant hazels at a later stage in our area. During this time, when the sea was advancing, Mesolithic men particularly collected as food the many kinds of shellfish which would have abounded in the shallow waters. Their tools, particularly very small pointed flints usually under a centimetre long – microliths – have been found in their bases at Corfe Mullen, Ulwell near Swanage, Blashenwell in the Purbecks and in the Stour valley. It was during the Mesolithic period that the advancing seas after a succession of storms broke through the chalk hills to the south, forming in time the Needles and Old Harry Rocks and turning the fresh-water lakes and swamps into Poole Bay and Poole Harbour.

During the Neolithic (New Stone) Age from, perhaps, 4,000-2,000 B.C. small groups of immigrants from the Continent reached the south coast bringing with them the new techniques of grinding and polishing flint implements – polished axes fixed to wooden handles, and arrowheads – the knowledge of how to make pottery, how to spin and weave, how to plant seeds and cultivate grain and how to rear domesticated cattle, sheep and goats. When Neolithic man arrived here, the vegetation of the Poole basin consisted of open, heathy woodland and the soils were already acid, so that there was little cultivation of the favoured Neolithic crops, wheat and barley, since these were intolerant of acid soils. In fact the large proportion of arrowheads among the Neolithic artefacts found in the Bournemouth and Poole area suggests that there was a very sparse settlement and that it was possibly in the main a hunting area. Neolithic men here were probably semi-nomadic, but some settlements accompanied by finds of Neolithic implements have been found in the Stour valley. Sites near East End, Corfe Mullen, and Moortown have yielded some two hundred flint implements, some pounding stones for crushing grain as well as fragments of pottery. Excavations at Moortown, east of Canford, in 1984 revealed small pits from which were recovered several characteristic round-bottomed bowls, shaped like the leather bags, which they doubtless replaced. The decline in the number of elms by about 3,000 B.C. may be due to Neolithic men feeding the leaves of deciduous trees to their cattle – a practice which still survives in Europe. The most permanent Neolithic remains on the landscape, the communal graves or family vaults called long barrows, are not well represented in the area, the nearest to Poole being the Holdenhurst long barrow, excavated in 1936, and Ailwood Down, near Corfe Castle.

Towards the end of the Neolithic period circular structures and sometimes circles of stones were erected, presumably for some kind of religious purpose and perhaps for the promotion of fertility, and these continued to be used into the early Bronze Age. South-east Dorset has nothing to compare with Avebury and Stonehenge in Wiltshire, but there is a small incomplete stone circle at Rempstone on the south side of Poole Harbour, whilst the Knowlton Circles, seven miles north of Wimborne, are, like Avebury and Stonehenge, excellent examples of a 'henge' monument, a circular sacred site surrounded by a ditch and a bank *outside* the ditch. Evidently the area within the main Knowlton circle was regarded as holy ground long after the Bronze Age, for in Norman times a church, now ruined, was constructed within it. A few arrowheads and other flint tools of late Neolithic or early Bronze Age date, from Moortown and a site in Arrowsmith Road, are the main indications of settlement in the Borough of Poole area at this time.

By about 1,900 B.C. a knowledge of using copper and later making bronze implements – axes, spearheads, arrowheads, daggers and rapiers – spread to south-east Dorset. Early in the Bronze Age (*c.*2,000-600 B.C.) the climate became warmer and drier and, whilst human settlement tended to be at a lower altitude, the burial mounds of the Bronze Age period – the round barrows, in each of which just one person was buried, were constructed at a higher level. By the Bronze Age the original heathlands which were lightly forested were cleared for farming, and this process resulted in a rapid deterioration of the soil and the open, very acid heathland of today was created.

Pollen analysis of soil in the later Bronze Age revealed very low amounts of tree pollen. Some oats, tolerant of acid soils, may have been cultivated, but the area was probably more important for pastoral farming. The building of the very large number of round barrows, for example, on Canford Heath would have involved substantial joint effort and those

would have been used only for the leaders of society such as chieftains and priests. Changes
in fashion and perhaps a growth in population later led to the spread of cremation. People
of the Deverel-Rimbury culture, so named after the Deverel barrow in Milborne St Andrew
and the Rimbury urn-field near Weymouth, cremated their dead, and, doubtless after
burning on a ceremonial pyre, the remaining bones and ashes were placed in bucket urns,
barrel urns or globular urns and placed in large cemeteries or urn-fields as well as in
barrows. The Deverel-Rimbury folk were thought to have belonged to the late Bronze Age,
but carbon-dating of the urns, if accurate in heathland areas such as the Knighton Heath
cemetery in Poole and the Simmonds Ground cemeteries in Hampreston, suggests that these
urns were present through much of the Bronze Age. At Moortown two pits containing
Deverel-Rimbury pottery could be all that remains of a small farming settlement with a
round house, and, close by, a cemetery with cremation urns of much the same date.

   From about 600 B.C. successive bands of immigrants or invaders from Europe landed in
Britain bringing with them the knowledge of the use of iron, a harder metal than bronze,
for weapons and implements, though bronze continued to be used widely especially for
making buckets, tankards, brooches and many other everyday articles. The newcomers
spoke a Celtic language, as probably did the late Bronze Age peoples, and were organised
into tribes among whom there was considerable rivalry – a factor which may have helped
to produce the Iron Age hill-forts, of which Dorset has so many magnificent examples like
Maiden Castle. A hill-fort was a strong defensive enclosure constructed on an easily
defensible position such as a hill-top, or on a promontory as at Hengistbury Head, where
most of the ramparts were constructed across the isthmus on the landward side. In the early
Iron Age – before 250 B.C. – the hill-fort was mainly univallate, that is, it was defended
by a single rampart fronted by an outer ditch as at Dudsbury, occupying a semi-circular
area on the north side of the Stour overlooking Kinson to the south. To the west of Lytchett
Minster is another single-rampart hill-fort, Bulbury Camp, sited on a hill-slope. Other
hill-slope forts are Buzbury Rings (Tarrant Keyneston) and Spetisbury Rings, also known
as Crawford Castle. The most important hill-fort in the vicinity of Poole was undoubtedly
Badbury Rings, which, like Woodbury outside Bere Regis, is a contour hill-fort where the
site was a natural isolated hill and the ramparts and ditches followed the contours of the
land. At an earlier stage Badbury Rings consisted of two ramparts and ditches, but later a
third outer defence-line was added, possibly in order to deal with the growing use in native
warfare of the sling, a stone from which in the hands of a skilled operator could stun or kill
at a distance of 100 yards. Thus the depth of the defences seems to be directly related to
the range of the sling and to the steepness of the slope of the hill. Early in the Iron Age
hill-forts may have been refuges to which people from nearby farmsteads could retreat with
their animals and most prized possessions in times of trouble, but later many developed
into more permanent urban centres – towns or *oppida* as the Romans called them. Hengistbury was certainly a major manufacturing centre and port.

   The Britons of the later Iron Age produced much improved pottery turned on the wheel,
used lathes to fashion wooden vessels, developed light-wheeled vehicles and employed
rotary querns to grind their corn. They made fine iron swords, but also bronze shields,
mirrors and harness fittings often gaily ornamented with red, yellow and blue enamel and
vigorous curvilinear designs. Trade developed extensively and thus arose a need for money.
At first this took the form of iron 'currency bars' looking like rough-outs for sword blades
in six standardised weights. A hoard of currency bars was discovered in 1970 in a defensive
V-shaped ditch at a settlement excavated at Bear Wood. Later there came into use circular
coins in silver and bronze which were imitations of well-worn coins used for centuries by
Greek merchants in the Mediterranean and Gaul. These portrayed a wreathed head on one
side and two horses and a chariot as well as an inscription on the other side. The coins of

2. A Celtic
currency bar
as found at the
Bear Wood
site.

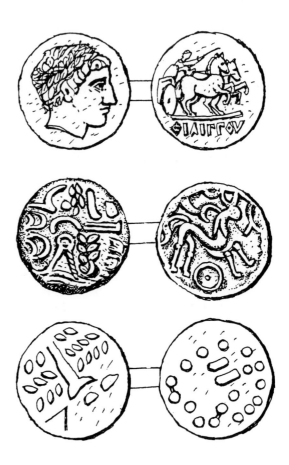

3. The evolution of Celtic coins: (*top*) a stater
of Philip II of Macedon; (*centre*) a Durotrigian
coin; (*bottom*) a debased coin found at
Hamworthy.

the Durotriges, the Celtic tribe occupying Dorset, had no inscriptions and showed little more than a wheatsheaf or the remnants of the wreath round the head of the god Apollo on one side and a few blobs or dumb-bells, or at best a caricature of a horse, on the other. Large numbers of such coins were found and were probably minted at Hengistbury and indeed were still being produced after the Roman occupation.

Out in the countryside would have been several farmsteads the chief feature of which – within a strong pallisade – would have been a large circular thatched farmhouse. A small

Iron-Age farmstead has been excavated at Bear Wood, whilst excavations south of Magna Road, where quarrying is being developed, promises to yield not only a Bronze Age urn-field but also another Iron Age farmstead. Iron Age settlements at Hamworthy and on Green Island indicate that Poole Harbour was by 100 B.C. developing as a centre for trade. A log-boat, 33 feet long, hollowed out of a single oak log, which would have weighed 1.7 tons, was dredged out of Poole Harbour in 1964 and has been carbon-dated to 295 B.C. + or − 50 years. It would probably have been used to ferry people and to transport clay, corn, peat or stone across the harbour. At Hamworthy and Green Island, as at Hengistbury, vessels of a particular 'cauldroned' type have been found and these also abound at various sites in north France – sure evidence of a growing cross-Channnel trade. Strabo, the Greco-Roman geographer (c.63 B.C.-A.D. 19) wrote of Britain exporting corn, cattle, gold, silver, hides, slaves and hunting dogs. Among the Celtic tribes in Gaul in his time which may well have been trading with the Poole area were the Veneti, a seafaring people of south Brittany of whom Julius Caesar spoke as accustomed to sail to Britain and as using great flat-bottomed boats made of oak fastened with 'iron nails and equipped with leather sails' and also 'anchors fastened to iron chains rather than ropes'. Among the tantalising finds excavated over a century ago at Bulbury Camp were an iron anchor and iron chain now exhibited in the Dorset County Museum together with many iron nails over six inches long and as 'thick as a thumb'. It is tempting to think that these objects were of Venetic origin, perhaps part of a store of scrap metal obtained by a Durotrigian smith, but there is just a possibility that, after Caesar defeated the Veneti, some of these tribesmen escaped by sea to Poole Harbour and may just possibly have been allowed to establish a refugee camp at Bulbury.

Excavations by Professor Barry Cunliffe and his teams in recent years have revealed the unique importance of Hengistbury Head in the late Iron Age. About 100 B.C. a group of traders seem to have occupied the Hengistbury promontory hill-fort, particularly attracted because it had the tranquil waters of Christchurch harbour to the north, and was protected to the south by the sea and to the west on the landward side by the 'Double Dykes', which were further strengthened about this time. Here the occupants established a busy settled community, as far as can be judged the first industrial town in Britain. Hengistbury had obvious advantages for overseas trade situated as it was immediately north of the Cherbourg peninsula from which it was only some seventy miles distant and twelve sailing hours in good weather. Strabo spoke of traders setting out for Britain from the mouth of the Loire and the Garonne and it seems likely that the trading route ran from Hengistbury across to the Cherbourg peninsula round the coasts of Normandy and Brittany, up the river Garonne along the line of the Canal du Midi and so to the southern shores of Gaul and the Mediterranean, thus avoiding the long and hazardous sea-journey round Spain and Portugal. And what in

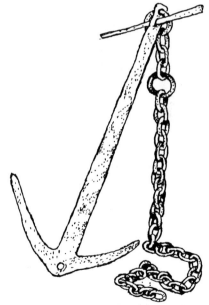

4. The Late Iron Age anchor and chain from Bulbury Camp, now in the County Museum, Dorchester.

return for the goods that Britain had to offer would these traders be bringing back to Hengistbury and Poole Harbour? Undoubtedly Italian wine, for a large quantity of amphorae, large two-handled jars for holding liquids, of a distinctive Dressel 1A type, associated with the wine-producing areas of Italy, has been found at Hengistbury and to a lesser extent at sites on Green Island in Poole Harbour. As Professor Cunliffe argues, the sheer quantity of Dressel 1A amphorae found at Hengistbury, far exceeding that from all other sites together in Southern England, leaves no doubt that Hengistbury was the principal port of entry for Italian wine in the first century B.C. Fish paste and probably olive oil were also imported. Green Island may have been an alternative port, or British coastal vessels may have transported the amphorae laden with wine from Hengistbury into Poole Harbour. It would mean that Celtic aristocrats, living in the hill-forts up the Stour and further west in Dorset and beyond, developed a passion for Italian wine and fish paste. Much pottery was imported at Hengistbury from Brittany (Armorica) and, of 25 imported coins found at Hengistbury, 21 came from Brittany and Normandy, but all well before 50 B.C. Yet this flourishing trade between Hengistbury and Gaul and Italy seems suddenly to have ceased by 50 B.C., for virtually no amphorae of the type in use after 50 B.C. (Dressel 1B) have been found at Hengistbury and the explanation may well be that, when the Veneti of Brittany rebelled in 56 B.C. as a result of Caesar's drive into north-west Gaul and Caesar then destroyed the Venetic navy and slaughtered or enslaved a large part of the population, the whole of this flourishing trade with Hengistbury was disrupted. Just possibly a few of the Veneti managed to escape to Poole Harbour and Bulbury.

5. A coin of the Emperor Vespasian.

For nearly a century after Caesar's two re-connaissance raids, 55 and 54 B.C. on Kent, Roman expansion in north-west Europe was halted, although commercial contacts with south-east Britain continued and the Belgae, Celtic tribesmen from the area now called Belgium, moved across to Britain bringing with them improved techniques of producing pottery, tilling the soil and using the wheel. Then in A.D. 43 the Roman emperor Claudius, probably in the hope of strengthening his personal position, mounted a full-scale invasion of Britain. The Roman historian, Suetonius, related that the general Vespasian (later to be emperor from A.D. 69 to 79) in command of the Second Legion Augusta, conquered two formidable tribes and over twenty towns together with the Isle of Wight. The two tribes could have been the Belgae of Hampshire and the Durotriges and the 20 *oppida* would have included great hill-forts like Badbury Rings, Hod Hill and Maiden Castle. It is tempting to think that Vespasian crossed from the Isle of Wight to Hengistbury, but even though Hengistbury was much less important than it had been a century earlier, Vespasian may well have preferred not to make a frontal attack on the formidable 'Double Dykes', but to outflank Hengistbury by landing at Hamworthy within a sheltered harbour, especially if traders had informed him of its location and potential. Excavations by H. P. Smith at Hamworthy near Carter's tileworks brought to light fragments of black Iron Age C pottery and briquetage (bits of coarse brick-like burnt clay containers and props) indicative of a salt-boiling industry.

H. P. Smith's discovery of two coins of the Emperor Claudius dated by the British

Museum to A.D. 41-42 and fragments of brick-red Samian ware from Europe dated A.D. 40-50 provide evidence of Roman occupation at the time of the invasion. A further clue to the status of Hamworthy is provided by the fact that in the mid-19th century a Roman mill of a definitely military type of hard grit rock from the Rhineland, now in the British Museum, was discovered there. It could well have been used to grind corn for invading Roman legionaries. H. P. Smith also traced part of a Roman road north-westwards from the Hamworthy site and then to the west of Holes Bay turning due north towards the Stour, doubtless following an earlier pre-Roman trackway heading towards Badbury Rings. The probable nature of Vespasian's invasion campaign was clarified by N. H. Field's discovery in 1959 of part of a Roman fortress at Lake Gates at the northern end of this road and just south of the Stour. When the Wimborne by-pass was about to be constructed right across where the fort appeared to be, the Poole Museum Archaeological unit under K. S. Jarvis and I. P. Horsey undertook further excavations, which revealed – with the help of a magnetometer survey indicating soil disturbance – a fortress of some 30 acres designed to

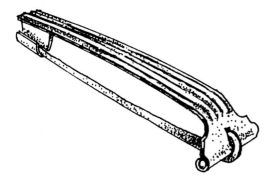

6. (*above*) Roman bronze fibula found near Wimborne.

7. (*right*) Roman amphora excavated at the Lake fort.

accommodate half a legion. A full legion was composed of between five thousand and six thousand heavy infantry, accompanied by a similar number of auxiliaries such as slingers, archers and light infantry and cavalry. The site yielded the foundations of barrack blocks, a fine amphora now in Scaplens Court museum, two coins of Augustus and several of Claudius, Samian ware and other pottery of the invasion period, fragments of metallic military equipment, a bronze statuette of a lion, another of the war-god Mars, iron nails, a crowbar and gaming counters. The pattern that emerges, therefore, is that Hamworthy was a supply base and that the Lake fort was in occupation from about A.D. 45-47 to A.D. 65. After the hill-forts of the Durotriges had been captured the fort at Lake would have been invaluable in the consolidation of Roman control. Only large-scale excavations can reveal whether Badbury was the scene of fierce resistance or of tame surrender. Presumably the Roman forces advanced up the Stour valley to seize Spetisbury Rings, Hod Hill, and

Hambledon Hill. When in 1857 a railway cutting was being dug across the north-eastern part of Spetisbury Rings, some 120 skeletons, showing signs of violent death, were brought to light as were several Roman weapons. Clearly the Romans encountered resistance at Spetisbury as they did at Hod Hill, although there the bombardment of the British commander's dwelling with ballista bolts produced a rapid surrender. Aerial photography during the dry summer of 1975 revealed the outline of another small Roman fort of only about six acres at Crab Farm, Shapwick, a mile to the south-west of Badbury Rings on a broad spur of land giving a good view of both Spetisbury and Badbury Rings and of the Stour almost as far east as Lake. It lies outside the Roman road which was constructed from Badbury to Dorchester (Durnovaria) probably after this little fort was built. After the suppression of Queen Boudicca's rebellion against Roman oppression (A.D. 61-62), Britain south and east of a line from the Bristol Channel to the Wash was pacified. The Second Legion moved to Exeter and later to Caerleon in South Wales to keep watch over the wilder Celtic regions. The Celtic aristocrats of the south-east became Romanised. Some of them settled down in the new Roman towns such as Durnovaria (Dorchester) or in Roman-style country houses (villas). Peasants would have continued to live in thatched farmhouses with cob walls – but with a rectangular instead of circular plan as previously. Such a farmhouse at Woodhouse Hill, Studland, was excavated by N. H. Field in 1952-8. Its occupants would have had a life-style differing little from that of the pre-Roman period.

A priority task during the period of the Roman conquest was the construction of roads to facilitate quick movement of troops to trouble spots. Sometimes existing trackways may have been improved, but new routes would also have been laid out by the Roman military engineers in a series of straight sections. The main consideration in the construction of the Roman road was adequate drainage, since lying water on the surface, if it froze in winter, could easily break up the surface. Thus essential features of a Roman road were two drainage ditches, one on each side of the road. The road itself would normally be on top of a causeway or *agger*, which could be quite high – in the case of Ackling Dyke, north of Badbury Rings, in places as much as five or six feet above the adjacent land level. The causeway could be as much as twenty yards wide, though five yards was a more normal width – just wide enough for two vehicles to pass if they were moving slowly. The lower layers of the road would be of large stones, if available, then came small pebbles at a higher level, and on top fine gravel. Flat stone slabs were only very rarely used for surfacing – because of the labour and expense involved and then only if stone like limestone slabs were locally available. The Lake-Hamworthy road is a turf bank with gravel on top.

The major Roman road in East Dorset was Ackling Dyke running southwards from Old Sarum, whence it is linked with London, and then across Bokerly Dyke, the defensive earthwork which follows the present Dorset boundary, and so on south-south-west through the parish of Witchampton to Badbury Rings. Just north of the hill-fort the Roman road continues in a south-westerly direction to Dorchester – and then on to Exeter. Another Roman road ran south-eastwards from Badbury to a ford across the Stour to the Lake Gates fort. During a drought in 1934 H. P. Smith located this road, before, of course, anything was known of the Lake Gates fort. 'It showed', he said, 'as a low bank about 22 feet wide and was as distinct as if it had been a newly formed gravel road, the yellow, burnt-up grass standing out against the green of the meadows'. By the Lake fort the road turns southwards alongside Corfe Hills, and following the western boundary of the Borough of Poole underneath what is still called Roman Road in Broadstone. Later, west of Holes Bay, it turns south-eastwards into the Hamworthy peninsula to what was Vespasian's invasion port and supply base near the modern power station. H. P. Smith traced some of its course in Hamworthy, at one stage along a garden path, but because of modern building its original course cannot easily be traced. In 1928 Colonel Drew located a small section of Roman

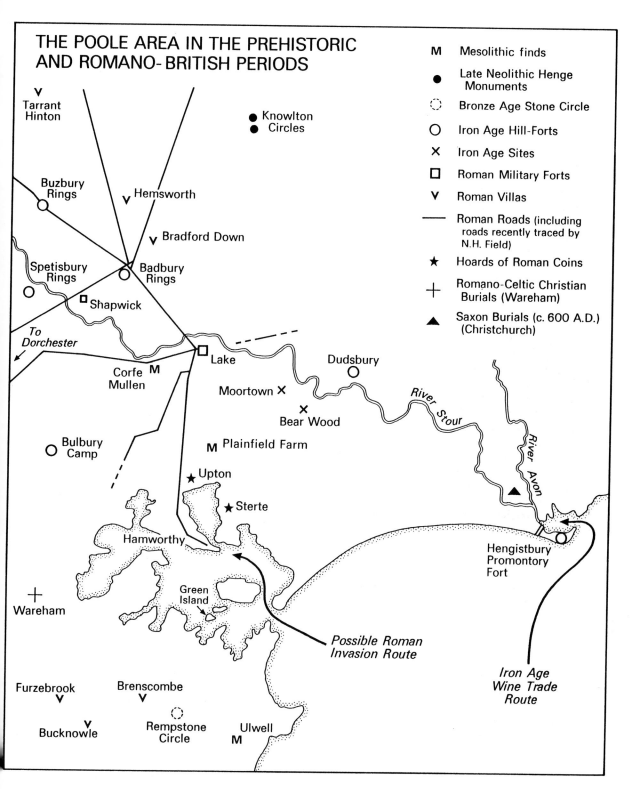

THE POOLE AREA IN THE PREHISTORIC AND ROMANO-BRITISH PERIODS

Legend:

M	Mesolithic finds
●	Late Neolithic Henge Monuments
◌	Bronze Age Stone Circle
○	Iron Age Hill-Forts
×	Iron Age Sites
□	Roman Military Forts
V	Roman Villas
—	Roman Roads (including roads recently traced by N.H. Field)
★	Hoards of Roman Coins
+	Romano-Celtic Christian Burials (Wareham)
▲	Saxon Burials (c. 600 A.D.) (Christchurch)

V Tarrant Hinton

● Knowlton Circles

Buzbury Rings

V Hemsworth

V Bradford Down

Spetisbury Rings

Badbury Rings

□ Shapwick

To Dorchester

Corfe Mullen M

Lake

Moortown ×

Dudsbury

× Bear Wood

M Plainfield Farm

Bulbury Camp

River Stour

River Avon

★ Upton

★ Sterte

Hamworthy

▲

Green Island

Hengistbury Promontory Fort

+ Wareham

Possible Roman Invasion Route

Furzebrook V

Brenscombe V

Iron Age Wine Trade Route

V Bucknowle

◌ Rempstone Circle

Ulwell M

8. Map of the Poole area in the prehistoric and Roman periods.

road just south of the first milestone on the Ringwood road east of Wimborne running westwards towards Lake and eastwards towards Winchester. N. H. Field has undertaken much research into identifying additional stretches of Roman road in this area, such as one running north-westwards from Badbury via Buzbury to Hod Hill and beyond, and another branching off the Lake-Hamworthy road and probably continuing across Holton Heath to Wareham and southwards to a point where one road could have forked eastwards towards Roman Purbeck marble workings, whilst another continued to Flowers Barrow.

The Roman road system covered the whole area from the south of Britain to Hadrian's Wall and so during the three centuries of the Pax Romana these roads became arteries of trade. Thus in the late 1960s detailed examination of the mineral content of the black-burnished pottery used on Hadrian's Wall revealed that it originated in the Poole area! Since then production sites have been located at Redcliffe, Wareham and Ower, where kilns must have turned out a steady stream of pots for export and for the use of legionaries defending the Province of Britain against the Picts. A small late Roman pottery industry also developed at Corfe Mullen. Salt production was also a major industry on the coast of Poole Harbour. Briquetage from salt containers has been found at several sites in Hamworthy as well as in 1985 at a large site at Boat-house Clump near Upton House. There is, however, no evidence of Roman settlement on the peninsula where later the old town and port of Poole were to develop. East of Holes Bay at Sterte a hoard of 965 Roman coins stored in a jar was discovered in 1932, probably part of the same hoard as 300 coins found there nearly a century earlier. Romano-British pottery has also been discovered in the same meadow. The 1932 hoard consisted of base coins with very little silver content issued by various short-lived emperors and pretenders spanning the period A.D. 238-274. The emperor Aurelian in 273 had declared all these debased coins to be of no monetary value and the owner had possibly buried them in the hope that later on he might be able to dig them up and pass them off as good money. Alternatively, there might have been some unrecorded outbreak of disorder or brigandage which caused some merchant to bury his money. In 1986 yet another hoard of some 1,600 coins dated as between A.D. 310-318 was unearthed on farmland at Upton.

The acid heathland around Poole had few attractions in Roman times, although there must have been many farm sites in the Stour valley. Immediately to the west of Badbury Rings there seems to have been a substantial settlement and excavations there have brought to light stone roofing slabs, painted wall-plaster, a wide range of pottery, glass beads, bronze pins, a bracelet, a brooch and 21 Durotrigian coins of the first century A.D. and over 185 Roman coins, minted throughout the occupation period but mainly in the fourth century. It seems likely that here was a staging-post at the junction of several roads where travellers could change horses and obtain refreshment, and there is a strong case for identifying it with Vindocladia, one of the road-stations mentioned in a list of landmarks in Britain compiled by an anonymous seventh-century geographer of Ravenna. If so, Vindocladia would be appropriately named since it would seem to be a Latin form of two Celtic words meaning 'white ditches', an apt description of the chalk defences of the hill-fort on this settlement. A market could well have been held there to meet the needs of local farmers, but Badbury was never developed as a Roman town as was Dorchester (Durnovaria). Just to the north of Badbury on the chalkland there were several farms and some, as at Hemsworth, Bradford Down and Tarrant Hinton, were of villa status. The Hemsworth villa, excavated in 1905, though without the sophisticated techniques of modern archaeologists, yielded a plunge bath, a hypocaust (under-floor central heating) and two outstanding mosaics, one (now in Dorchester Museum) showing the bust of a sea or river god and the other depicting the well-known theme of the goddess of love, Venus, rising naked from the waves surrounded by a border of five dolphins, scallops and smaller fish.

This is now a major exhibit in the British Museum. The remains of this villa showed several signs of destruction by fire and a burnt patch blotted out the upper part of Venus. The Tarrant Hinton villa, excavated since 1968, yielded a twin-cylinder pump and an inscription on a stone block from the adjacent cemetery recording that 'Cupitius Vep. . . died on August 26th in the consulship of Tuscus and Bassus [i.e. A.D. 258] in his 39th year'. 'Vep. . .' was probably a Celtic name and so he may well have been the only Romano-Briton to have lived and died in Dorset, whose name, or part of whose name, has come down to us.

In the later fourth and early fifth centuries, the most outlying province of the Roman Empire suffered increasingly from raids by Picts from the north, Irish pirates from the west and Saxon plunderers from the east. In A.D. 410 the Emperor Honorius told the Britons that, because of attacks by German invaders on Rome itself and on provinces nearer Rome, they must organise their own defence. Already regular Roman troops had been withdrawn in stages. Thus without central direction from Rome, it fell to retired military men or Romano-British gentry to cope with any incursions. What happened in south-east Dorset from 410 till about 660, when it had become part of the West Saxon Kingdom – a period of two and a half centuries – we can only guess at, with the help of all too few clues.

Roman mosaic of a water god, Hemsworth villa.

Chapter Two

The Saxon Take-Over and the Norman Conquest

The English historian, Bede (*c.*673-735), writing after Dorset had been swept into this West-Saxon state centred on Winchester, related how, after an initial period of defeat, the Romano-Britons began to fight back under the leadership of a commander named Ambrosius Aurelius. 'Sometimes the natives and sometimes their enemies prevailed till the year of the siege of Baddesdown hill, when they made no small slaughter of the invaders, about forty-four years after their arrival in England', i.e. about A.D. 493, but this approximate date may be some ten or twenty years too early. The much later *Anglo-Saxon Chronicle* records: 'This year Cerdic and Cynric undertook the government of the West Saxons; the same year they fought with the Britons at a place called Cerdicesford'. This can be identified with Charford on the river Avon, four miles north of Fordingbridge. If the Saxons having overrun most of Hampshire advanced 10 more miles to the west from Charford, they would have reached the point where the Roman road, Ackling Dyke, crossed the Bokerly Dyke, the fortification along the north-east border of Dorset constructed, to judge from some excavated finds, in the fourth and fifth centuries to keep out invaders from the north and east. A short march farther down Ackling Dyke would have brought them to Badbury Rings. Was this fort the Baddesdown Hill, where, according to Bede, the advancing West Saxons suffered a severe set-back? The *Anglo-Saxon Chronicle* makes no mention of such a defeat, but that is not surprising for national or tribal historians not uncommonly omit or conveniently forget humiliations and inglorious episodes in their accounts of the past. By contrast, Celtic writers made much of a great military triumph at Mount Badon which halted the Saxon advance and guaranteed independence to the Romanised Celts in some areas for another two centuries or more. This 'Mount Badon' could well have been our Badbury Rings, the Iron Age hill-fort, which was still of great strategic importance placed as it was at the junction of important Roman roads.

The British monk, Gildas, writing between 540 and 545 *De Excidio et conquestu Britanniae* (Concerning the Ruin and Conquest of Britain), was preaching a sermon and chiding the British princes for their sinfulness or for squabbling among themselves. He was probably not attempting to write an historical account. Gildas did, however, praise Ambrosius, who rallied the Britons and added 'by God's aid, victory came to them. From that time onwards sometimes the Britons, and sometimes the enemy were victorious . . . up to the year of the siege of Mount Badon'. Gildas does not name the British leader at Mount Badon, but his implication seems to be that after that battle the British successfully held their own against the Saxon invaders.

A much later Welsh chronicler, Nennius, in his *Historia Brittonum*, compiled in the early ninth century, declared: 'Then Arthur fought against them [i.e. the English or Saxons], together with the Kings of the Britons, but he himself was *dux bellorum* [that is, just a military commander] . . .'. Nennius then listed the 12 battles which Arthur fought and concluded: 'The twelfth battle was on Badon Hill and in it 960 men fell in one day, from a single onslaught by Arthur and no one save he alone laid them low; and he was victorious in all his campaigns'. Another Welsh source, the *Annales Cambriae* (Welsh Annals) recorded against the date 516 'The battle of Badon in which Arthur carried the Cross of our Lord Jesus Christ for three days and three nights on his shoulders [or more likely his shield since

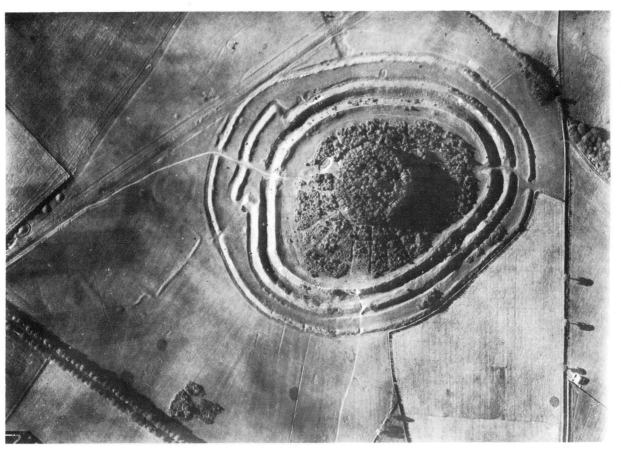

9. Badbury Rings, the possible site of the battle at Mount Badon, viewed from the south and showing the Roman road running diagonally from W.S.W. to E.N.E.

the translator probably mistook *scuit* (the Welsh for shield) for *scuid* (shoulder)]; and the Britons were victors'.

Where was this Badbury, Baddanbyrig (that is 'the fort of Badda'), where Arthur's great victory was fought? Several suggestions have been made – Bath, and sites in Gloucestershire, Wiltshire and even Lincolnshire – but the most feasible site for Mount Badon is Badbury Rings in Dorset. A pertinent clue is provided by a further entry in the Welsh Annals: '665 The second battle of Badon'. Evidently this second battle was fought at the same place as Arthur's well-remembered victory. It is not stated whether this second battle was a victory or a defeat for the Britons but it was probably a defeat. That being so, the site is unlikely to have been Bath or in Gloucestershire or Wiltshire since other evidence shows these places to have fallen into Saxon hands long before 665. On the other hand it seems that after the first battle of Mount Badon most of Dorset and certainly East Dorset remained Welsh for several generations. Pagan Saxon burials occur mainly to the north and east of Bokerly Dyke, rather than on the Dorset side, whilst in St Mary's Church, Wareham, five Christian

10. Seventh-century Christian inscriptions, St Mary's church, Wareham.

tomb slabs, dated to the seventh and eighth centuries, have Latin inscriptions, but commemorate people who seem to have Celtic names – evidence therefore, of the continuous presence of a Christian Welsh community on the western side of Poole Harbour.

Moreover, the *Anglo-Saxon Chronicle* has the entry: 658. This year Cenwealh [King of the West Saxons] fought with the Welsh at Pen [believed to be Pen Selwood on the north-west Dorset border, although it could well have been the South Cadbury hill-fort] and pursued them to the Parret'. It looks very much as though the Britons, protected by Bokerly Dyke and the great belt of forest, Selwood or, as the Welsh called it, Coit Maur (the great wood), were left alone, maintaining Christianity and using a little Latin, until King Cenwealh encircled north Dorset and secured this victory.at Pen Selwood (or South Cadbury) in 658. What more likely than that the Saxons then moved south-eastwards and overcame the remaining Celtic resistance in a second encounter at Badbury Rings seven years later – in 665? Some day no doubt sufficient funds will become available to conduct a substantial excavation of Badbury Rings, which could reveal whether the Durotriges resisted Vespasian's advance in

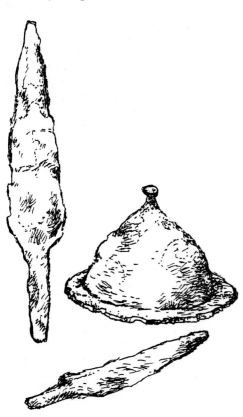

11. Pagan Saxon grave finds, Christchurch.

the period A.D. 43-48, whether Badbury like South Cadbury 25 miles to the north-west in Somerset was massively strengthened in the late fifth century to maintain the frontier against the Saxon invaders, and whether about 490-520 a great battle took place here between the Germanic interlopers and the revived Romano-British resistance movement under the great war leader Arthur – the basis of the later medieval stories about 'King' Arthur and his Knights of the Round Table.

What evidence of early Saxon settlement have we? Very little, in fact, apart from the thirty or so Saxon warrior burials located by the excavations of K. S. Jarvis and his team at Bargates, Christchurch. Bones had not survived because of the acidic soil, but the graves, estimated to be late sixth or seventh century in date, yielded nine spearheads, 23 knives, several buckles (probably of waist-belts), besides a number of shield bosses and handles. The indications are, therefore, that there was a pagan Saxon incursion and settlement about A.D. 600. Whether this Saxon presence at Christchurch was maintained throughout the next century until all Dorset came under the control of the West Saxon king only further excavation can reveal.

It seems likely then that from the time of Arthur's victory at Mount Badon (say A.D. 516) until Cenwealh's triumph 'aet Peonnum' (at the hills) in 658, Dorset remained a Celtic state or group of states free from Saxon control. With the second battle of Mount Badon (665), assuming it to be a defeat for the Welsh, the West Saxons would be consolidating their hold on Dorset and the entry in the *Anglo-Saxon Chronicle* under 681 that the King of Wessex, 'Centwin pursued the Britons to the sea' may relate to a final southward drive across Dorset from the north. Thereafter under the political control of the King of Wessex no doubt old established Welsh communities, as at Wareham and probably Lytchett and Crichel, co-existed with new Saxon settlements as the newcomers infiltrated perhaps from the sea by way of Poole Harbour, Christchurch Harbour and the river Stour. Accustomed to tilling the heavy soils of north-west Germany, their homeland, and possessed of improved ploughs, the Saxon infiltrators would have been able to clear many sites in the Dorset river valleys. A study of the place-names of the Poole area suggests that the Saxons were soon predominant here. The river names, Frome (meaning perhaps 'fair' or 'fine'), Stour (the strong or powerful one), and Tarrant ('the trespasser', i.e. 'a river liable to flood') are all Celtic, as too are the village names Lytchett (the grey wood) and Crichel (literally Celtic *cruc*, a hill, to which has been added the duplicating A.S. *hyll*, having the same meaning) and, farther north, Pimperne (probably Celtic for 'five trees'). If the Saxon immigrants referred to the Pool (A.S. *pol*), the native Welsh would have understood the term for the distinctive large stretch of water that was the harbour, for they had the word *pwll* with the same meaning. However, the Poole area abounds in place-names incorporating many common Anglo-Saxon elements. Whatever its Romano-British inhabitants may have called it, Wareham at the earliest stage at which we can identify it was known by a thoroughly Saxon name, i.e. the *ham* (homestead or village) by a *waer* (weir). Doubtless there was a weir and a fishery here on the river Frome. Sandford (= sandy ford), Holton (a *tun*, i.e. 'homestead' or village in a *hol* or 'hollow'), Upton (= higher homestead), Slepe (A.S. *slaep*, a slippery place), Steıte (A.S. *steort*, a tail of land), Longfleet (longflete in 1230 from A.S. *lang* (long) and *fleot* (inlet), i.e. a long creek or inlet), Fleets (= inland creek). Parkstone (mentioned as early as 1326 and presumably meaning the stone at an entrance to a park), Holdenhurst (the *hyrst* or copse where *holegn* or holly grows), Throop (A.S. *throp* an outlying farm or settlement), Hurn (*hyrne*, an angle of land, a reference perhaps to a piece of land between the Stour and the Moors river), Parley (the *leah*, A.S. for wood where the *peru* or pear-tree grows), Oakley (mentioned as early as 1327, the *ac* (or oak-tree), *leah* (wood or clearing), Leigh (*leah*, the wood or clearing in a wood), Ashington (Ashamton in 1327, probably meaning the *tun* or farm of the *haeme*, 'dwellers', by the *aesc*, 'ash-tree'), Longham (a long enclosure or river-meadow from the A.S. *lang* and *hamm*), Horton (muddy farm from the A.S. *horo* and *tun*), Holt (A.S. *holt* or wood, earlier called 'Winburneholt', the wood near Wimborne), Knowlton (the *tun* or farm near a *cnoll* A.S. for hillock), Colehill, Colhulle in 1431, possibly where *col* (A.S. for charcoal) was produced, Stanbridge (Stanbrig in 1230, the stone bridge or causeway from A.S. *stan* and *brycg*, meaning probably a stony raised ·track across marshland by the river Allen), Walford Walteford in Domesday Book from *wealt* (Anglo-Saxon shaky or unsteady ford), Wimborne (Wimburna in A.D. 705. 'meadow stream' from A.S. *winn* 'meadow' and *burna* 'stream'), Witchampton perhaps the *tun*, village of the *haeme*, dwellers by a *wic*, a dairy farm). Shapwick (A.S. *sceap* 'sheep', *wic*, 'farm'), Spetisbury (A.S. *speoht*, 'green woodpecker', A.S. *burh*, 'fort' – a reference to the adjacent Iron Age hill-fort), Almer (eel-pool from A.S. *ael*, eel, and *mere*, 'pool'), Morden (hill in marshy ground from A.S. *mor*, 'moor or marshy ground' and A.S. *dun*, 'down' or 'hill'), Studland ('a tract of land where a herd of horses is kept' from A.S. *stod* and *land*), Rempstone (probably the farm where wild garlic grows from A.S. *hramsa* and *tun*), Ower (A.S. *ora*, 'bank or shore') and Goathorn (Gotowre) in 1286, probably the bank or shore where goats are kept, from A.S. *gat*, goat – all these are thoroughly Saxon names – an indication of the very substantial Saxon occupation of the Poole area which, because of the poor or heavy nature of the soil, had hitherto attracted little settlement. Some place-names provide a clue to the name of the original settler or to a later owner. Canford probably means 'the ford of a man called Cana', Bloxworth, 'the *worth* (A.S. for enclosure or farm) belonging to a man named Blocc', and Brownsea (formerly Branksea) Island, probably Brunoc's island, Bere Regis means what Thomas Hardy called it King's Bere (Anglo-Saxon *bearu* 'wood', Latin *regis* 'of the king'), for there was formerly a royal forest here. Sturminster Marshall (Sturminstre, 1086) is derived from *mynster* (A.S. 'monastery church' or 'missionary church') on the Stour. The addition of Marshall is a reminder that the manor was held in the early 13th century by William Marshall, Earl of Pembroke. Charlton Marshall, Charlton meaning 'the *tun* or village of the peasants' from A.S. *ceorl* (peasant), presumably also obtained its additional name from the Marshall family. Nearby Tarrant Keynston was the *tun* (or estate) on the river Tarrant held by the Cahaignes or Keynes family in the 12th, 13th and 14th centuries. Kingston Lacy was the *tun* (or estate) of the king (from Saxon times) which was granted in 1230 to John de Lacy, Earl of Lincoln. The second part of Lytchett Matravers refers to the Norman-French Maltravers family which held the estate from the Norman Conquest for some three centuries. It is always wise in tracing the derivation of a place-name to study earlier forms of it. Kinson, for example, was Kyneston in 1431, Kinstanton in 1407 and Chinestanestone in 1086, so that it has lost two or three syllables over the centuries, thus concealing its original meaning, the *tun* (or farm) of a Saxon landowner named Cynestan. Likewise Hengistbury is not what it seems for, though it is featured as Hengestbury Head on Speed's 1610 map, it was Hensbury in 1540 and Hedensburia in the 12th century and so it may be a fortified place (A.S. *burh*) associated with a man named Heddin. At a much later stage when it was known that Hengest was the Jutish leader who conquered Kent in the fifth century and that the Jutes also conquered the Isle of Wight, the proximity of the Isle of Wight to Hengistbury seems to have taken the Germanic conqueror of Kent on a quite unauthenticated voyage along the Channel to the mouth of the Stour. In 1949 a group of Danish enthusiasts commemorated the 1500th anniversary of Hengist's arrival in Kent by sailing across the North Sea to Kent in a replica of a Viking ship not dissimilar to the vessel in which the Angles, Saxons and Jutes came to Britain. This ship was then sailed and rowed along the south coast to Poole Harbour, where it spent some weeks undergoing an overhaul at Poole. Christchurch, of course, takes its name from the priory church, but it was originally Twynham or Tweoxneam in the 10th century, meaning '(the place) betwixt the streams' from A.S. *betweaxn* and *earn* (dative plural of *ea*, river), i.e. between the rivers Stour and Avon. Some earlier forms of place-names may be much briefer than their modern equivalents. Hampreston and Hamworthy were both known just as Hamme in 1204 and 1236 respectively. The meaning (from Anglo-Saxon *hamm*), would seem to be 'the enclosure' or 'river-meadow', a very appropriate description of Hampreston alongside the river Stour. Meadows adjacent to water would be a similarly apt description for Hamworthy. The fuller name, Hamworthy, is first recorded in 1463, worthy from A.S. *worthig* meaning 'enclosure', but in very modern times the inhabitants of the Hamworthy peninsula have often called it just 'Ham'. The full name Hampreston was mentioned in 1244 and 1299, the additional Preston meaning 'priest-farm' from A.S. *preost* and *tun*, probably a reference to the fact that lands there belonged to the college of Wimborne Minster. Sometimes Hamworthy was called South Ham to distinguish it from Hampreston, North Ham. Often a place-name very accurately describes a location. Corfe, for example, comes from A.S. *corf*, 'a cutting, gap or pass'; Corfe Castle is situated in a very important gap in the Purbeck Hills, and Corfe Mullen denoted the original situation of the village between two hills or the pass between the Corfe Hills and the Stour, or, even more likely, the gap in the belt of woodland. The additional Mullen from the

French *moulin* refers to the very valuable mill on the Stour here, recorded in Domesday Book as yielding a revenue of 20 shillings a year.

However many bands of blond Saxons, perhaps under such leaders as Cana, Cynestan and Blocc, were moving into south-east Dorset in the late seventh century, the majority of Dorset's inhabitants would have been Britons or, as their new Saxon masters called them, Welsh or *wealh*, that is foreigners who did not speak the Old English language. Proof of this is contained in Laws 23, 24, 32 and 33 promulgated about A.D. 690 by King Ine of Wessex, and referring to Welshmen of various ranks. This seems to indicate that whole Welsh communities, including gentry, had been more or less peacefully absorbed into the West Saxon state. Thus Law 23 stated that 'The *wergild* [that is the compensation to be paid if a person is killed] of a Welsh taxpayer is 120/-; of his son, 100/-' and Law 24 said that 'the *wergild* of a Welshman who holds five hides of land shall be 600/-'. The holder of an estate of five hides would rank as a thegn or minor nobleman and so it would appear that Welsh aristocrats were allowed to keep their higher social status, but it is interesting to note that the *wergild* of Saxons of corresponding rank would have been twice that of the Welshman. So the Saxon holding five hides of land had a *wergild* of 1,200 shillings, not 600 shillings, and throughout a Saxon seems to have been rated at twice the amount of a Welshman. Thus Welsh landowners in, say, Wareham, Lytchett or Crichel were treated as second-class citizens, though due regard was paid to men of high rate rank and substantial property.

It was not until 634 that Christianity was brought to Wessex and so some of the earlier settlers in south-east Dorset may well have been pagans, worshipping the old Germanic gods, Tiw, Woden, Thunor and Frey, after whom four of the days were named. King Ine in his laws tried hard to enforce baptism and respect for the Sabbath. Thus Law 2 stated 'A child shall be baptised within 30 days. If this is not not done [the guardian] shall pay 30 shillings as compensation', and Law 3 declared: 'If a slave works on a Sunday by his Lord's command he shall become free and the lord shall pay a fine of 30 shillings. If, however, a slave works [on a Sunday] without his master's knowledge, he shall undergo the lash or pay a fine'.

King Ine's right-hand man in spreading Christianity to Dorset was his kinsman, St Aldhelm, whom in 705 he made bishop of the newly-conquered Celtic and pagan region of Dorset, West Somerset and east Devon. Aldhelm made Sherborne the centre of his diocese. Already Aldhelm had come into the Poole area, when about A.D. 700 he went on a pilgrimage to Rome and set sail from Wareham, then the chief port of the area. Indeed, whilst he was held up by rough weather at Wareham he built a church, which could well have been on the site of St Martin's, which, although its architecture is mainly Norman, contains several Saxon features. At this time Aldhelm would have been over sixty and was described as white-haired but agile with 'keen eyes, red cheeks, excellent hearing and wonderful hands', and he could well have visited some of the settlements to the north of Poole Harbour, bringing the teachings of Jesus to the pagans, but telling the Celtic Christians that they must accept the leadership of the Pope (the bishop of Rome) and observe Roman regulations, such as a different method of calculating the date of Easter. Doubtless he won over his audience by music on his lute and by posing some of his riddles, of which he left behind him a collection of 104, of which the following provides some insight into contemporary conditions by referring to things that would have been familiar in Dorset in 700. The following are some examples:

> Of willow-wood and tough bull-hide am I,
> And I can stand the sharpest knocks of war,
> With my own frame I guard my master's trunk,
> Protecting him from death. Who like myself

> Has felt so oft the deadly blows of war
> And known as many wounds, a soldier bold?

The answer was a shield.

> Of furrowed body and blue steel am I,
> By rubbing I the formless metal shape,
> Gold I can polish and make rough things smooth;
> I have no voice, yet can I chatter well,
> And with hoarse screeching make a hideous din.

The answer was a file.

> We are twin sisters sharing a common lot,
> Who by our labours furnish food for all,
> Equal our toil, unequal is our task,
> One sister runs, the other never moves,
> And yet we feel no envy, each for each.
> We chew our food but never swallow it,
> We break it up and give it freely back.

The answer was a pair of mill-stones, very familiar to the Saxon villagers of Corfe Mullen, Canford, Kinson and Witchampton.

> Once I was water, full of scaly fish,
> My nature changed, by changed decree of fate,
> I suffered torments torrid by the flames,
> My face now shines like whitest ash or snow.

The answer was salt, made by the evaporation of sea-water as took place at Studland, where 32 salt-houses were recorded in Domesday Book (1086).

In 705 Bishop Aldhelm granted liberty of election to all congregations under his control and expressly to the monastery seated by the river called Wimburnia over which Cuthburga presided. Cuthburga, sister of King Ine, had been married to King Ealdfrith of Northumbria but, having no liking for the married state, she obtained a separation to enable her to train as a nun, after which she founded at Wimborne a 'double monastery' consisting of two sections, 'one for men and the other for women, both surrounded by strong and high walls', wrote Rudolf of Fulda in his life of St Lioba, one of the Wimborne nuns who later spent her life in missionary work in Germany. From the beginning of the foundation the rule firmly laid down was that '. . . no woman was allowed to go into the men's community, nor was any man permitted to enter the women's; apart from priests who used to enter the churches solely to celebrate Mass; even so, when the service was concluded the priest must withdraw . . . The mother superior of the community spoke through a window when it was necessary to send for something outside and to conduct the business of the convent'. Rudolf added that any woman who wished to renounce the world and to join the community did so on the understanding that she would never leave it, unless in the opinion of the abbess there was a very good reason or some great advantage could thereby accrue to the monastery. In fact under the first abbess, St Cuthburga and her successor and sister, Cwenburga, it was decided that great good could come from selected nuns leaving Wimborne after special training to go across to Germany to help the English St Boniface to convert to Christianity the Old Saxons living there, who spoke virtually the same language as West Saxon. St Lioba (700-780) was one of these Wimborne missionaries and she herself became abbess of Bishopsheim and a close friend of Hildegarde, the wife of the Emperor Charlemagne. Other such Wimborne missionaries who went to Germany were St Agatha and St Walburga, on the eve of whose feast-day (1 May), Walpurgis night, witches were said to ride on broomsticks, and he-goats to cavort with the Devil.

Aldhelm may well have visited the Wimborne monastery. Somewhere, however, Aldhelm saw some nuns, who shocked him by their interest in their coiffure and in colourful dress, for in a treatise 'On Virginity', which he dedicated to the Abbess of Barking under whom St Cuthburga trained, Aldhelm explained that, whereas a married woman was busy plaiting her hair or tinting her cheeks with rouge, a virgin preferred to let her hair be unkempt and her locks unbrushed. Yet, he wrote in horror, he had actually seen nuns wearing purple under-clothes, red tunics with long sleeves trimmed with silk stripes, and shoes of red leather. Their hair was elegantly curled with irons, he said: 'they wore, instead of a black veil, a coloured and white head-dress with ribbons attached passing round the hair and hanging down to their ankles, whilst their nails were pared to a point like the claws of a falcon'. It is unlikely that such worldliness prevailed among the nuns at Wimborne, at any rate when princess Tetta, another sister of St Cuthburga, was abbess, for she would never allow her nuns to approach priests nor permit any male, even a bishop, to set foot inside the women's section. Under Tetta there were said to be 500 nuns at Wimborne. One nun who acted as prioress was such a fanatical disciplinarian that she was loathed, especially by the young nuns, so much so, wrote Rudolf of Fulda, that when she died and was buried, the young nuns climbed on to her grave and cursed her for her cruelty. Abbess Tetta then noticed that the earth heaped over the corpse had subsided and lay about six inches below the surface of the surrounding ground (perhaps because the young nuns had jumped up and down in delight on the grave!). Tetta, however, thought that the subsidence was a sign of divine wrath, and urged the young nuns to let bygones be bygones, reminding them that Christians should love their enemies and ordered the nuns to fast for three days and to pray for the soul of the bullying prioress. Then, as the abbess was praying, the hole on top of the grave began to fill up and the grave became level with the surface of the ground, a sign, it was believed, that Tetta's prayers had helped to secure the forgiveness of the sins of the old nun who had made the lives of the novices such a misery.

About the same time that the Wimborne 'double monastery' was established, a priory for nuns was founded at Wareham, and a monastery for Secular Canons of the Holy Trinity was set up at Christchurch, with nine separate chapels or cells – perhaps an indication of the Celtic influence. From the eighth century until the Norman Conquest the three major towns in the area, though small by later standards, were Wareham, Wimborne and Christchurch and in all three the presence of monasteries will have encouraged the growth of trade in the adjacent area. The *Anglo-Saxon Chronicle* recorded that Beorhtric, King of Wessex (786-802) was buried at Wareham, perhaps an indication of its growing importance, and that 'in his days first came three ships of Northmen from the land of robbers' – a reference to a Viking visitation at Radipole – and 'These were the first ships of the Danish men that sought the land of the English Nation'. During the next three generations the Viking coastal raids developed into full-scale campaigns of conquest and during one of these, as the *Anglo-Saxon Chronicle* related under the year 871: 'King Ethelred [I] and Alfred, his brother, fought with the [Danish] army at Marden [identified with Martin, in Wiltshire, near the Dorset border at Bokerly Dyke] . . . enjoying the victory for some time during the day, and there was much slaughter on either hand; but the Danes became masters of the field; and there were slain Bishop Heahmund (of Sherborne) with many other good men . . . And after Easter of this year King Ethelred died . . . and his body lies at Wimburn – minster. Then Alfred, his brother . . . took to the Kingdom of Wessex'. The probability is that Ethelred was mortally wounded at the battle of Martin and that Alfred withdrew with him towards the royal residence of Kingston near Badbury Rings, recently identified by David Smith, the Kingston Lacy estate warden. Strong tradition associates Ethelred I with Witchampton. Either he died there or his bier rested there on the way to Wimborne Minster, where his body was buried. A 15th-century brass in the Minster recorded Ethelred's death and burial. Thus it was almost certainly in Wimborne Minster that Alfred the Great was proclaimed King of Wessex. In 876 a Viking fleet moved into Poole Harbour and the Danish 'army moved into Wareham, a fort of the West Saxons . . . The King made peace with them and they gave him hostages . . . and swore with oaths on the holy bracelet . . . that they would withdraw from his Kingdom'. In fact the next year the Danes moved westwards to Exeter and their 'fleet sailed west about until they encountered a great storm at sea and there perished 120 ships at Swanage'. Despite this setback the Danes overran much of Wessex, including Dorset, but in 878, when the struggle against the invaders seemed lost, Alfred counter-attacked, defeated Guthrum, the Danish leader, and prevailed upon him to embrace Christianity and to withdraw to the north-eastern half of England.

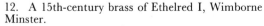

12. A 15th-century brass of Ethelred I, Wimborne Minster.

13. *The Hugin*, the Viking ship replica with steerboard, in Poole for overhaul in 1949.

Alfred then embarked upon a programme of post-war reconstruction. He built up a navy, modelled on that of the Danes, reorganised the army, rebuilt churches destroyed by the Vikings and ordered that certain towns be designated as *burhs* and fortified with earthworks and ditches. Wareham was one of these *burhs* and the 'Walls' were the result of this

strengthening of its defence. Alfred's grandson, King Athelstan, was to confirm the importance of Wareham in this area by giving it the right to coin money. One such silver penny
struck by a Wareham moneyer included the inscription 'Verham'. Alfred also revised the
code of laws, particularly to deal with crimes of violence which had doubtless multiplied
during the period of the Danish invasion. Thus, if a couple of Canford men had a quarrel
and came to blows and a front tooth was knocked out, a fine of 8s. would be imposed, 15s.
if a canine tooth was dislodged. Breaking a man's chin-bone in two attracted a fine of 12
shillings. If knives or daggers were drawn, and injuries were sustained, an elaborate tariff
of fines would apply, of which the following are examples; wounding in the stomach, 30s.;
cutting off a thumb, 30s.; a middle finger, 12s.; little finger, 9s.

On the death of Alfred in 899, the Witanagemot, the council of nobles and bishops, met
to decide, as was the customary rule regarding the succession, which member of the royal
family was best fitted to become king. Alfred's son, Edward, was chosen. Edward's cousin,
Prince Ethelwald, son of King Ethelred I, probably disgruntled because Alfred had left
him only three estates in his will, decided to make a bid for the throne, as the *Anglo-Saxon
Chronicle* related:

> Prince Ethelwald ... seized the residences at Wimborne and Twynham (Christchurch) without
> permission of the King and his councillors. Then the King rode with the army until he encamped
> at Badbury, and Ethelwald stayed inside the residence with the men who had submitted to him and
> he had all the gates barricaded against him, and said he would either there live or there die. Then
> in the meantime he slipped away during the night and came to the Danish army in Northumbria.
> The King gave orders to ride after him, but he could not be overtaken. Then they pursued and
> captured the wife whom Ethelwald had taken without the King's permission and against the orders
> of the bishops, for she had previously been consecrated a nun.

Evidently Ethelwald had hoped that, if he attempted his coup d'état in the area of Wimborne
where his respected father was buried, he might win popular support, but abducting a nun
(possibly from the Wimborne convent) was expressly forbidden by Alfred's law and should
have involved him in a fine of 120 shillings. It is easy to see why the bishops passed over
this anti-clerical prince and had no sympathy with the young lovers. Incidentally the
residence at Wimborne where Ethelwald threatened to hold out could almost certainly
have been the royal hall at Kingston where the ramparts and ditches can still be seen.
Ethelwald was killed four years later fighting on the side of the Danes, whom he had
persuaded to go to war with King Edward. After intermittent war over the next half-century,
the West Saxon kings conquered the Danelaw, the north-eastern half of the country where
the Danes had settled and ruled. The entry in the *Anglo-Saxon Chronicle* for the year 961,
'King Sifferth killed himself, and his body lies at Wimborne' perhaps refers to a Danish
leader, who could not stand being a prisoner and therefore committed suicide.

Under King Edgar (959-975) the whole of England was united but, after his death, the
nation was shocked when his son and successor, young Edward (later called the Martyr),
after a day's hunting and whilst he was drinking a goblet of wine, was stabbed to death by
one of the retainers of his step-mother, Elfthryth or Elfrida, at a hunting lodge at Corfe
where the castle now stands. And the *Anglo-Saxon Chronicle* commented

> ... This year [978] was King Edward slain, at eventide, at Corfe-gate on the fifteenth day before
> the calends of April [18 March] And he was buried at Wareham without royal honour. No worse
> deed was ever done by the English nation since they first sought the land of Britain.

The murder of Edward led to the enthronement of his half-brother, Elfthryth's son,
Ethelred II the Unready (that is, without council). It was during his reign (978-1016) that
England had to face another wave of Danish invasions for which Ethelred's only remedy
was to try to buy off the Danes by paying them Danegeld, large sums of silver pennies, to
stay away, although like most blackmailers they came back again for more and more, so

that the *Anglo-Saxon Chronicle* recorded: 'A.D. 998 This year coasted the [Danish] army back eastwards [into Poole harbour] to the mouth of the Frome and went up everywhere as widely as they pleased, into Dorset' and again, 'A.D. 1015 . . . King Knut [the Danish leader] . . . went into Wessex until he came to the mouth of the Frome, and then plundered in Dorset, in Wiltshire and in Somerset'. In a life of St Ethelwold it was stated that 'Canute having spoiled the church and monastery of Cerne took himself to the port of the Frome's mouth [Wareham] and sailed thence to Brunkesy, that is, to Brunk's island' – the earliest reference to Brownsea Island.

It is likely that Knut, then a pagan, in this 1015 raid destroyed the monastery at Wimborne as well as Canford Church and St Martin's, Wareham. In 1016 both the ineffective Ethelred II and his capable and energetic son and successor, Edmund Ironside, died, and Knut was left in control of England. Turning Christian, Knut speedily restored order and pursued a policy of rebuilding the churches. Examples of Saxon architecture in the Poole area probably date from the half-century 1016-66. These include the stair turret on the west side of the north transept at Wimborne Minster, and the chancel of Canford Magna church, including a round-headed opening into the former south chapel. The nave, round chancel arch and chancel, some narrow windows and external typical Saxon 'long and short' work on the south-east corner of the nave at St Martin's, Wareham, have in the past been judged to be Saxon, but recently some authorities prefer to date it to about 1080.

When the deeply religious King Edward the Confessor, of the restored West Saxon royal family, died in January 1066, the Council elected as king Edward's brother-in-law and chief adviser and general, Harold II, whose mother, Gytha, was a cousin of King Knut and whose father, Godwin, may have been a descendant of that Ethelred I buried in Wimborne Minster. The choice was at once challenged by Edward's cousin, William, duke of Normandy, who with an army of land-hungry adventurers from Normandy and other parts of France invaded England, defeated and killed Harold II at Hastings (October 1066) and cowed the Council into accepting him as king, though it took another five years to bring England completely under his control.

The Normans were French-speaking descendants of Vikings from Norway, who were skilful exponents of the arts of war, ardent upholders of the Pope, and energetic builders in stone. Before the Norman Conquest most buildings were of timber (the Anglo-Saxon word *getimbran* means 'to build') and the dwellings of the common people long continued to be wooden, but stone was increasingly used in the construction of churches and fortresses. Just across Poole Harbour at Studland and Worth Matravers both dedicated to St Nicholas, and mainly built about 1080-1150, are two almost perfect, unaltered examples of the typical Norman village church. The massively thick stone walls, the small round-topped windows set high above the ground level, are a reminder that at that time the church was not only the place of worship but also a place of refuge in times of trouble for the whole village population. Worth Matravers, Steeple and Hinton Parva churches all have Norman round chancel arches ornamented with the characteristic Norman zig-zag or chevron design. At Canford the original Saxon church, now the chancel, was enlarged in the Norman period with the addition of most of the present nave with the massive round Norman pillars and round arches and the north and south aisles incorporating round-headed Norman windows and round-topped Norman north and south doorways. In Hinton Parva church (north of Wimborne), though rebuilt in 1860, there is a restored Norman round chancel arch and reset over the southern doorway a carved stone panel showing an angel with book and cross, probably 12th century. Norman fonts survive in the parish churches of Almer, Studland, Shapwick, West Parley and Lady St Mary, Wareham. The font at St Mary's, Wareham, is of lead and hexagonal and on each of the six sides are two bays of arcading with round

14. A Saxon window, Canford church.

15. Column of about A.D. 1200 by the north door, Canford church.

16. Canford church with its four-stage Norman tower.

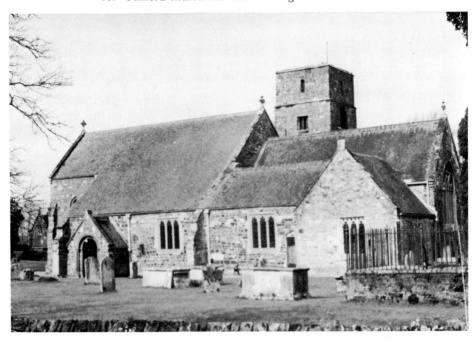

arches, under each of which is a figure with a halo, holding a book. The figures are presumed to represent the 12 apostles and one with a key is clearly identifiable as St Peter.

The Purbeck marble font of Wimborne Minster is probably late Norman and indeed Norman architecture is exemplified on a grand scale in the minster both by the central tower (*c.*1120) with its four stages, its massive piers, round-headed arches and, on the top stage on each external face, a wall-arcade of seven bays with interlacing semi-circular moulded arches; and by the nave with its typically round columns with plain capitals and bases supporting slightly pointed arches whose chevron decoration shows them to be Norman, too, although the combination of pointed arches with zig-zag ornamentation is most unusual. The earliest style of Gothic architecture, the Early English, is represented by the east windows (*c.*1230), consisting of three separate graduated lancets with a quatrefoil over the middle light and with sexfoil openings over the side lights. The crypt beneath the chancel also has pointed

17. Wimborne Minster, Saxon stair turret and Norman square tower.

arches of the 14th century. The central tower at one time supported a magnificent spire said to have rivalled that of Salisbury Cathedral, but, despite repairs carried out in 1547, it suddenly collapsed during a service in 1602 and miraculously, though the streets were full of people, no one was injured. The western tower had been added in 1464 as the central tower was thought not to be strong enough to carry a peal of bells, and its Perpendicular style with slightly pointed arches contrasts sharply with the rest of the building.

After the Danes destroyed the Wimborne nunnery it was replaced in 1043 by Edward the Confessor with a College of Secular Canons, consisting of a dean, four prebends, four vicars, four deacons and five singers. These non-monastic clerics did not stay within the precincts of the Minster, but went out and ministered to the needs of the surrounding district. For the next five centuries the minster was the church of these secular canons. Some ten miles to the east at Twynham (or Christchurch) there was another college of secular canons and the extortionate Ranulf Flambard, right-hand man of William II (1087-1100), was made its dean. He pulled down its little Saxon church and began to construct a much larger building in the Norman style with many similarities to Durham Cathedral with the building of which Flambard was involved when he was bishop of Durham. In 1150 Flambard's church became the church of the priory of black-robed Augustinian Canons, who used the Norman nave with its imposing round arches as a parish church for the people of Christchurch and appointed one of their priests as vicar, whilst they used the choir as their own church. A quite unique example of Norman architecture is the stair turret with its richly decorated wall arcading on the exterior of the eastern angle of the north transept. Later in the Middle Ages the roof of the priory was raised and in the 15th century impressive additions were made in the Perpendicular style, in the choir and the western tower.

The Normans were energetic builders in stone not only of churches but also of castles to replace the timber defences usual at the time of the Conquest and for many years afterwards. Christchurch, recognised as a *burh* at least since the early 10th century, was granted by Henry I (1100-35) to Baldwin de Redvers whose descendants were earls of Devon for the next 200 years. They raised a large artificial mound or motte on which was constructed within a wooden palisade a timber fort, which in turn was restored by 1300 with a square stone keep with walls 10 feet thick, the ruins of which still survive. Nearby already a much more comfortable stone hall (the so-called Constable's House) was constructed beside the mill stream. This is now roofless but is a rare example of Norman domestic architecture

18. Norman arcading on the exterior of the north transept, Christchurch Priory.

19. Norman architecture: Christchurch, the 'Constable's House', with a glimpse of the castle keep.

complete with rounded-headed windows and doorways and, to serve the upper floor, a large fireplace and chimney.

At Wareham alongside the river Frome in the grounds of Castle House excavations in 1950 by H. J. S. Clark brought to light the massive foundations of the square keep with walls over twelve feet thick enclosing an area 37 feet square, constructed it would seem in the early 12th century. Sadly only the foundations of Wareham Castle remain today. To the south of Wareham to control the gap in the Purbecks the structures on the isolated hill, where Edward the Martyr was slain, were replaced about 1080 by a new 'ring and bailey' castle. The 'Old Hall' some 58 feet by 34 feet, built of Purbeck stone in 'herringbone' design, and the inner ward wall are surviving features of this. To this was added about 1105 the square keep (a 'King's Tower'), the most dominating feature of Corfe Castle even in its present ruined state. Round-headed doorways and windows indicate its Norman origin. Within a few years stout stone walls enclosed the area of the Keep, the 'Old Hall' and the adjacent area, the south-west 'Bailey' – strong enough to keep Henry I's rebellious elder brother, Robert, Duke of Normandy, securely incarcerated here after his defeat at Tinchebrai (1106). He would have been equally secure inside Wareham Castle, where, according to another authority, he was imprisoned.

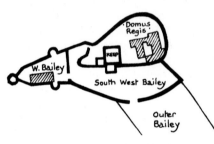

20. Plan of Corfe Castle.

The Norman Conquest, in addition to the stimulus it gave to the building in stone of churches and castles, also established a new military aristocracy, speaking Norman-French. Latin, then an effective international language, was used for administrative purposes, whilst Anglo-Saxon, which had been widely employed in the business of government, continued as the speech of the peasantry, who ploughed the land with the oxen, harvested the crops and cared for the beasts in the fields – the cows, the sheep and the swine (all English words!), but the Norman lords controlled government, justice and war and expected what was served at table to be identified as beef, mutton or pork (all French words). The evidence contained in Domesday Book, the survey of all the estates or manors conducted by William the Conqueror in 1086, shows very clearly that virtually every Anglo-Saxon lord in the Poole area in 1066 had by 1086 been replaced by a Norman. Any Saxon lord, who had supported Harold II at Hastings or who had not unequivocally accepted William in the next few years, forfeited his lands, which were bestowed by the Conqueror on those Norman-French followers who had helped him gain control of the English realm. Two of the new Norman land-owning families in south-east Dorset continued to hold these lands for several generations. Hugh de Maltravers acquired the manor of Upper Lytchett after the Conquest and his descendants still held it two centuries later. Another Norman, Walter de Claville, secured five estates, among them Morden and, in the Isle of Purbeck, Afflington and (Church) Knowle. The Saxon lord of the latter before 1066 was Beorn and he gave his name to Barnston (Beorn's farm) in Knowle, where the manor-house retains much 12th-century masonry. The Claville (later Clavell) family continued to hold lands in the Purbecks. John Clavell in 1427 succeeded to the estate of Barnston and Smedmore and although his descendant, George Clavell of Smedmore, died in 1774, leaving no children, his sister's descendant, Major John Clavell Mansel, still owns Smedmore and has been very active maintaining the house and opening it to the public. One very small estate – one of six manors in Wimborne St Giles – was held by one of the king's thanes with the very Saxon name of Wulfgeat and he held it before 1066. Again another small estate in Morden – one of five manors there – was held by Wulfric in 1086 and Domesday Book tells us that his father held it before 1066. So clearly these two Saxon thanes, Wulfgeat and Wulfric, had switched their loyalty to William immediately after the Conquest and had been allowed to keep their land. Godwin the huntsman, who held Walford on the north side of Wimborne in 1086, was another Saxon who had speedily sworn allegiance to William and was able to take over Walford, whose lord before 1066, Almar, had died or been dispossessed. Godwin the huntsman held another small Dorset estate which had been held by his father before the Conquest. We shall never know which of the Saxon thanes, who no longer retained their family estates in 1086, were killed at Hastings or had been dispossessed because they fought there or continued to resist afterwards, but by 1086 the vast majority of those who held estates in south-east Dorset were Normans.

Apart from this transfer to French-speaking lords, who may well have been more harsh and less considerate to their Saxon peasants, the way of life in the countryside continued very much as before, despite the Norman take-over. Already in the later Saxon period there had been established the system known as feudalism by which manors and estates were held in return for military service – and from time to time taxes – to the king, whilst on each estate the mainly unfree peasantry, who were tied to the manor, provided agricultural labour for the lord and rendered to him various other services and payments in return for his protection. The hard lot of the average peasant had been indicated in the Colloquy written by Aelfric the Saxon schoolmaster abbot at Cerne Abbey some two generations before the battle of Hastings, in which the ploughman explained woefully, 'I am not free' and so 'I have to work far too hard; I go out at dawn, driving the oxen to the field and yoke them to the plough and I dare not in the most severe weather lie hid at home for fear of my lord'.

Domesday Book, from which we derive so much of our knowledge of the country after the Norman take-over, was the product of an extraordinarily detailed and well-organised survey carried out in 1086 to determine and put on record who held each estate and who held it before the Conquest and what was its value in 1086 and 1066. Then commissioners were sent into areas 'which they did not know and where they themselves were not known in order to check the first survey', wrote the contemporary bishop of Hereford, so that concealment or falsification would have been difficult. William I wished to have detailed information about the resources of his new realm, an accurate list of all land-holders and a precise account of the assets of each estate (or manor) as a basis for any reassessment of liability to pay tax (geld) which he might wish to make. The *Anglo-Saxon Chronicle* noted that 'not a single hide or yardland (a quarter of a hide), nor indeed – shame to tell . . . – an ox nor a cow nor a pig was left out and not entered in his (the king's) record. The so-called Exeter version of Domesday Book contains fuller entries for some manors in Dorset, giving details of th animals on each estate, such as were collected in the original survey.

The following are extracts from Domesday Book as translated in Phillimore's *Domesday Book: Dorset* (1983). *Villani*, traditionally rendered as 'villeins', unfree peasants normally holding 30 acres of arable each with right of inheritance in return for three days' labour each week on the lord's land, are translated as 'villagers'. The lesser peasants with smaller holdings in return for probably one day's labour a week, *bordars*, *cotsets* and *cottars*, are rendered as 'smallholders' and 'cottagers' respectively.

Edward of Salisbury [Sheriff of Wiltshire – a Norman, despite his English name] holds CANFORD [Magna] from the King. Wulfwen [a Saxon lady] held it before 1066. It paid tax for 25 hides. Land for 18 ploughs [i.e. 2,160 acres of arable, i.e. 8 times 120 acres], of which 11½ hides are in lordship; 3 ploughs there; 9 slaves; 35 villagers and 40 smallholders with 15 ploughs.
2 mills which pay 15s; meadow, 118 acres; pasture 2 leagues [3 miles] in both length and width; woodland 1 league long and ½ league wide.
At Wimborne (Minster) 3 smallholders and a house belong to this manor; water-meadow, 1 league there.

21. Domesday Book entries for Canford and Kinson.

Edward also holds KINSON. Wulfwen held it before 1066. It paid tax for 13 hides. Land for 9 ploughs [i.e. 1,080 acres of arable], of which 5 hides and 1 virgate of land are in lordship; 2 ploughs there; 7 slaves;
18 villagers, 14 Cottagers and 4 cottagers with 7 ploughs.
A mill which pays 5s; woodland, 1 acre; meadow, 100 acres, less 5; pasture 3 leagues long and 2 leagues wide, less 3 furlongs.
Value of these two manors when he acquired them £50; now £70.

There is no mention of any port or even a fishing hamlet on the peninsula where the town of Poole was to grow up and no hint of any salt-pans here or at Hamworthy, but the Wiltshire section of Domesday does mention that 'Nobody has rendered an account of one manor [of Woodchester], held by Edward of Salisbury' to the King's Commissioners. Thus Edward of Salisbury (lord of Canford) was trying to conceal the existence of this Wiltshire estate, but this attempt at tax evasion failed, since its value was declared to be £7.

The manor of Canford was one of the most extensive as well as one of the most valuable in all Dorset. It probably included approximately the whole area of the present borough of Poole, that is the modern parishes of Canford Magna, Canford Parva, Parkstone, Longfleet, Poole and Hamworthy. On the basis of the proportion of hides and population in Canford and Kinson, Canford would seem to have been valued at about £46 out of the £70 quoted as the value of the two manors together. Clearly the two manors had over two hundred acres of meadow alongside the Stour, 3,240 acres of arable, a great belt of woodland, and a vast area of heathland, used as rough pasture extending from three to four and a half miles southwards to the sea. Scholars are unsure what exactly was the status of the 'cotsets' (cottage dwellers), of whom 14 were said to live in the manor of Kinson. Since there are no bordars (smallholders) mentioned among the Kinson inhabitants, probably they were much the same as the bordars. Indeed a 10th- or 11th-century document said that cotsets had five acres of their own land each and were expected to work each Monday for the lord and three days a week at harvest time. It is generally believed that the *servi* (slaves) were enumerated as individuals, whereas the number of villagers, smallholders and cottagers referred to peasant households. If a household was reckoned on average to consist of five people, then the population of the manor of Canford would have been nearly 400 and that of Kinson about 190, by comparison with about 140 at Lytchett Matravers, 125 at Corfe Mullen and just 15 to 20 at Walford. After the royal manors of Puddletown (with 1,600 sheep) and Portland (with 900 sheep) valued at £73 and £65 respectively, Sturminster Marshall ranked next at £55 and Canford possibly fourth at £46. The Domesday accounts of some of these estates in the Poole area were as follows:

Roger [of Beaumont, one of the leading Norman landholders] also holds
STURMINSTER (Marshall). Archbishop Stigand [friend of Harold II] held it before 1066. It paid tax for 30 hides. Land for 25 ploughs [3,000 acres of arable], of which 12½ hides are in lordship; 3 ploughs there; 8 slaves;
64 villagers and 26 smallholders with 15 ploughs.
2 mills which pay 28s; meadow, 124 acres; pasture 3 leagues long and 1½ leagues wide; woodland 1 league long and ½ league wide.
Value when he acquired it, £66; now £55.

Hugh [de Maltravers] also holds LYTCHETT (Matravers) from William [Count of Eu, who later rebelled against William Rufus and was blinded and mutilated as a punishment]. Toli [a Saxon] held it before 1066. It paid tax for 12 hides. Land for 8 ploughs [960 acres of arable] . . . 3 slaves;
16 villagers and 11 Cottagers with 5 ploughs.
Meadow, 40 acres; pasture, 11 furlongs; woodland ½ league in both length and width; water-meadow(?), 1 league in length and width; in Wareham 2 gardens and 1 smallholder.
The value was £9, now £10.

Robert son of Gerald holds CORFE [Mullen] from the King. Wada and Aethelric [two Saxons] held it before 1066. It paid tax for 10 hides. Land for 10 ploughs [1,200 acres of arable] . . . 4 slaves;
12 villagers and 12 smallholders with 5 ploughs.
A mill which pays 20s; meadow, 102 acres; pasture 2 leagues in length and width; woodland 2 leagues long and 1 league wide. The value was and is £15.

Godwin Hunter holds WALFORD. Aelmer held it before 1066. It paid tax for 1 hide. Land for 1 plough [120 acres of arable], which is there, with
3 smallholders.
Meadow, 7 acres; pasture 5 furlongs long and 2 furlongs wide; woodland, 1 furlong.
Value 15s [i.e. one-tenth the value of Corfe Mullen].

One large grouping of royal manors described as Wimborne Minster, Shapwick, Crichel and Up Wimborne All Saints, rendered to the king one night's revenue, which originally meant providing the food needed to support the king and his whole household for one night, equivalent after 1066 to about £100. Of these four manors the king had 63 villagers, 68 smallholders, seven cottagers, 15 slaves and, according to the Exeter Domesday which gives details of the stock, three pack-horses, 30 pigs, 250 sheep and 44 goats. The manor of Stollant (Studland), held by Hamo from Robert, Count of Mortain, half-brother of King William, who also held 70 other Dorset manors from the king, was valued at £8, of which 40 shillings was yielded by 32 salt-houses.

Chapter Three

The Early Lords of Canford Manor and the Emergence of Poole

The borough of Poole grew up on a peninsula on the southern shore of the very large manor of Canford Magna, held in 1086 at the time of the Domesday survey by Edward of Salisbury. Before the Norman Conquest Canford and the adjacent manor of Kinson had been held by a Saxon lady, Wulfwen (Ulwen), who obviously supported King Harold II when William of Normandy invaded England in 1066, for both her manors were confiscated and handed over, presumably to one of William's Norman companions, Walter of Evreux, whose son, Edward of Salisbury, later inherited them. This Edward, probably named after King Edward the Confessor, was reputed to have been born in England. So perhaps his father was one of those Normans already living in England and paving the way for the Norman take-over before 1066. Edward of Salisbury held vast estates outside Dorset and was Sheriff of Wiltshire, where he held 38 manors. Edward's son Walter of Salisbury inherited Canford and founded a priory at Bradenstoke in Wiltshire to which he retired after his wife's death. The church of Canford and the chapel of St James, Poole, were later given to Bradenstoke Priory. Walter's son Patrick was a staunch supporter of the Empress Matilda, the only surviving child of King Henry I, to whom he bequeathed the English throne, and who led the rebellion against her cousin, Stephen, whom a majority of the English barons proclaimed king in 1135. William de Cahaignes, one of Matilda's supporters and lord of Tarrant Keynston and several other Dorset manors, took King Stephen prisoner at the battle of Lincoln (1141). Patrick of Salisbury served as a steward of Matilda's household and was created Earl of Salisbury by her. During the reign of her son, Henry II (1154-89), Patrick went on a pilgrimage to the shrine of St James at Compostella in North Spain, as did many later men of Poole, but was killed on his way home in 1167 in the south of France in a scrap with Guy de Lusignan, who later became a crusader and King of Jerusalem and Cyprus. Patrick's son, William, second Earl of Salisbury, bore the golden sceptre at the coronation of Richard I and had an only daughter and heiress, Ela, whom King Richard married off to his half-brother, William Longsword (Longespée), who became Earl of Salisbury in her right, and at the beginning of John's reign Sheriff of Wiltshire. William's mother, 'Fair Rosamund' Clifford, was the mistress of Henry II, who is said to have constructed a hideout for her in the middle of the maze at Woodstock, where however Henry's formidable wife, Queen Eleanor, is supposed to have tracked her down eventually and packed her off to a nunnery.

William Longespée entertained his half-brother, King John, at Canford Manor House in 1200 and 1204 and yearly from 1210 to 1215. These royal visits were a doubtful boon to the inhabitants of the manor, for even though each visit lasted no more than two days all the local food resources would have been commandeered to ensure that the king and his considerable retinue were suitably entertained.

During King John's protracted quarrel with the ambitious Pope Innocent III, even when England was placed under an Interdict, William Longespée loyally supported his half-brother and when John finally in 1213 accepted the Pope's peace terms – the surrender of England to the Pope followed by its restoration to John as the Pope's vassal and in return for an annual tribute to the Pope – Longespée was one of the witnesses to the agreement. Perhaps he had recommended it to John. A year earlier Longespée had brought to John a hermit named Peter of Wakefield, who prophesied that by the following Ascension Day

John would cease to be king. John had meanwhile thrown Peter and his sons into a dungeon in Corfe Castle and, by the time Ascension Day came round, John had indeed given up his crown to the Pope, but nevertheless he had the prophet Peter dragged on a hurdle to Wareham and back to Corfe Castle and there hanged outside the castle gate.

Philip II, King of France, who had been commissioned by the Pope to depose John, continued his preparations to invade England, despite the agreement between John and the Pope. The lord of Canford manor was put in command of an English fleet to prevent this invasion and ships from Poole may well have been in this fleet which inflicted a major naval defeat on the French ships off Damme on the Flemish coast (1213). Longespée, however, was the commander of an English army which, in conjunction with German and Flemish forces, suffered a decisive defeat at the Battle of Bouvines (1213), which effectively made Philip of France the dominant leader in Western Europe. Longespée himself was captured and released only in the following year. Weakened by this setback, John had to give way to the mounting opposition of English churchmen, barons and merchants against his financial exactions and attempts at arbitrary rule and agreed in 1215 to affix his seal to Magna Carta (the Great Charter) by which he guaranteed the rights of the Church and barons and undertook that no freeman should be tried or punished except by his equals and the law of the land. One of the leading barons who forced John to accept the charter at Runnymede was William Marshall, Earl of Pembroke, lord of the manor of Sturminster Marshall, five miles from Canford. At this stage Longespée was still supporting John and was indeed described by the barons at Runnymede as one of the king's evil counsellors. When, however, John with the backing of the Pope repudiated the Great Charter, Longespée had had enough and joined the opposition to the extent of being prepared to put Louis, son of the French king, on the English throne. Further civil war was averted by the death of John in 1216. Both Marshall, who became regent, and Longespée rallied to the support of John's young son, Henry III.

The restless warrior lord of Canford then went off to Palestine to do battle with the Moslem Arabs and to be defeated at the battle of Damietta in North Egypt. He finally settled down to more peaceful pursuits. He and his wife, Ela, threw themselves with enthusiasm into a project initiated by Richard Poore, Bishop of Sarum, to build a new cathedral just south of Old Sarum in Salisbury. On 28 April 1220 Bishop Richard Poore laid three of the foundation stones of what was to become the country's finest example of the Early English style of architecture – one on behalf of the Pope, a second for the Archbishop of Canterbury and a third for himself. William Longespée laid the fourth and the Countess Ela, his wife, the fifth. Bishop Poore did not live to see the completion of Salisbury Cathedral and it was his successor, another Dorset-born cleric, Bishop Giles de Bridport, who was present at the new hallowing of the great church in 1258. Bishop Richard Poore was closely associated with the founding of a hermitage for three nuns at what became the Abbey of Tarrant Kaines and he himself died in 1237 nearby in what seems to have been his native village. There he was buried and a tomb slab in Tarrant Crawford church may well be his. Another coffin slab there probably covered the grave of the young Queen Joan of Scotland, Henry III's sister, who died there in 1238. William Longespée, Earl of Salisbury, had died in 1226 and his imposing tomb surmounted by his effigy in chainmail and with his long sword, for which he was famous, extending to his spurs is now on the south side of the nave of the new Salisbury Cathedral, which he helped to found.

His widow, Countess Ela, refused to remarry. She served on three occasions as Sheriff of Wiltshire – an indication no doubt of her strength of character – and then founded Lacock Abbey and served as its abbess for some 18 years. Her youngest son, Nicholas Longespée, was Bishop of Salisbury from 1291 to 97.

William Longespée II (c.1200-50) seems never to have had the title of Earl of Salisbury bestowed upon him by the king, probably because his mother, Countess Ela, outlived him. William inherited his parents' piety and his father's desire to fight Moslems in the Middle East. The Crusaders were motivated by a strange mixture of piety, fanaticism, adventure and greed. The first Crusade had been successful in effecting the recapture of Jerusalem from the Moslem Arabs in 1099. The Crusaders celebrated their victory by massacring all the Moslems in the city and engaging in an orgy of land-grabbing by setting up estates carved out of the ancestral lands of the Palestinian Arabs. Jerusalem was regained by the Arabs in 1187 and during the following century further futile attempts were made by Western European Crusaders to recapture it. William Longespée II made a pilgrimage to Palestine in 1240 and once again in 1247 took the cross. Longespée received the Pope's authority to embark on a campaign of collecting money to fit out an English expedition to join the French king, Louis IX, in his attack on northern Egypt in what was known as the Seventh Crusade. It was fortunate for him that on the southern edge of his Canford estate a prosperous trading community had grown up over the past century – Poole. Some time, it is believed, in the year 1248 William Longespée bestowed a charter of self-government on his borough 'La Pole' or Pola in return for the very substantial sum of 70 marks – 11,200 silver pennies – no doubt after a great deal of haggling between Poole's shrewd merchants and their crusade-crazed lord.

Matthew Paris related that some two hundred English knights prepared to set out on their journey to Jerusalem. Dissensions soon broke out between the French and the English, partly because the French King's arrogant brother, the Count of Artois, kept referring to Longespée and his men as 'those tailed English' (a reference to the current rumour that because of the murder of Thomas à Becket the English had had tails fixed to them as a divine punishment!).

Meanwhile, the Sultan, hearing through spies of the bickering among the Christians, surrounded the troops under Artois and Longespée on all sides and particularly cut off their retreat to the river which they had just crossed. Then, according to Matthew Paris, 'Count Robert, seeing William Longespée surrounded on all sides by the enemy in a dense mass, sustaining the whole weight of the battle, shamelessly called, "William, God fights against us . . . We can no longer resist . . . Escape alive while your horse can carry you away". To this William replied briefly, as well as was possible in the midst of such noise. "God forbid that my father's son should flee from any Saracen; I would rather die than live unhappily". But Robert of Artois, seeing himself already hemmed in by his enemies turned his horse's head and suddenly took flight. Mounted on a swift horse, he sped towards the river and plunged in, hoping to swim the river, since he knew that his horse was a very strong one. This he was unable to do weighted down as he was with iron armour and weapons. Thus perished this proud man, mourned by no one's tears'.

Meanwhile the French retreated in disarray. 'Seeing which', wrote Matthew Paris, 'William, on whom all the Saracens had rushed, found that it was a matter of life and death. Yet he bravely withstood all their blows, and sent the souls of many of his enemies to hell, and although at last his horse became weak and had his feet cut off, William himself even then cut off the heads, hands and feet of some of his assailants. At length after receiving many blows and wounds, and overwhelmed by a shower of stones, William began to fail from loss of blood, and breathed forth his spirit to receive the crown of martyrdom'. Ironically his Moslem opponents, if they too believed that they were fighting a holy war (Jehad), will have been quite sure that in giving their lives for Islam, they would go straight to Paradise, presided over by the same God, worshipped both by Moslems and Christians. The lord of Canford manor, the donor of Poole's first charter, died on 7 February 1250 at Mansoura, Egypt. No one can doubt his extraordinary personal courage. One can but regret the futility of this sacrifice, indeed of the whole expedition, for King Louis was later captured by the Arabs and had to be ransomed. The only beneficial side-effect was that it facilitated the development of the emerging port of Poole. The Moslem Arab civilisation, which the Crusader aggression was trying to destroy, was manifestly superior to anything then existing in Western Europe in the arts, the crafts, science, mathematics and medicine.

It was related that the night before Longespée's death his mother at Lacock Abbey saw in a vision the heavens opening and her son, fully armed and bearing his familiar shield, being received joyfully by angels. When six months later, she received news of her son's death, she bore it with equanimity and rejoiced that she had given birth to such a martyr and champion of Christianity. Two years later the Sultan, in conversation with the Christian envoys negotiating the release of prisoners, said, 'I am surprised that you Christians who venerate the bones of the dead have not enquired about the remains of the illustrious William Longespée. We hear various stories, whether authentic or not we cannot say, about his bones; for example that on dark nights, there have been appearances at his tomb and that many benefits have been conferred by Heaven on those who call upon his God at that place. Accordingly, as he was slain in battle and on account of his excellent qualities and noble rank, we have buried his body with due respect. Impressed by the honour shown by the Moslems to Longespée, the French envoys therefore collected his remains and had them reinterred in the Church of the Holy Cross at Acre. The sepulchral effigy of a cross-legged crusader clad in chainmail at the west end of Salisbury Cathedral is believed to commemorate William Longespée II.

His son and heir, William Longespée III, inherited Canford but died in 1257 as a result of severe injuries sustained in a tournament. His widow, Maud, complained to Henry III that John, Lord Giffard, had carried her off by force from her manor-house at Kaneford to his castle in Gloucestershire and had there kept her in restraint. Giffard denied the charge, saying that she had come quietly and willingly but did confess to marrying her without the king's consent, for which offence the king agreed to accept a fine of 300 marks, provided that she did not complain again. Her only child by William Longespée, Margaret Longespée, was a

22. Drawing based on the sepulchral effigy of William Longespée II, Salisbury Cathedral. The Salisbury effigy does not carry the arms on the shield.

valuable property, for in 1256 when her father was dying and she was only two years old, she had been given in marriage to Henry de Lacy, in respect of which his father paid the king 10 gold marks – a good investment since the lord later inherited through his wife the title of Earl of Salisbury – and of course Canford manor, where there was 'a capital messuage and garden of yearly value 6s. 8d. . . . 120 acres of arable yearly value 20s. at 2d. per acre, a separate pasture, yearly value 20s., three parks . . . yearly value 60s. a dove-house, yearly value 3s., and a water-mill yearly value 30s.' He also held the manor of Kingston to which he gave his family name, Lacy. He was also Earl of Lincoln and, for a time, Governor of Corfe Castle. His daughter, Alice, Countess of Salisbury, who was on one occasion abducted from Canford by a knight named Warren, married three times and was claimed by yet another man as his wife, but she left no children – and Canford ceased to belong to the descendants of the Longespées.

In the survey of the resources of Henry de Lacy, when he was lord of Canford, it was further stated that he received the considerable sum of £8 13s. 4d. as yearly rent paid at Christmas, Midsummer and Michaelmas by free burghers at La Pole belonging to the manor of Canford.

How and why had Poole grown up into a substantial port by the mid-13th century? Although the peninsula on which it developed was part of the manor of Canford, there was, as we have seen, no mention of it in the Domesday survey of 1086. There is little archaeological evidence of settlement on the Poole peninsula in the Roman or Saxon periods, but by 1086 there may have been a few fishermen's cottages. The discovery of two oyster middens, attributed on the basis of radio-carbon dating to the period 1050-1100, confirms this view.

In May 1988 whilst sorting through fragments of pottery found during the 1987 excavations of the Poole Foundry site, Mr. Keith Jarvis identified one potsherd as dating from the Saxon period and coming from Quentovic in North France. Another sherd found in Thames Street was a piece of 10th-century English shell-tempered ware, so perhaps there were four or five households settled in late Saxon times on this south shore of the Poole peninsula where it would have been convenient for captains of ships on their way to and from Wareham and the harbour mouth to anchor.

The two major ports within a 10-mile radius of Poole were Wareham and Christchurch (or Twineham). By the time of the Norman Conquest Wareham had 285 houses and a population of perhaps 1,400, and also the distinction of having two moneyers authorised to mint the king's coins. Wareham was heavily punished perhaps for complicity in a rising against William I, so that Domesday Book records that over half the houses standing in 1066 were then in ruins. During the civil war of King Stephen's reign (1135-54), Wareham seems to have suffered massive destruction again; it changed hands at least five, and probably seven, times. In 1137, when Stephen captured Wareham from Matilda, he set fire to the town. In 1139 Baldwin de Redvers, one of Matilda's main henchmen, arrived by sea and regained it, only to be driven out at a later stage, when most of what was left of Wareham was burnt down. When the supporters of Matilda were temporarily ousted, it would be natural for those who could escape by boat to retreat to Christchurch, De Redvers' stronghold, or indeed, since the lord of Canford, Patrick, was Matilda's steward and indeed raised by her to the dignity of Earl of Salisbury, might not the manor of Canford have been a convenient place of refuge for Matilda's supporters when Stephen was in control in Wareham? Perhaps it was at this stage that the value of the deep-water channel along the southern edge of the Poole peninsula came to be appreciated, especially as the process of silting was probably reducing the depth of the river Frome at Wareham. When peace was finally restored no doubt many of these uprooted Wareham merchants decided that Poole, surrounded by the sea on all sides, apart from a narrow causeway leading northwards to Canford, was a much safer place in which to store their merchandise; and the lord of the manor would be happy to have them, especially if they would pay him something for the harbour facilities.

The earliest documentary references to the growing port as a place-name or surname came from the Pipe Roll, containing the yearly accounts of sheriffs, 1179-80 – Rogerus de Poles and 1182-3 – Pole. The Curia Regis Rolls, 1199, refer to Pola and the Patent Rolls of 1224 to La Pole. The latter reference is part of a record of letters sent to 'the bailiffs and trusty men of Portsmouth, Southampton, Seaford and Poole' to keep their ships in readiness for the king's service. The Feet of Fines 1227 refers to a grant by Ela, Countess, of 50s. of land in Kaneford and Pola to a tenant Thomas de Kaneford in return for two pounds of pepper and one pair of gilt spurs, or 6d. for all service each year. The Patent Rolls for 1230 mention four traders or sea-captains of La Pole – William Curneis, Peter de la Chaene, Walter Stanhard and Luke Wulwy, and a writ of 1230 required that all ships in the port of La Pole big enough to transport 16 horses should proceed to Portsmouth by St Michael's Day. William Curneis in fact duly went to Portsmouth and accompanied the King across the Channel to Brittany. At least one merchant from Poole engaged in lucrative

23. A 'long-cross' silver penny of Henry III, 1247.

coastal trade along the southern and eastern coasts of England and established himself in Hull as one of that port's wealthiest merchants. This was William de la Pole and his son, also William de la Pole, was soon supplying the king's army with wine and provisions, lending the king £1,000 in gold and serving as a baron of the Exchequer. His son Michael became Earl of Suffolk. A descendant, John de la Pole, Duke of Suffolk, married the sister of King Richard III and his son John de la Pole was nominated heir to the throne by Richard. In fact had Richard III won the battle of Bosworth, the name of the English royal family would have been Poole!

24. The Longespée Charter (1248).

Recent research by the present Town Clerk, Mr. I. K. D. Andrews, has revealed that a royal charter dated 20 October 1239 to William Lungespee (*sic*) authorised him to hold a weekly market at Poole on Tuesdays and a yearly fair there on the Vigil and Feast of St Margaret (20 July) and the two days following – obvious proof of the growing importance of Poole by 1239. Certainly by the mid-13th century, when William Longespée II was trying to raise funds for his crusading enterprise, the merchants and ship-owners of Poole were sufficiently affluent to raise 70 marks to obtain a very favourable charter of liberties. A mark consisted of 160 silver pennies, 11,200 of which would have been weighed out and bagged up to pay for the charter. This 1248 charter set out on parchment 28 cm by some 18 cm, with the neat handwriting clearly legible, is preserved in the Poole archives.

The following is a slightly abbreviated translation of the medieval Latin wording of this document:

I, William Longespée on behalf of myself and my heirs have granted to my burgesses of Poole and their heirs all kinds of liberties as regards their persons as well as their goods, and exemptions from tolls due to me, with the exception of two shillings to be paid to me in respect of every ship sailing overseas to foreign parts.

The same burgesses may choose from among themselves as often as may be necessary for the government of my said borough of Poole six burgesses, and I will appoint one of these who seems to us worthy as port-reeve [head man], and he shall promise to preserve our rights and those of our burgesses. If later he is found not to be conscientious in our business, we shall replace him by someone else.

However, I will appoint a beadle who upon his oath shall swear that he will present to the port-reeve or to my bailiffs, if they should be present, all attachments [i.e. all legal seizure of persons or property] touching my rights. Moreover, six times each year, i.e.

On the Morrow of the Circumcision [2 January]

The Octaves of the Blessed Mary [9 February]

The Morrow of the Annunciation of the same [26 March]

The Saturday following Hockday [the second Saturday after Easter]

The Wednesday after the feast of the Holy Trinity [the second Wednesday after Whitsun] and the third day before St Peter ad Vincula [29 July], my bailiffs shall hold in the said borough our pleas for the breaches of measures and assize and all other things rightly belonging to me . . . and when these cases are presented and brought to judgment, any fines arising from them shall be taken by my bailiffs for my use.

Moreover, if it should happen that any of our burgesses are unable to attend the court at these fixed times through the hindrance of the sea, the bailiffs shall not charge them with deliberately failing to appear in court; instead when they do return and any pleas have been opened against them, they shall be compelled to appear before the bailiffs.

Moreover, when any merchants whose home is elsewhere, come to the port of our said borough and wish to return quickly, but meanwhile have committed any offence with which the port-reeve and burgesses can deal, then the latter shall try the case, repaying any fines to the bailiffs, and the said merchants shall freely and quietly depart, except that there shall be paid to me in respect of every foreign ship bringing corn for sale, one bushel of corn for the use of the measure belonging to my court at Canford.

Moreover, whenever the King imposes tallage on his cities and boroughs, it shall be lawful for me to take tallage of my said burgesses. I wish also that the burgesses shall be free to put their cattle out to pasture on my heath, as they have always been accustomed, and also shall have what they need for fuel from my heaths and turbaries under the supervision of my bailiffs.

And for the grant of this charter the aforesaid burgesses have given me seventy marks, wherefore I and my heirs are held to guarantee the said liberties for ever to the said burgesses and their heirs. . . . I have given corroboration to this charter by attaching my seal.

These witness: Lords Everard Cevonicus, Thomas of Hyneton, Roger of Leburne, John of Barentine; Knights, Ralph de Aungers, Thomas of Hyneton the younger; Master Walter Salsator, Peter de Salcetus, Lord Simon Berenger, Ralph (parson of Up-Wimborne), Thomas Makerel and Valentine, clerks, and many others.

If the Longespée Charter is stripped of its legal jargon, what in fact was its significance for the townsfolk of Poole? In the first place they obtained a limited form of self-government in that they could elect six burgesses to form a borough council, though the lord of the manor retained the right to choose the head-man (or port-reeve) from among these six and to replace him by someone more amenable if he turned out to be a trouble-maker. Secondly, some long-standing grievances were redressed. Instead of having to trek five or so miles out to the lord's hall at Canford – and five miles back – to have some minor case settled, in future a court would be held approximately every two months on the spot in Poole itself where such grievances as overcharging, selling underweight loaves or giving short measure of ale could be dealt with. Again in the past some merchants had clearly been fined for contempt of court, when bad weather prevented them from getting home in time to answer some charge. Henceforth they were just to appear at the next meeting of the court. Moreover, merchants from other ports, English or foreign, had complained about having to stay around for weeks on end waiting to have some petty offence or dispute, such as the payment of a debt, settled. Henceforth such a case could be settled immediately by the port-reeve and his council and the 'stranger merchant' could be on his way home – quite a consideration since there seem to have been no regular court meetings for five months (August-December). The charter also defined the respective rights of the lord and the Poole burgesses. On the one hand he was still to collect a toll of 2s. from each ship leaving the port of foreign parts, whilst on the other the Poole townsfolk, despite their new status, were still to be able to put their animals out to graze on the manorial common and to dig peat for fuel, as in the past.

Early English window,
Steeple church.

FAMILY LINKS BETWEEN THE LORDS

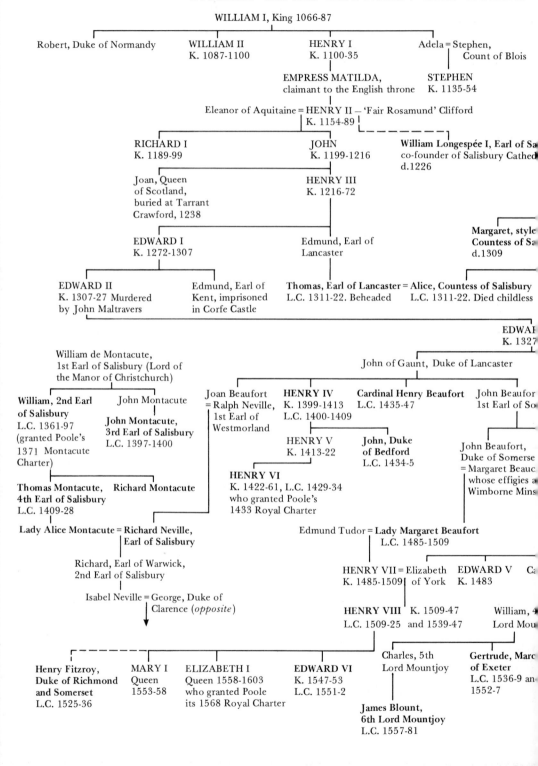

WILLIAM I, King 1066-87

Robert, Duke of Normandy

WILLIAM II
K. 1087-1100

HENRY I
K. 1100-35

Adela = Stephen,
Count of Blois

EMPRESS MATILDA,
claimant to the English throne

STEPHEN
K. 1135-54

Eleanor of Aquitaine = HENRY II — 'Fair Rosamund' Clifford
K. 1154-89

RICHARD I
K. 1189-99

JOHN
K. 1199-1216

William Longespée I, Earl of Sa
co-founder of Salisbury Cathed
d.1226

Joan, Queen
of Scotland,
buried at Tarrant
Crawford, 1238

HENRY III
K. 1216-72

EDWARD I
K. 1272-1307

Edmund, Earl of
Lancaster

Margaret, style
Countess of Sa
d.1309

EDWARD II
K. 1307-27 Murdered
by John Maltravers

Edmund, Earl of
Kent, imprisoned
in Corfe Castle

Thomas, Earl of Lancaster = Alice, Countess of Salisbury
L.C. 1311-22. Beheaded   L.C. 1311-22. Died childless

EDWAR
K. 1327

William de Montacute,
1st Earl of Salisbury (Lord of
the Manor of Christchurch)

John of Gaunt, Duke of Lancaster

William, 2nd Earl
of Salisbury
L.C. 1361-97
(granted Poole's
1371 Montacute
Charter)

John Montacute

John Montacute,
3rd Earl of Salisbury
L.C. 1397-1400

Joan Beaufort
= Ralph Neville,
1st Earl of
Westmorland

HENRY IV
K. 1399-1413
L.C. 1400-1409

Cardinal Henry Beaufort
L.C. 1435-47

John Beaufor
1st Earl of So

HENRY V
K. 1413-22

John, Duke
of Bedford
L.C. 1434-5

John Beaufort,
Duke of Somerse
= Margaret Beauc
whose effigies a
Wimborne Mins

Thomas Montacute,
4th Earl of Salisbury
L.C. 1409-28

Richard Montacute

HENRY VI
K. 1422-61, L.C. 1429-34
who granted Poole's
1433 Royal Charter

Lady Alice Montacute = Richard Neville,
Earl of Salisbury

Edmund Tudor = Lady Margaret Beaufort
L.C. 1485-1509

Richard, Earl of Warwick,
2nd Earl of Salisbury

HENRY VII = Elizabeth
K. 1485-1509   of York

EDWARD V
K. 1483

Ca

Isabel Neville = George, Duke of
Clarence (*opposite*)

HENRY VIII   K. 1509-47
L.C. 1509-25 and 1539-47

William, 4
Lord Mou

Henry Fitzroy,
Duke of Richmond
and Somerset
L.C. 1525-36

MARY I
Queen
1553-58

ELIZABETH I
Queen 1558-1603
who granted Poole
its 1568 Royal Charter

EDWARD VI
K. 1547-53
L.C. 1551-2

Charles, 5th
Lord Mountjoy

Gertrude, Marc
of Exeter
L.C. 1536-9 an
1552-7

James Blount,
6th Lord Mountjoy
L.C. 1557-81

Walter d'Evreux, of Rosmar, Normandy

Edward of Salisbury, Sheriff of Wiltshire L.C. 1086

Walter d'Evreux, founder of Bradenstoke Abbey

Patrick d'Evreux, Steward of the Household to Matilda,
who created him 1st Earl of Salisbury

William d'Evreux,
2nd Earl of Salisbury

K. = King
L.C. = Lord of Canford

ountess of Salisbury
8, Abbess of Lacock, 1240 d.1261

n Longespée II L.C. 1226-50 who granted the 1248 Longespée Charter

Nicholas Longespée,
Bishop of Salisbury 1291-7

n Longespée III L.C. 1250-7

ry de Lacy,
of Lincoln
1257-1311

Ela = James, Lord Audley

William de la Pole (from Poole),
a rich Hull merchant

Hugh de Audley,
Earl of Gloucester

William de la Pole,
Baron of the Exchequer

Ralph, 1st Earl = Margaret
of Stafford

Michael de la Pole,
1st Earl of Suffolk

Edmund, Duke of York

Hugh, 2nd Earl of Stafford

Richard, Earl of
Cambridge

Katherine = Michael de la Pole,
2nd Earl of Suffolk

ward, Duke
Somerset
C. 1447-55

Richard, Duke of York

William de la Pole,
4th Earl of Suffolk

y, Duke   Edmund, Duke   EDWARD IV   George, Duke of Clarence   RICHARD III   Elizabeth = John de la Pole,
merset   of Somerset   K. 1461-83   L.C. 1471-8 = Isabel Neville   K. 1483-5   Duke of Suffolk
1455-64   L.C. 1464-71

John de la Pole,
Earl of Lincoln,
declared heir to the throne

Edward, Earl of Warwick   Margaret, Countess of Salisbury
L.C. 1478-85   = Richard Pole, Lord Montacute

Villiam Courtenay

Henry, Lord Montagu   Sir Geoffrey Pole   Reginald, Cardinal Pole

Francis, 2nd Earl = Katherine
of Huntingdon

Elizabeth = Sir William Neville

Henry, 3rd Earl   George, 4th Earl
of Huntingdon   of Huntingdon
L.C. 1581-95   L.C. 1595-1604

Margaret = William Constantine

ry, Marquis
xeter
1536-9

Henry Constantine, of Merley

Francis   Henry Hastings,
Squire of Woodlands

Henry, 5th Earl
of Huntingdon
L.C. 1604-11

William Constantine,
M.P. for Poole 1640-3
Recorder of Poole,
1639-43 and 1660-2

Chapter Four

Medieval Poole

Towards the end of the 13th century in the reign of Edward I, Poole and its harbour were much involved in the strengthening of Corfe Castle. The outer gateway was being constructed about 1280-5 and the Compotus Rolls of 1280-92, when the Constable of Corfe Castle was Richard de Bosco, feature these items of expenditure:

12 quarters of lime purchased at Poole	7s.	2d.
Carriage of the lime from Ower to Corfe	1s.	0d.
200 lbs. of iron for the gate	6s.	8d.
92 pieces of timber from Hampshire, landing the same at Ower and transporting them to Corfe	£5 9s.	0d.
For a rope made at Studland for landing the timber		3d.
Expenses of Brother Henry journeying to Twyford [between Winchester and Eastleigh] to prepare the timber and returning with it	£3 12s.	1d.
Paid to Adam Bureis for making two great hinges and hooks for the outer gate and nails for the same	5s.	0d.
Paid to Master Ralph de Totewys preparing the places where the hinges were to be hung and for cutting the same	2s.	0d.

The Rolls give an indication of the value of money at this time in the wages of the various categories of workmen. Labourers got 2d. per day, carpenters from $2\frac{1}{2}$d. to 3d. per day, masons $3\frac{1}{4}$d. and surveyors 1s. 0d. per week.

Evidently the quays at Ower and Poole were considered not large enough to deal with the increased volume of traffic and the Patent Rolls of 1286 contain proposals for the construction of an entirely new town on the south side of Poole Harbour to provide for the needs of Corfe Castle. King Edward I commissioned the Constable of Corfe Castle and a priest, Walter de Marisco: 'To lay out a new town with a harbour and sufficient streets and lanes as well as adequate sites for a market and church, and plots for merchants and others in a place known as Gotower-super-Mare [Goathorn] in the parish of Studland and on the King's land, the King being prepared to grant the lands and tenements of this Newtown to merchants and others willing to take them'.

Had such a Newtown or Goathorn become fully established, such a competitor handling trade to and from Corfe Castle and the Isle of Purbeck could have ruined the prospects of the rising town of Poole. As it was, the scheme seems never really to have got off the ground, although the names Newton, Newton Heath and Newton Bay remain as reminders of this abortive attempt at town planning.

The growing prosperity of Poole brought with it additional responsibilities, especially in time of war. Thus in 1295 Poole responded to the request of King Edward I by providing three ships with 59 mariners towards the fleet that he was fitting out to go to Guienne, the area near Bordeaux, to confront the King of France. The men of Poole, like those of other south coast ports, were well aware of the danger of attacks by the French, but they were not convinced of the need to help the king in his wars against the Scots living so far to the north. Thus in 1301 a writ from the king to the bailiffs and honest men of 'La Pole', requiring them to send one ship to Berwick for service in the king's war against the Scots, was just ignored. Consequently the next year Thomas de Verblyngton and Peter de Donewych were authorised to punish in an appropriate manner Poole and other southern ports which had sent no ship for the king's service, to the great contempt of the king and manifest delay in concluding the war. A writ of 16 March 1303, directed to the bailiffs and men of Pole, Warham and Brunkeseye, took note that Peter de Donewych had explained that they had after all provided the required naval aid, exhorted them to provide suitable tackle and men-at-arms for the king's service at the place and on the day fixed by the king's clerk. This early reference to Brownsea (Brunkeseye) suggests that it already had a quay and settlement. However, when Edward I thought he had subdued the Scots, he had to face a new rebellion led by Robert Bruce, and his son, Edward II, had to continue the struggle. Consequently in 1310 the new king called upon Poole to send one ship to help in transporting troops to wage war against Robert Bruce, who, however, was to win a decisive victory at Bannockburn in 1314.

25. (left) Seal of La Pole (c.1320-25).

26. (above) Early 14th-century Poole ship, based on the seal.

About this time the men of Poole and adjacent ports from Southampton to Lyme were much more interested in a feud with the south-eastern Cinque Ports, for in 1321 Edward II wrote to his brother, Edmund, Earl of Kent, Keeper of the Cinque Ports, about the 'murders, depredations, burnings of ships and very many other injuries' suffered by Poole and other Dorset towns at the hands of the men of Kent and Sussex and required him to 'give full justice for all injuries' and to ensure that the disputes be speedily settled. The men of Poole were likewise ordered to do no damage to the mariners of the Cinque Ports and to send two representatives to a meeting to settle the disputes. Three years later Edward II called upon Poole and other south coast ports (including several of the Cinque Ports) to bring their largest ships to Portsmouth, manned and provided with gangways, landing bridges and 'clays' for the purpose of transporting troops and horses to Aquitaine at the king's expense. Poole actually sent four ships to join this fleet. It is to be hoped that the bitter feud between the Cinque Ports and the men of Dorset had indeed been ended by then, since otherwise this expedition could well have been torn with dissension. There was also dissension in royal circles. The French king, Charles IV, had summoned Edward II, his brother-in-law, to do homage or else forfeit all his possessions in France, such as Aquitaine. Edward sent his estranged French wife Isabella to deal with her brother, the French king. In fact, once in France she joined her paramour, Mortimer, and ·the two of them plotted Edward's overthrow. It was doubtless in order to counteract their intrigues that Edward ordered Poole in 1326 to examine all letters coming from foreign parts, to seize all correspondence that might be harmful to the king and to arrest all suspicious persons. However, the next year Isabella and Mortimer deposed Edward and set themselves up as regents for Edward III, the 14-year-old son of Edward and Isabella.

The unfortunate Edward II after his deposition was handed over to Sir John Maltravers of Lytchett Matravers, and Sir John Gurney who were empowered to enter any strong place in the kingdom and to take control of it for as long as they pleased. Travelling along unfrequented roads and by night they took the wretched ex-king to Corfe Castle and after a short stay there took him to Bristol and then to Berkeley Castle in Gloucestershire, where he was confined in a small foul-smelling room and subsequently murdered by Maltravers and Gurney in a particularly brutal manner, so that his agonised shrieks were heard throughout the neighbourhood.

Maltravers for some time went unpunished but rather rewarded, being made Constable of Corfe Castle in 1330 and summoned to Parliament as Lord Maltravers. He seems to have aided Mortimer in tricking Edwards II's brother, Edmund, Earl of Kent, into involving himself in a scheme to release Edward II. Apparently Maltravers had a hand in inducing the Earl of Kent into believing that Edward II was still alive and confined in Corfe Castle. The earl fell into the trap and wrote a letter addressed to his brother, promising to restore him to the throne. As a result of this he was arrested, accused of plotting to overthrow the king and executed. In the same year Mortimer was overthrown and young Edward III assumed control. Perhaps, because of remorse over the murders of his father and uncle, Edward III ordered Maltravers to be tried on a charge of luring the Earl of Kent into writing the fatal letter by inducing the Earl to believe that Edward II was still alive. Maltravers did not appear to stand trial, but in his absence he was found guilty and condemned to be hanged, drawn and beheaded. Maltravers fled to the continent. It was only in 1351 that the judgment was reversed and he recovered his lands. He fought for the king against the French at the battles of Crécy (1346) and Poitiers (1350) and on his death in 1365 he was buried in Lytchett Matravers church, where the remains of his tomb slab is still to be seen. Originally it was inlaid with a brass fret, the Maltravers heraldic device. In the 18th century a larger portion of the surrounding inscription, including the words in medieval French, *Sage chyvaler en gere* (wise knight in war) could be read.

In 1337 Edward III embarked upon a new war with France, a conflict which, because it was to continue sporadically until 1453, was later to be known as the 'Hundred Years' War'. Edward's main concern was to protect the profitable export trade in English wool, on which a 20s. 0d. duty was collected for the king, to the cloth-manufacturing cities of Flanders, whose independence was being threatened by his cousin, the new French king, Philip VI. For good measure Edward claimed that he himself had a better claim to the French throne on the grounds that he was the son of the heiress of the last French king, his mother, Isabella. Consequently in 1338 Poole provided six ships in a fleet of 200 to transport an English army to Flanders. The war went well for the English, who won a great naval victory off Sluys in 1340 and a decisive triumph on land at the battle of Crécy (1346) when English longbowmen proved their superiority over the heavily armoured French cavalry and crossbowmen. Poole contributed four ships and 94 mariners to the expedition which led to the capture of Calais in 1347.

The growing importance of Poole in these opening years of the Hundred Years' War was confirmed by the contents of an enquiry made in 1341 on the petition of the Earl of Surrey, lord of the manor of Canford and William Montacute, his designated successor before a royal official. On the oaths of 12 local men it was confirmed that (1) Poole was a free borough. (2) the burgesses were entitled to be paid coming to the port of Poole twopence for anchorage and twopence for dockage, (3) merchants were to pay to the borough the customs duties set out below when these goods were imported, i.e.:

For every last of herrings	4d
hundred of salt fish	4d.
salmon	¼d.
bundle of staves	¼d.
quarter of salt	¼d.
quarter of corn	¼d.
jar of oil	½d.
ox-hide	½d.
sarplar [bale] of wool	4d.
sarplar of undressed skins	4d.
hundred of iron or poles	½d.
hundred of cod fish	½d.
vessel of nuts	½d.
dozen bags of rosin	½d.
quarter of coals	¼d.
barrel of tar	2d.
barrel of pitch	2d.

and that these duties were intended to be used towards paying the fee-farm rent payable each year to the lord of the manor; (4) the port of Poole extended from the North-Havensford (Sandbanks) as far as the place called Redcliff Atwell (on the Arne peninsula up the Wareham Channel) and extended to the middle of the water between the port of Poole and Brownsea Island.

Two other documents giving interesting information about Poole and neighbouring villages and towns in 1327 and 1332 are the Dorset Lay Subsidy Rolls of those years, which provide lists of those people who were called upon to pay a special tax to the king, together with the amounts they were asked to pay. Portions of the parchment of the 1327 roll are in poor condition and it is incomplete and so examples will be quoted from the 1332 roll. The tax was imposed on movable property (one fifteenth of the value in rural areas, and one tenth in the boroughs), but poorer people were exempt. Thus those whose property was worth less than ten shillings (in rural districts) and under six shillings (in the boroughs) were not called upon to pay the tax. In addition much property was exempted from assessment for tax. In rural areas the riding horses, armour and clothing of knights and gentlemen and their wives, together with jewellery and vessels of gold, silver and brass were disregarded as were the household goods of peasants and craftsmen, the foodstuff in their larders and the tools of their trade. In urban areas the property exempted from taxation included one garment each for a man and his wife, their bed, a drinking cup of silver or mazer, one ring, one clasp of silver or gold, and a girdle of silk. The items which were assessed for taxation in the rural areas were farm animals, grain, hay, honey and other farm produce, whilst in urban areas household goods, some merchandise, items of luxury and some of a craftsman's tools were taxed.

27. Cruck roof construction in a medieval Poole house, now demolished.

In the town of Poole (Villa de la Pole) 27 people were assessed for tax and the total tax due from Poole was 48s. 10d. By contrast 119 people were assessed in the mother community of Canford, the total tax from which amounted to £10 10s. 3d. In Canford the highest tax was placed on the lord of the manor, John de Warenne, assessed at 13s. 4d. – 200 silver pennies, and next in wealth came a lady called Alicia Pleycy, assessed at 6s. 8d. In Poole those listed in order of wealth as taxpayers were as follows: tax due, 7s. 6d., the wealthiest merchant, Henry Dodde; 6s. 6d., Walter le Blower; 3s. 6d., Nicholas Utward; 3s. 2d., Roger Swayn; 2s. 6d., Hugh Huberd; 2s. 2d., William le Couk; 2s. 0d., Joanna Wyndelsor; Stephen le Threscher and Richard Justice; 22d., Roger Warkman; 20d., Peter Bount; 12d., the widow of Robert Goudrich, Robert Blakeman, John Cole, William le Taillur, Edward Corthevyle, John Goudrich, Robert Nicole, Robert de Oure [Ower], Roger Sprake and John Shupman; 8d., Edith Maundevyle, John Bosse, Thomas le White, Richard Mone (Moon), Edward Freer and John Goudgrom (Goodgroom).

These, of course, were just the wealthier householders and the Lay Subsidy Roll does not say how many householders were below the tax threshold. Wareham, taxed on the same basis as Poole, that is, as a borough, had the same number of taxpayers, 27, but the total tax due was £6 0s. 4d. Other neighbouring villages listed, with the number of taxpayers, the total tax and the wealthiest taxpayer were: Hamme (Hamworthy) 25, 36s. 3d. (Robert Toly, 3s. 6d.); Lytchett Minster, 37, £4 0s. 1d. (Andrew Peverel, 6s. 8d.); Lytchett Matravers, 14, 19s. (the lord of the manor, John Maltravers, father of the murderer of Edward II, 3s. 4d.); Corfe Mullen, 33, 47s. 8d. (Egidius de Erdington, 6s. 8d.); Sturminster Marshall, 46, £4 1s. 8d. (Christina de Mohon, 6s. 8d.); Shapwick, 68, £6 0s. 4d. (John, Earl of Warenne, 13s. 4d.); Kingston Lacy, 139, £7 8s. 10d. (Ebulon le Straunge, 20s.); Hampreston, 30, 67s. 2d. (Robert Lacy, 4s. 10d.); Wimborne Minster, 71, 63s. (Thomas Clutkerver, 3s.); Leigh in Colehill, 87, £4 10s. 2d. (John de Grymstede and Ralph atte Hyde, each 4s.). So, of these 13 local communities analysed, Canford emerges as the wealthiest with the highest total tax: £10 10s. 3d.

A study of the Christian names in the Lay Subsidy Roll shows how thoroughly old Anglo-Saxon names have been replaced by the names of saints or Biblical characters, e.g. John, Nicholas, Simon, Matthew, Peter and Adam, and also by Norman-French names such as William, Henry, Robert, Roger, Hugh, Walter and Richard. The second names of taxpayers also throw interesting light on the development of surnames, although we cannot be sure that in 1332 in this area these second names were the same as those of the fathers and were no longer appropriate descriptions of the sons. For example, if Robert Blakeman of Poole, was fair, then 'Blakeman' ranked as a surname. However, the four main types of surnames are potentially to be found in the Poole (P) and Canford (C) lists:

1. *Occupational.* William le Taillur, William le Couk (P), William le Muleward (Millward) (i.e. mill-keeper), Walter le Blower (i.e. of a horn or bellows), Matthew le Cartere, Richard Ridere (horseman), Nicholas le Akerman (literally acre-man, i.e. ploughman or cultivator), John Herdman, Walter le Yrmanger (i.e. ironmonger), Peter Potter (C), John le Smyth of Sturminster Marshall, John le Haiward (Hayward) (official in charge of hedges), Lytchett Matravers, Peter le Tenner of Wimborne.

2. *Indicating an ancestor's first name* (much less common in 1332 than today), such as Dodd (descendant of a Saxon named Dodda), John Goudrich or Goodrich (descendant of Godric, the typical name for an Englishman), Henry Huberd or Hubert (son of Hubert) (P), Edward Josep (son of Joseph), William Gibbes (son of Gilbert), of Corfe Mullen, William Davy (son of Davy), Robert Cobbe (descendant of a Saxon named Cobba) (C).

3. *Area or place of origin or location of home.* Richard Waleys (Welsh), John Norys (Norris = Northerner) (C), Joanna Wyndelsor (Windsor) (P), Walter in the More (on the moor), Adam Wyke, of Wimborne, George de Caneford, Thomas atte Nywelond (at the newly-cultivated land) of Leigh, William Philipp (son of Philip), of Canford.

4. *Nicknames.* Descriptive of appearance or character. Robert Blakeman (man of dark hair or complexion) (C), Thomas le White (of very fair hair or pale complexion) (P), Nicholas le Rede

(red), Richard le Fox, John Stout, William Blakarmeys, Walter Barfot, whose surname presumably originated with some ancestor who preferred (like Zola Budd) to go bare-footed. This unusual and uncommon surname extant in Canford in 1332 is represented by 27 entries in the Bournemouth area telephone directory of 1987 (22 in one Poole area) (C). Peter Whitlock (Whitelock), of Shapwick, Richard Jolyf (cheerful), of Wimborne. It is likely that Thomas le White was a member of a family of merchants in Poole for many centuries down to the late 16th, if not early 19th century. This Thomas le White is likely to have been the ancestor of three generations of merchants named Thomas White, who served as Mayors of Poole in the years 1504, 1510, 1511, 1517, 1531, 1538, 1545 and 1551.

In 1348-9 life in both town and countryside and also the war with the French were suddenly disrupted by the epidemic of bubonic plague, commonly known as the Black Death. Spread by the bite of fleas infesting the black rat, this frightening disease, with a very brief incubation period, was characterised by a rapid pulse, severe headache, aching limbs, giddiness and swellings or buboes under the arm and in the groin. Victims could be dead only three days after showing symptoms of the disease. It first arrived in England at Melcombe Regis in late June 1348, probably introduced by a sailor from Gascony, and rapidly spread throughout Dorset and the rest of the country. Records of the replacement of priests through death in the diocese of Salisbury provide clues to the routes by which the pestilence spread. It is estimated that on average at least a third of the population died from the plague and priests ministering the last rites to the dying were particularly exposed to infection. In November three priests and a prior at Wareham and priests at Winterborne Zelston and East Morden all died and, as the winter advanced, the mortality increased. Spetisbury lost two rectors and two vicars, whilst Wimborne Minster lost two of its deans, and Witchampton, Wimborne St Giles and Wimborne All Saints also lost their clergy.

The impact of the plague was catastrophic. Since it was spreading rapidly at harvest-time, much of the corn was not gathered in. Animals went untended. Trade was disrupted. Burying the dead constituted a major problem. Contact with the plague victims or the buildings where they had languished seemed to involve a high risk of infection. There is a strong tradition that in Poole a special field on the relatively remote Baiter peninsula was set aside for the burial of those who died of the pestilence. Some villagers and townspeople fled in panic, thereby often spreading the infection. A writ, directed to the bailiffs of Poole and to the authorities in many other ports, stated that a large part of the kingdom's population had died and many people were trying to go abroad taking with them all the money that they could collect. Consequently the king required the Poole authorities to stop any such people leaving for foreign parts unless they were merchants, notaries or accredited messengers. Some communities were afraid to go on living in houses where people had died of the plague – with good reason, even though it was not then known that it was spread by the bite of fleas on black rats which preferred to live in houses. In some villages, such as Lytchett Matravers, it seems that the community moved away from the old plague-ridden site and built afresh some distance away, especially after a further severe outbreak of the plague as in 1361, when Lytchett's rector, Henry Tingewyke, died. Thus today the church is noticeably remote from the village of Lytchett Matravers.

In 1361, too, the vicar of Canford who had survived the 1348-9 epidemic was carried off, as was William Bembre, Dean of Wimborne and founder of the Great Chantry there. Hinton Martell and West Almer lost their priests and two vicars died at West Parley within a month. Likewise, the abandonment of the Leaze quarter of medieval Wimborne occurred in the mid-14th century. 'It is hard to resist the idea', writes N. H. Field, 'that the main cause was the Black Death.'

The Calendar of Fine Rolls noted in July 1349 that at Bere Regis 'the mortality of men in the present pestilence is so great that its lands remain untilled'. The drastic decline in the population meant a reduced demand for corn and encouraged a marked decrease in the amount of arable land and a corresponding increase in large-scale sheep-farming which could be undertaken with a much smaller labour force. Doubtless some unfree villagers fled from their manors and set themselves up as free labourers demanding higher wages. Parliament tried to restrict the rise in wages without much success. In the long run manorial lords seem to have preferred to accept money rents from their dependent villagers in lieu of labour services reluctantly and carelessly performed. The process of the commutation of labour services for money rents was, however, a gradual process. The earliest recorded commutation at Kingston Lacy occurred in 1408-9, when 17 out of 78 villagers were allowed to pay a rent in lieu of labour services. Nevertheless at Kingston Lacy tenants were performing their 'winter works according to custom', possibly some ploughing and cutting of timber, as late as 1485.

Despite the jolt to the economy caused by these outbreaks of bubonic plague, the port of Poole continued to obtain documentary recognition of its importance. According to the Winchelsea Certificate (1364), one of the most important documents in the Poole archives, the Mayor of Winchelsea – in medieval French – recognised that 'the water between Redcliff Attwell and North Haven Orde (Sandbanks) constituted the haven of Poole and belonged to no other place than the said town of Poole'. The Certificate confirmed that Poole officials were entitled to collect customs duties from ships within this haven. Seven years later the lord of Canford manor (1361-97), William Montacute, Earl of Salisbury, granted Poole an additional charter. Under this Montacute Charter of 1371 the head officer of the borough was to be known as mayor instead of port-reeve. (In fact he was referred to as 'Mair de la Ville de Pole' in the Winchelsea Certificate.) The Longespée Charter was confirmed and in addition the burgesses of Poole were henceforth to receive the fine imposed for the breaches of assize of bread and ale, which hitherto had gone to the lord of the manor. In return the burgesses were to pay to the lord half a mark (6s. 8d.) on the first Court Day and 18d. at the commencement of each of the other five courts in the year for the attendance of the lord's steward. The Montacute Charter also specifically confirmed the right of turbary – the right of the Poole townsfolk to dig for peat on Canford Heath. The charter was written in chirograph, that is, twice on the same parchment, the lower half sealed by the lord, the other (upper) half with the common seal of the 'mayor and burgesses', with the word *cirographum* inscribed between the two entries. The parchment was then cut in two and the burgesses kept the lower half with the earl's seal attached.

One further financial obligation of the burgesses of Poole was the payment of an annual fee, the farm rent, to the lord of the manor. This was fixed at £5 17s. 5½d. (including 10d. for a pound of wax and a pound of cummin), so that together with the waits payment of 14s. 2d. Poole paid the lord of the manor £6 11s. 7½d. annually – right until the Enclosure Act of 1805.

28. Jean de Vienne on a 1942 French stamp.

The fact that the English king ruled Aquitaine (south-western France) provided ports like Poole with substantial trading opportunities, but, when the Hundred Years' War was resumed, Poole was exposed to attacks by the French across the Channel. Thus in 1377 the great French admiral, Jean de Vienne, attacked and devastated several south-cost ports. Among these was Poole. 'The Earl of Salisbury was unable to prevent the partial destruction by fire of Poole, Dorset, situated on a flat peninsula . . . accessible by means of a narrow channel.' However a quarter of a century later many expeditions were setting out from Poole Harbour to attack the French. For example, in 1403, Richard Bylle, of Wareham, master of a Poole vessel, captured a French ship, the *Saint Croys* of Nantes, 'contrary to the form of treaty between the King and the French' (a truce in the Hundred

Years' War). Bylle was ordered to make restitution. In the same year Henry Cotillen, master of an armed vessel of La Pole, captured a consignment of wine from a Flemish vessel.

The most formidable Poole sea-captain to attack the French in the reign of Henry IV was Harry Paye. The Spanish chronicle, *La Cronica del Conde don Pero Niño*, wrote of him as a 'Knight who scours the seas as a corsair with many ships, plundering all the Spanish and French vessels that he can encounter. This Arripay often raided the coast of Castile and carried off many ships. He scoured the channel of Flanders [the Straits of Dover] in such strength that no vessel could pass that way without being captured. This Arripay burnt Gijon and Finisterra [in North Spain], carried off the crucifix from Santa Maria de Finisterra . . . the holiest in all those parts . . . and inflicted great damage in Castile, taking many prisoners and extorting many ransoms.' Back in England Harry Paye was charged with piracy and cross-examined about a French barque, the *Seint Anné*, and the seizure of its cargo of wine by 'Harry Paye of Pole', but the next year he was authorised to fit out privateers to harass the French. A French account of one of his exploits in 1404 related how the French captured the large ship of the warden of the Cinque Ports, Harry Paye, and that Paye himself, 'the most implacable of the enemies of the French' was on board. The French went below in search of booty, leaving their English prisoners in charge of a few guards. Suddenly Harry Paye's war-cry was heard. He and his fellow-prisoners broke free, attacked their guards and slew the rest of the French, who had gone below, as hearing the din they emerged from the hatchway. Paye then seized two French vessels and, flying the French flag, sailed up the Seine, plundering several ships with impunity. In 1405 he was one of the captains of an English fleet which burnt 40 towns and villages in Normandy. However, in an earlier exploit Paye had seized a Spanish vessel and its cargo of iron and, although he was forced by the English king to set it free, he had understandably antagonised Enrique III, King of Castile and Leon (central and northern Spain).

The Spanish monarch agreed to supply naval aid to France and a combined Franco-Spanish force of five galleys and two smaller vessels with crossbowmen on board was assembled. The French contingent was commanded by Sieur Charles de Savoisy, whilst the Spanish forces were led by Don Pero Niño. The account of the expedition has come down to us in the chronicle bearing his name. On arriving within the vicinity of Poole Harbour and learning that he was near the home-port of 'Arripay', Pero Niño resolved to return the visits which the English pirate, as he regarded him, had made on the Spanish coast. The chronicle continued: 'Accordingly they entered the harbour and at dawn were in sight of Poole. The town was not walled and there was a fine tower with a cupola [of St James's church]'. The French commander deemed it unwise to attempt a landing and forbade any of his men to go ashore, but the Spanish leader, feeling that his country's honour was at stake and that vengeance must be sought, sent a raiding party ashore under the command of his cousin, Fernando Niño, with orders not to encumber themselves with plunder, but to set the houses on fire. 'One large building [probably on the site of 'The Town Cellars', now the Maritime Museum] was defended successfully for a time until after stout resistance the Spaniards forced an entrance and the defenders escaped through the back of the building, which was found to contain arms and all kinds of naval stores. The attackers carried off what they could and then set fire to the store-house. By this time the English had gathered together longbowmen and men-at-arms, who, having positioned themselves, then came so close that it was possible to see which of them were of a ruddy complexion and which were swarthy. They had removed the doors of several houses and managed, with the help of stakes, to place them as shields in front of themselves as protection from crossbow bolts. Thus protected, the Poole longbowmen discharged shower after shower of arrows so that the Spanish crossbowmen dared not expose themselves by stooping to draw their crossbows.

Many were wounded and those who were protected with armour were fledged with arrows like so many Saint Sebastians. The Spaniards retreated three paces and then Pero Niño came ashore with the rest of his soldiers and his French troops, despite their former reluctance, landed to support them. With shouts of Santiago! [St James – patron saint of both Spain and of Poole] the Spaniards surged forward and the Poole defenders, who even by the admission of the Spanish chronicler had fought with great courage, were forced to retreat and to leave behind among those slain, a brother of Arripay'.

Harry Paye himself was away from Poole on another mission at the time. The invaders withdrew to their ships, taking with them some prisoners, and sailed eastwards towards Southampton. Despite their success in sacking and setting on fire the quayside storehouse, this Franco-Spanish raid of 1405 was far from being an unqualified success, for the Poole men clearly had both the resources and spirit to put up a vigorous defence of the port. Despite this onslaught on Poole, Harry Paye is on record as continuing active in his career of plunder. In 1406 he had to be ordered by the king to hand back a vessel laden with wine since its owner was a London merchant. After another expedition in 1407 Paye brought into Poole Harbour 120 vessels laden with iron, oil and salt captured off the coast of Brittany, but after 1407 there are no further references to Harry Paye's activities in this area. A damaged memorial brass in Faversham church, Kent, near the Cinque Ports with which he was associated, records that there lies Henry Paye. He seems to have died in 1419.

He may well have been active in the renewed war with France as a result of which young King Henry V was able to conquer the northern half of France. The lord of Canford manor, Thomas Montacute, Earl of Salisbury, who in 1411 granted Poole a further charter confirming all its existing privileges, was very active as a military commander in France and died there in 1428 after being wounded in the face by a cannon ball at the siege of Orleans. For the greater part of the next century the manor of Canford was held by one or another close relative of the reigning monarch. Then it was held briefly (1433-5) by John, Duke of Bedford, brother of Henry V and grandson of John of Gaunt, Duke of Lancaster.

29. Etching of John of Gaunt's Kitchen, Canford House.

30. (*above*) Fifteenth-century Poole seal of the
Wool Staple.

31. (*right*) Fragment of the town wall,
St Clement's Alley.

At this time part at least of the surviving medieval portion of Canford manor house would
have already been constructed. This was the kitchen wing – the so-called 'John o' Gaunt's
Kitchen', but John of Gaunt himself never lived here, though several of his descendants
were to be lords of the manor. It may have been the influence of the Duke of Bedford, regent
for his young nephew, Henry VI, that caused Letters Patent dated 8 July 1433 to be issued
noting that the port and town of Poole was inhabited by a great multitude of people and
was secure and sufficient for ships going there, whereas Melcombe Regis was weak and
depopulated, and ordaining that in the future Melcombe should be reduced to the status
of a creek, whilst Poole should be raised to the rank of a Port of the Staple, that is one of
an exclusive group of ports through which alone staple goods, mainly wool, woolfells and
hides, could be exported. Four-fifths of the customs revenue of this time was derived from
duties on the export of wool, and the brass matrix of the 15th-century Seal of the Staple is
still preserved by the Borough as is the matrix of the Seal of the Comptroller of Customs
of Poole. The prosperity of Poole will have been greatly boosted by this 1433 grant and
great quantities of wool from the growing number of sheep-farms in the hinterland of Poole,
especially on the chalk downs, will have been sent to Poole for export.

  Much valuable produce will have been imported through Poole by merchants both
English and foreign. The 1433 grant also authorised the Poole authorities 'to wall, embattle
and fortify' the town. The Spanish chronicler of the 1405 raid had noted the absence of a town
wall. However, despite the 1433 grant it was apparently not until the reign of Richard III

that work began on constructing a wall on the seaward side and the remains of this wall with a small gateway and surmounted by battlements may be seen at St Clement's Alley near the Quay. The rebuilding of the 'Town Cellars', gutted in the 1405 raid, probably took place soon after 1433 to provide a storehouse for the large stocks of wool, as would be indicated by its alternative name the 'Woolhouse', first used in a document of 1512. Yet another name for it, 'the King's Hall', may be derived from the fact that the manor of Canford reverted to the Crown from 1429-33 and 1464-71. Excavations suggest that the earliest foundations, nearly five feet below the present street level, belong to the 13th century and that the 15th century saw substantial alterations, including the complete rebuilding of the south wall. At present 70 feet long, it once extended for a further 50 feet across what is now Thames Street, a portion now enclosed by the Harbour Office and *King Charles* Inn. The recently restored open timber roof is a particularly fine example of 15th-century design.

32. A 13th-century Early English Purbeck marble font, Canford church.

In 1453 – the year which saw the end of the 'Hundred Years' War' and also the capture of Constantinople by the Turks – Henry VI granted a further charter to Poole establishing the right of Poole to hold a weekly market each Thursday and also two fairs, one to be held on the feast-day of St Philip and St James (1 May), and the seven days following, and the other to be held on All Souls' Day (2 November) and the seven days following. It was also stated that the mayor and his two bailiffs during the time of the fair could hold a special summary court (Pie-powder Court) to deal with any commercial disputes, so that traders could go speedily on their way after the settlement of any dispute over a transaction. As already mentioned, as early as 1239 a royal grant permitted William Longespée, lord of the manor of Canford, to hold a weekly market at Poole every Tuesday and a yearly fair on 20 July.

From 1453 onwards until 1885 the borough of Poole was regularly invited to send representatives to Parliament (two M.P.s to each parliament until 1867). From 1295 kings – at irregular intervals – had called upon each shire to elect two knights to represent it and also requested a variable number of boroughs to send representatives – usually two for each borough – so that he might explain the need to go to war with the French and/or Scots and to win approval for special taxes. M.P.s brought petitions for the redress of various grievances and in time presented their suggestions for legislation in the form of draft laws or bills. After some bargaining the king might get the money he wanted, and the M.P.s might secure his consent to new laws. In 1302 and

1349 Blandford was invited to send M.P.s but never again; in 1307 and 1308 Christchurch was called upon to send representatives but excused itself on grounds of poverty and only regularly elected M.P.s from 1572. Wareham elected two M.P.s from 1302 onwards. Poole was invited to send two representatives in 1341 to a Council to discuss naval matters and actually elected John Goodrich and Edward Triscote. Two M.P.s were also elected to the parliaments of 1363 and 1369, but it was only from 1453 that Poole was put on the permanent list of boroughs invited to elect two members to each parliament. Corfe Castle elected two M.P.s to each parliament from 1572 to 1832.

However much the townsfolk were preoccupied with trade and the villagers with farming, religion played a most important role in their lives. The Church was the main employer of architects, masons and woodcarvers, and local churches provide many good examples of the different style of Gothic architecture, which followed the Norman between 1200 and 1600. Thirteenth-century Early English pointed windows are represented at Steeple and in the east window of Wimborne Minster, and a 13th-century font may be seen in Canford church. The Lady Chapel of Wimborne Minster is of the 14th century in the Decorated style, as is the piscina, the small basin in which holy vessels could be cleansed, in Tarrant Rushton church. The fonts at Lytchett Matravers and Corfe Mullen are of the 15th century, when the Perpendicular style, with its large windows and flattened pointed arches was developing. Fine examples of the Perpendicular style are the west tower of Wimborne Minster and the lady chapel and choir of Christchurch Priory, the latter being dated to about 1520. Corfe Mullen church has a plastered barrel form roof of about 1480. At Christchurch Priory the misericords – the brackets on turn-up seats to provide some support for aged or infirm monks during the long services – provide magnificent examples of wood-carving as well as an insight into medieval humour. They date from 1200 to 1515 – one misericord with tri-lobed carving being the oldest in the country – and include such varied themes as the Devil on a woolsack, an emaciated dog gnawing a bone, a contortionist, rabbits and a crowned king believed to represent Richard III. At Wimborne Minster the astronomical clock constructed about 1320 illustrated the Medieval Church's belief that God had created the universe with the earth at its centre and the moon, fixed stars and the sun all moving round it.

South-east Dorset had two contrasting examples of the monastic life. At Tarrant Crawford a nunnery following Cistercian rules was established, and linked to it originally was a community of three sisters living in strict seclusion, for whom Bishop Richard Poore, founder of Salisbury Cathedral, may well have written (c.1220) a handbook in a form of English intermediate between Anglo-Saxon and the Middle English of Chaucer, entitled the *Ancren Riwle* or Rule of the Anchoresses. The recluses were required to spend much of their time on religious services and meditation and were enjoined to accept much bodily discomfort. 'Next to your flesh', said the Rule, 'wear no flaxen cloth except it be of hards and coarse canvas.' On the other hand harsh mortification of the flesh was frowned upon. 'Wear no haircloth nor hedgehog skins and do not beat yourselves therewith nor with a scourge of leather nor leaded; and do not with holly nor with briar cause yourselves to bleed without the approval of your confessor. . . . Let your shoes be thick and warm.' Contact with the outside world must be minimal. Their maidservants, who must be 'very plain and of sufficient age' must not allow any man to see them unveiled. Nor must they 'look fixedly at any man nor romp nor frolic with him'. The recluses were warned against engaging in trade or in keeping herds of cattle, but they were allowed one concession: 'Ye shall not possess any beast, my dear sisters, except only a cat'.

By contrast the Augustinian Canons of Christchurch Priory had many contacts with the outside world. Although they distributed food to the local poor, the canons also entertained many travellers, often unruly guests. The porch of the Priory church was the largest in the country because the prior had so much daily business to conduct with the townspeople. There were rents to be collected from tenants, tithes of grain, wool, geese, calves, cows, fruit, fish and salt to be collected; barns to be repaired and workmen to be supervised. Worldliness and gossip were the order of the day. And the Priory was generally popular with townsfolk and pilgrims. People came from far and wide to venerate the Priory's holy relics, which included what were alleged to be the bones of five assorted saints, the sandals and cowl of St Thomas à Becket, pieces of wood from the cradle of Christ and stone from his sepulchre.

Going on pilgrimages was a popular pastime in the 15th century – not only to Christchurch and Canterbury but also to shrines abroad. Spain in particular was a tourist attraction for people in the Poole area, for in 1428 John Davey, of Poole, had a licence to transport 80 passengers on the *Nicholas* to the shrine of St James of Compostella in northern Spain, and for the same purpose in 1434 Robert Owen was authorised to transport 70 on the *Bernard*, and John Mower was licensed to take 60 on the *Michael* from Poole to Compostella – all doubtless motivated by a mixture of piety, superstition and sheer love of adventure.

Early in the 15th century there were a few people who disapproved of the veneration of images and relics. For example, the lord of the manor of Canford 1397-1400, John Montacute, Earl of Salisbury, was a Lollard, a follower of Wycliffe, the pioneer of Protestantism, and abhorred superstition and the material wealth of the Church. He was reputed to have destroyed most of the images in one of his chapels. He was executed on a charge of disloyalty to Henry IV. The Lollards, who like the Earl of Salisbury, criticised the doctrines and practices of the Roman Catholic Church, were persecuted and driven underground for a century.

33. Medieval niche in the wall of St George's Almshouses.

Meanwhile in the later Middle Ages many pious people with charitable motives, instead of bequeathing property to the monasteries where bequests were so often misused, endowed chantries, chapels within churches, where priests were to chant masses and pray for the souls of the founder of the chantry and others. For example, Thomas de Bembre founded in 1354 the Great Chantry in Wimborne Minster, whilst John Radcotts endowed a chantry attached to the hospital of St Margaret and St Anthony, founded for the treatment of lepers on the outskirts of Wimborne. Since there was a firm belief in the efficacy of prayers for the dead in reducing their suffering in Purgatory, people, unable to afford to endow their own chantries, banded together to establish a co-operative guild for such a purpose. An example of such a forerunner of the friendly society was Poole's Guild or Fraternity of St George, founded about 1400. The objects of the Fraternity were:

1. to provide masses for the souls of deceased members of the guild, especially those who had made particular gifts;
2. to keep a light constantly burning on the altar of St George in the parish church;
3. to maintain an almshouse for necessitous members in need of food and accommodation, and to distribute alms.

It was particularly appropriate to dedicate the Guild to St George, the patron saint of

England and protector of the weak. A candle was kept burning on the altar of St George in a special chapel in the parish church and on St George's Day members of the Fraternity would process to St George's Chantry for divine service, probably adjourning afterwards for a feast in the hall of the Fraternity, which could well have been located in a wing of Scaplan's Court. The almshouses of St George were established at least as early as 1429 on the site where they still stand in Church Street. Originally a hall-type structure with partitions inside, the building was probably enlarged in the 17th century to provide additional upper rooms. In 1904 the Almshouses were drastically altered and improved, but deteriorated during the 1960s. Providentially in 1970 a solicitor, Howell Dawson Mundell, whose grandfather had founded a bakery in Poole, bequeathed £30,000 for the benefit of the old people of Poole and this was used to renovate the Almshouses and, whilst preserving the external appearance, to provide sheltered accommodation in four modernised, self-contained units. In the south wall there is still a medieval niche, which may once have housed an image of St George.

During the 15th century the Poole area was closely associated with that branch of the royal family known as the House of Lancaster. Kingston Lacy was one of several manors held by John of Gaunt, Duke of Lancaster, the fourth son of Edward III, and five members of the Beaufort branch of the House of Lancaster – descendants of John of Gaunt and his mistress, Katherine Swynford, whom he later made his third wife – were lords of the manor of Canford between 1435 and 1509. Thus during the spasmodic Wars of the Roses, a struggle between the rival houses of Lancaster and York which arose out of the incompetence and mental instability of the Lancastrian Henry VI, the sympathies of Canford and Poole were with the Lancastrians, though, after Henry VI's final overthrow and death in 1471, Canford was bestowed by the victorious Yorkist claimant, Edward IV, upon his son, George, Duke of Clarence who was followed from 1478 to 1485 by Clarence's son, Edward, Earl of Warwick. Edward IV died young in 1483 and his son Edward V was removed from the throne by his

34. Lady Margaret Beaufort.

uncle, who installed himself as Richard III (1483-5). As opposition to Richard mounted, discontented Lancastrians looked to the son of Lady Margaret Beaufort, wife of Edmund Tudor – Henry Tudor, Earl of Richmond – as the Lancastrian claimant to the throne. One of his main supporters was the Dorset cleric, John Morton, formerly Rector of Bloxworth, who had become Bishop of Ely. He joined Henry Tudor in exile in Brittany. In October 1484 Henry set sail from St Malo with a large army of mercenaries in 15 ships making for Poole, hoping that, if he could effect a landing, an insurrection planned by the Duke of Buckingham would help him to overthrow Richard III. Possibly he made for Poole, because of the long-standing Beaufort associations of Canford and Poole, and because his grandparents, John and Margaret Beaufort, were buried in Wimborne Minster. A severe storm dispersed his fleet, but, wrote Holinshed, Henry's own ship 'cam at the last very early in the morning, when the winde grew calme, upon the south coast of the island, agaynst the haven caulyd Pole'. Henry saw the shore lined with soldiers. He accordingly waited in the hope that the rest of his ships would arrive, but meanwhile sent a boat towards the shore to try to ascertain whether the men on shore were friends or foes. The soldiers shouted out that they had been sent by Buckingham to welcome him. However, Henry suspected that he might be walking into a trap, and indeed, unknown to him, Buckingham had been captured and executed and the troops had been sent by Richard III to try to lure him ashore. The cautious Henry, finding that the rest of his ships had not arrived, prudently returned to France. Had he landed, he would have been caught and there would have been no Tudor dynasty. The next year he landed safely in Wales, the land of his Tudor ancestors, and went on to defeat Richard III at the battle of Bosworth and to seize the throne as Henry VII.

35. The Purbeck marble Beaufort tomb, Wimborne Minster with the alabaster effigies of John Beaufort, Duke of Somerset, and his wife, Margaret, grandparents of King Henry VII. Both wear the Lancastrian SS collar.

To consolidate the new king's position, his Dorset-born right-hand man, John Morton, soon to be Archbishop of Canterbury and a cardinal, arranged his marriage to Elizabeth, the Yorkist heiress, daughter of Edward IV. If her brothers Edward V and Richard, Duke of York – 'the princes in the Tower' – really were dead by this time, then the only surviving male member of the House of York – in fact the sole surviving Plantagenet prince –was Elizabeth's cousin, Edward, Earl of Warwick, lord of Canford manor. Henry duly imprisoned this potentially dangerous rival in the Tower of London and bestowed Canford upon his mother, the pious and scholarly Lady Margaret Beaufort. She very soon made her influence felt in the area, for she paid for the siting of the elaborate Beaufort tomb in Wimborne Minster, surmounted by exquisite effigies of her parents, John Beaufort, first Duke of Somerset and his wife, Margaret Beauchamp. She set up a chantry in the south chapel of the Minster alongside the font and provided that the chaplain should teach grammar 'to all who come for instruction according to the custom of the schools at Eton and Winchester'. Thus was launched the first grammar school in the area. Lady Margaret Beaufort came to be widely respected for her acts of charity and, when she died in 1509, the same year as her son, Henry VII, who was less than fourteen years her junior, her friend, Bishop John Fisher, preaching the funeral oration, declared that: 'All England for her death had cause for weeping . . . [such as] the poor creatures that were wont to receive her alms to whom she was always piteous and merciful . . . & all devout & virtuous persons to whom she was a loving sister'.

The Astronomical Clock of Wimborne Minster.

Chapter Five

The Tudor Transition

During the period of more than a century when England was ruled by the Tudor monarchs, the country underwent many important changes as it moved from the Middle Ages into the modern world. England broke away from the Roman Catholic Church and became a Protestant state. The authority of the monarch increased at the expense of the old medieval nobility, which was substantially replaced in influence and wealth by new men who served the king as lawyers and administrators. The expectation of greater internal stability not only encouraged trade and encouraged the middle classes, but also caused the new gentry to build unbattlemented houses intended for domestic comfort rather than defence. With knowledge of new lands beyond the oceans increasing yearly, Poole fishermen made their way to Newfoundland and traders sought new markets and sources of supply.

Because more documents covering the Poole area after 1485 are available – church records such as parish registers (from the earliest possible year, 1538, for Poole) and borough accounts, and a continuous list of mayors from 1490 – it is possible to have a fuller understanding of the Poole district in the Tudor period. The Privy Purse Expenses tell us that Henry VII on a tour of the south in 1496 was on 'July 25th at Christchurch, July 26th at Pole; July 27th at Corfe'. Unfortunately, we have no description of this particular royal visit, but clearly the king had to be feasted and accommodated in a suitably imposing building. Christchurch Priory could have provided lavish hospitality on the previous day and in Poole it could well be that Henry VII was entertained at the 'Old Town House' (Scaplen's Court). Eventually it formed a rectangle 80 feet by 61 feet and parts of the fine open roof may date from the late 14th century, though most of the building seems to belong to the late 15th century. It could well have been Poole's late medieval town hall and Henry VII might have stayed the night in the solar. When John Leland, the Tudor topographer, visited Poole between 1536 and 1542 he wrote:

> Pole is no town of auncient occupying in marchandise; but rather of old tyme a poor fisshar village ... There be men alyve that saw almost all the town of Pole kyvered with segge and risshes ... It is [within the memory of men] much encreasid with fair building and use of marchaundise. It standeth almost as an island in the haven, and hangith by N.E. to the mayne land by the space almost of a flite shot. And in this place is a dike, and to it often cummith through out the haven water, and here is an embattlid gate of stone to enter into the town. The length of the town liythe almost fulle by N. and S. *There is a fair town house of stone by The Key.*

Recent expert opinion pronounces Scaplen's Court to be 'one of the finest examples of a fifteenth century town house on the south coast'. There were probably other fine stone houses belonging to merchants by the quay, but in fact Leland referred just to one 'fair town house of stone' and so there is reasonable probability that this was what is now called Scaplen's Court. During the 17th century it became the *George Inn* and in the 18th it was purchased from Benjamin Skutt, four times mayor of Poole, by John Scaplen, whose name remains attached to it. Later the south front of the building partially collapsed and was faced with nine inches of brickwork which totally concealed its age and nature. Later it was converted into eight tenements which by the early 20th century had fallen into a bad state of repair. Considerable damage caused by a severe storm in 1923 exposed what H. P. Smith, local historian and headmaster of South Road School, recognised as part of a substantial late medieval structure. After many setbacks, including further damage caused by another

36. Scaplen's Court as revealed in the 1920s.

37. The roofing of Scaplen's Court.

38.   The roof of Bere Regis church with the 12 apostles.

gale in 1925, sufficient money to begin the work of restoration was raised, thanks especially to the efforts of H. P. Smith, Charles Carter, a former mayor of Poole, and the Society of Poole Men. It was taken over in 1931 by the Poole Corporation as a centre for a historical museum and, after further imaginative reconstruction of the High Street frontage in 1985-6, it now houses Poole's Museum of Domestic Life.

Henry VII and his chief adviser, Cardinal Morton, consolidated the position of the new Tudor monarchy by building up the Crown's financial resources, encouraging trade and shipbuilding, avoiding war and developing friendly relations with Spain, cemented by the betrothal of Henry's heir, young Arthur, Prince of Wales to Catherine, daughter of Ferdinand of Aragon and Isabella of Castile, whose marriage had united Spain. Morton himself accumulated considerable wealth as Archbishop of Canterbury and Lord Chancellor and drew on some of it to rebuild and beautify Bere Regis church, where the tombs of his mother's family, the Turbervilles, were located. The magnificent timber roof with 12 painted figures with the robes and beard styles of 1500, representing the 12 apostles, at the end of the hammer beams, form a lasting memorial to this great statesman from Dorset.

In Henry VII's reign there was an increasing volume of trade with Spain and the Studland Bay wreck, located in 1984, may well be that of a Spanish merchant ship trading with England. The shifting of sand as a result of storms early in 1984 exposed part of the timbers of this vessel so that they fouled a fisherman's nets. Investigation by the Hamworthy Sub-Aqua Club with the guidance and co-operation of the Poole Museum Service and the National Maritime Museum and with the help of sophisticated electronic equipment has made possible a provisional diagram of the nature of the wreck. What the divers have discovered seems to be one almost complete side of a vessel consisting of a number of strakes of planking some 75 feet in extent. The planking is carvel, that is, it consists of planks fitted edge to edge to provide a smooth outer surface – a method in general use in the Mediterranean, by contrast with the clinker-built construction of overlapping planks usual in Northern Europe. The lightness of construction suggests a late medieval merchant ship as does the cargo of pottery of between 1475 and 1525. Much of the pottery, though discoloured black by the sea-water, appears to be fine Spanish tri-glazed pottery with blue and purple decoration known as Isabella Polychrome. Also present is high quality copper lustre ware, Spanish coarse-ware and a jug from Saintonge in west France. These finds suggest that a ship trading between Spain and England or Flanders with a cargo of pottery was battered by storms and sank within sight of land. Whether it was making for Poole it may never be possible to determine. The wreck has been diagnosed as 'the sixth oldest so far discovered in British coastal waters and which has the most substantial surviving timbers'. It is older than the *Mary Rose*.

During Henry VII's one-day visit to Poole in 1496 he would have been introduced to many of the leading merchants, many of whom at one time or another

39. Isabella polychrome plate.

served the borough in the office of bailiff or of mayor. Particularly prominent at the time of Henry VII's visit were John Norton, mayor in 1496 and on at least three other occasions, John Bedford, mayor in 1493, 1499, 1503 and 1509, Thomas Whyte, mayor in 1504, 1510, 1511 and 1517, and James Havilland, mayor in 1494 and 1498. Thomas Whyte was probably the descendant of that Thomas le White who in 1332 was one of the 27 wealthier Poole men, assessed for taxation. A William White had been mayor in 1459, but Thomas was obviously the family's favourite Christian name. It was the son of Thomas White, mayor under Henry VII, who acquired land at Fiddleford, near Sturminster Newton, setting himself up as a country gentleman, but still heading the Poole merchant firm and serving as mayor in 1531, 1538 and 1545 and as M.P. for Poole in 1553. He was probably the 'old Thomas White, a great rich merchant and leader of the papists' who in 1553 led the opposition to the radical Protestant rector of St James. His son, Thomas White, junior had been mayor in 1551 and John Hanham, M.P. for Poole in 1547, evidently went along with the move to Protestantism and later acquired the Dean's Court estate, which the Hanham family have held ever since. Richard Phelips, of Charborough, M.P. for Poole in 1511 and Collector of Customs at Poole 1522-26, purchased the estate at Corfe Mullen in 1538 and his grandson John Phelips was M.P. for Poole in 1555. Perhaps the most remarkable of the Poole merchant families in the Tudor period was that of Havilland. In 1469 Edward IV had granted special trading privileges in Poole, Exeter and Dartmouth to 16 Channel Islanders, who had helped him to dislodge an invading French force from Mont Orgeuil Castle in Jersey. One of these was Thomas de Havilland, Sieur of Havilland in Guernsey, who despite his noble origins had no objection to involving the family in trade and accordingly sent his second son, James de Havilland, to Poole in 1471, where he soon became one of its wealthiest merchants and was twice mayor. James de Havilland and his wife, Helène de Beauvoir, also from Guernsey, were great benefactors to the town. They endowed a chantry and built the north aisle of old St James's church. In the 18th century there was a Gothic inscription cut in the stonework over the arches leading from the north aisle into the nave with the coats of arms of the De Havilland and De Beauvoir families on either side. It read: 'These six Arches made at the charge of James Havilland and Helene his wife, on whose souls God have mercy. Amen. Anno Domini m.cccccij'. Thomas de Havilland, the elder brother of James, who stayed behind in the Channel Islands, interestingly became the ancestor of Geoffrey de Havilland, the aviation engineer, and the film actress, Olivia de Havilland, and her sister, Joan Fontaine. Four sons of James (de) Havilland and a grandson served as mayors of Poole in the 16th century as did later descendants, Havilland Hiley and Peter Hiley in the 17th century. Another grandson, Matthew Havilland was Rector of St James's (1566-70). Helena, daughter of James de Havilland, married William Pitt of Blandford and became the ancestress of several worthy doctors and parsons named Pitt in the Blandford area, of 'Diamond Pitt', the highly successful East India Company trader and governor of Madras, two Pitt M.P.s for Wareham, William Morton Pitt, M.P. for Poole 1780-91, a great pioneer of agicultural reform, four British prime ministers – the elder William Pitt (Earl of Chatham), the younger William Pitt, Henry Addington (Lord Sidmouth) and Lord Rosebery – as well as the intrepid traveller in the Middle East, Lady Hester Stanhope, and the pioneer of modern archaeology, General Augustus Pitt-Rivers (1827-1900).

Surviving documentary evidence enables us to obtain a good picture of what the members of these and other families who accepted office in the borough or church did to promote and protect the interests of the community in the early 16th century. There are several impressive examples of their efforts to provide entertainment, to ensure adequate milling facilities and supplies of water and timber, to maintain practical means of punishing and deterring anti-social behaviour and to organise defence against any external attack upon the community.

40.   Probable appearance of the merchant ship wrecked in Studland
Bay, c.1500.

41.   Ships' timbers on the site of the Poole Foundry, excavated in 1987.

In this age before the advent of the gramophone, radio or television the arrival in the district of a group of minstrels or strolling players could be the occasion for great excitement. Indeed the annual statement for 1512 recorded that 'If . . . minstrels and players come to the town, then the mayor shall send for his brethren and by their advice shall reward them with such money as they think convenient and that money so given shall be at the town's cost'. Thus in 1515 6s. 8d. was paid 'to Cornish for the minstrel that went about the town in the morning and evenings'; in 1524 6s. 8d. was paid out as 'a reward to my Lord of Arundel's players' and 3s. 4d. as 'a reward to the King's minstrels' whilst in 1530 2s. 0d. was dispensed 'to the players that played at the Mayor's dinner'. The first reference to the mayor's annual dinner was in 1511 and among the items of expenditure were 13s. 4d. to the mayor for his dinner, 4s. 4d. for his costs, 20s. 0d. for a 'kercher' (a head-dress) for the mayoress and 20s. 0d. for minstrels.

Excavations in 1987 on the demolished Poole Foundry site between the quay and St James's church revealed a unique cache of some 50 ships' timbers, dating from about 1500 and including large stem and stern posts and Y-shaped mast crutches – probably part of the store of a family boat-building business – placed on a sandy beach for preservation until they were required in the repair or construction of future vessels. There may well be a connection between this unprecedented find and the shortage of timber in Poole which was behind a licence granted by Henry VIII in 1521 to permit the people of Poole to obtain as much wood for their ready money as they at any season shall need 'from Hampshire and Sussex' in view of the fact that 'the burgesses and inhabitants of the town of Poole . . . be destitute of wood'. Negotiations were opened up in 1524 with a Master Compton of Bisterne, a ranger in the New Forest, for the purchase of timber and these involved sending him presents of fresh fish and salted conger-eels and the mayor and his brethren riding out to Ringwood to meet Mr. Compton, who in his turn made them a present of a buck, for the bailiff's accounts show an allocation of 6s. 8d. 'to rychard allynys wyffe for ye bakying of a buke that m' compton send to m' mear & his bretheryn'.

In 1524 timber was needed for a new pillory and a new 'conking-stool' – or ducking-stool, in which a woman guilty of slandering her neighbours was firmly fastened and then with the stool attached to a beam projecting from the edge of the quay, where it was pivoted, the offending woman could be duly soaked in the waters of the harbour. The accounts of the bailiff, John Mann, show that the pillory and conking-stool were transported from Sturminster Newton castle, 8s. 0d. being paid for carriage, whilst a man named Lewis was paid 21s. 7d. for the timber and making the pillory and conking-stool, 1s. 4d. for food for himself and for the food and labour of an assistant, together with 2d. to Nicholas Howseck for half a day's work erecting the pillory. A further 5s. 3d. was laid out on ironwork for the conking-stool and for the hauling of the timber. Incidentally, the pillory stood in what was then called Pillory Street, now Upper Market Street, whilst the stocks were located on the north side of the Town Cellars. Poole's stocks have long since disappeared, but those of Wimborne are preserved in the garden of the Priest's House museum and those of Charlton Marshall are outside the church there.

In 1542 to provide two other vital amenities the burgesses obtained a licence from Henry VIII (1) 'to erect . . . upon the King's waste ground . . . called Bayter . . . one good and sufficient windmill to serve the said town and port . . . and to have one hundred feet of assize square of the said waste ground for a convenient hill to be made to set one windmill upon', and (2) 'to set one conduit head at Totnam [Tatnam], . . . for the conveying of fresh water for the serving of the said town'. This two-fold major construction enterprise cost the town £7 17s. 3d., but 21s. 5d. had to be borrowed from church funds to meet this expense. The mill was duly leased to James Mesurer at an annual rental of £3 6s. 8d.

The Borough obtained its income from various dues connected with the port's activities such as anchorage, poisage (payment for the use of the town beam to weigh goods), quayage (a pro rata tariff on all imports and exports), cellarage, cartage and the sale of ballast. The church derived revenues, totalling £3 19s. 8d. in 1530, from rents payable on seven houses, five shops and five gardens which had been bequeathed at various times in the past.

In view of Poole's coastal position adequate preparations for defence were important. In 1512 the town owed Richard Havilland 40s. 8d. for 5 cwt. 19 lbs. of gunpowder and in 1525 ran up a bill with his brother William for 20s. for 40 tons of wall stone and 3s. for 12 bushels of lime. In 1524 major repairs had been required on the town gate which controlled the narrow strip of land on the north side of the town between the two dykes which filled with tidal water. Thus the bailiff paid out

> for drink for the men that did carry up the stones at the Bulwark, and for them that did work at the Town's Gate . . . 2s. 5d., for resin for the gate, 4d.; for resining of the gate 2s. 5d. . . . and for making the iron-work of the gate, weighing 1 cwt. 3 qu. 20 lb., 36s.

although he obtained a rebate of 3s. 6d. for the old scrap iron from the gate. Also in 1524 the 'Quay Stairs' or steps were repaired and a wooden platform was constructed for mounting a number of guns on the quayside. This platform was ornamented with wooden lions and griffins – the supporters of the Tudor royal coat of arms – and a Christchurch artist, John Nightingale, was paid 13s. 4d. to paint the lions and griffins. It took Thomas, a carpenter from Wimborne, and his man 11 days to make the posts for the stairs and the covers for the guns and the carpenter was paid 11 shillings, that is, at the rate of 12d. a day as wages for himself and his assistant together. 49s. 6d. was also spent on gunpowder.

However, Poole men did not just rely on cannon. Perhaps remembering the effective use of the longbow in the 1405 raid, they maintained practice in archery.

42. Tudor arms in the mantelpiece in Poole Guildhall Museum.

In 1512 John Havilland was paid £1 'to buy 6 bows and 2 sheaf arrow-cases', whilst 30 years later 6s. 8d. was dispensed on the provision of 'ockey [oaken] piles for the town butts'. West Butts Street records the location on the west shore where on Sundays and Holy Days able-bodied men turned out for archery practice. When a French invasion was threatened in 1545, a chain of beacon fires was ignited along the south coast. A 1544 document referred to 'hoblers [ie. watchers light horses] to kepe the watche in the tyme of warre, at the bekon called Werybarowe'. This has sometimes been identified with Worbarrow in the Isle of Purbeck, but it must surely have been some high place close to Poole since in 1462 the mayor, William White, had been ordered 'to set the accustomed watches at Wyrebarowe by Pole, for the safety of the town and the adjacent country' – possibly on Constitution Hill.

In 1529 England like most of Europe acknowledged the Pope as head of the Church and had the same religious beliefs and ceremonial. 'Peter's Pence', a tax paid by England to the Pope since the reign of King John, was unpopular, especially since the Pope was usually an Italian and payment of this tribute involved a draining of wealth abroad. In 1529 Henry

VIII quarrelled with the Pope because of his refusal to grant the king a divorce from
Catherine of Aragon. Of the children of his marriage to this Spanish princess only one
daughter, Mary, survived and Henry wished to marry again in the hope of obtaining a male
heir. Henry VIII persuaded Parliament to transfer to him the taxes normally paid to the
Pope and to grant him authority over marriage and wills. Archbishop Cranmer granted
Henry his divorce and in 1534 Parliament accepted the Act of Supremacy recognising the
king as 'Supreme Head of the Church'. In 1538 Thomas Cromwell, Henry VIII's Vicar-
General, issued instructions that every officiating priest should keep a book in which he was
to register every baptism, marriage and burial – to the abiding delight of all future
genealogists. The Parish Register of St James, Poole, is one of the very few registers in the
country which have actually survived from 1538 onwards, although sadly many of the early
pages have been damaged by damp. One 1539 entry refers to the king's new status: 'Master
John Horssey, the son of sir John Horssey Knygtte of the paryshe of Clyffton was maryed
to Edythe Stocker the wyffe late off John Stocker merchawntt of pole the xiiij day of dec'ber
be privylegge gevyn by our *supreme hedd of the chyrche of Ingeland kynge henry the viijth*'.

43. Vatican stamp of 1946, portraying Reginald
Pole.

Sir Thomas More and Bishop Fisher
were executed for refusing to recognise
Henry as Supreme Head of the Church.
Other victims of Henry's suspicions were
certain surviving members of the House of
York, who might become claimants to the
throne and rallying points of resistance to
Henry's religious policies. Edward, Earl
of Warwick, had been executed in 1499,
but his sister, the last of the Plantagenets,
Margaret, Countess of Salisbury, who
held the manor of Christchurch, was arrested, accused of treason but given no
trial and beheaded in 1541 because her
son, Reginald Pole, Dean of Wimborne,
in 1535 wrote a booklet attacking Henry's
claim to be Head of the Church. The
beautiful Salisbury Chantry, built to receive her remains, was deliberately de-
faced so that her coat of arms and badges
were removed. The countess's cousin,
Henry, Marquess of Exeter, a grandson
of Edward IV and lord of the manor of
Canford (1536-9), was accused of plotting
to put Reginald Pole on the throne and
was executed in 1539. His wife, Gertrude,
Marchioness of Exeter, who had also been found guilty of high treason, was later pardoned
and lived on to end her days as lady of the manor of Canford (1552-7) and to be buried in
the Courtenay tomb in Wimborne Minster.

Henry VIII and Parliament dissolved the monasteries, which remained centres of Papal
influence. Commissioners were sent to report on each monastery and each one was closed
down; its buildings, lands and treasures were confiscated by the king, although the monks
and nuns received pensions provided that they did not resist the closure. Poole had no
monastery, but Christchurch Priory was both wealthy and famous. Its prior, John Draper,
one of the king's chaplains, wrote a persuasive letter to the king, pleading poverty in an

attempt to get the priory exempted from dissolution. He argued that it was the only church for miles around, that it maintained a school which taught Divinity and Grammar, that the local poor depended on alms from the monastery and that there was no accommodation available for travellers other than at the priory. All the pleading was of no avail, but the commissioners reported that they found the prior 'a very honest, conformable person' and he accordingly received a good pension. The report also noted that the house was 'well furnysshede of jewellys and plate whereof som be mete for the Kings majeste is use as A litill chalys of golde . . . two basuns doble gylt having the King's armys well inamyld'. The revenue of the priory amounted to some £600 a year. The priory church had always been the place of worship for the townspeople and so it continued for the king bestowed it upon 'the wardens and inhabitants of Christchurch for ever'. The Prior was granted a pension of £138 6s. 8d. per year and was allowed to continue to reside in the Prior's lodging. The canons received pensions ranging from £10 to £3 6s. 8d. The nunnery of Tarrant Kaines was duly surrendered without resistance by the abbess, Margaret Russell, and she was awarded a pension of £40 a year and the other 19 received pensions according to status and years of service ranging from £6 13s. 4d. down to £3 6s. 8d.

Under Henry VIII the doctrines and the ceremonial of the Church remained in the main Roman Catholic. In St James's church there were many images, venerated, as Protestant reformers saw it, with ignorant and superstitious awe. Above the gilded and painted rood-screen separating the nave from the more sacred choir area was the wooden Rood, a life-size figure of Jesus on the cross flanked on either side by figures of the Virgin Mary and of St John, and the Churchwardens' Accounts of 1530 recorded that 16d. was spent for 'four dozen images of wax to hang afore the Rood' and that a shilling was paid to Robert Smith, of Poole, for 'making of the candlesticks that standed in the window afore Saint Katherine'. An inventory of church vestments, plate and ornaments, made in 1545 referred to 'six candlesticks with branches of latten [fine brass] that stood afore images'; 'a spoon of silver to put in the frankincense to cense [burn] withal'; many different vestments, for example, 'a suit of blue velvet, embroidered', one of 'red velvet, embroidered', 'a suit of green bodkin' (rich embroidered silk), 'a suit of black damask' and 'a suit of vestments set with pearl the whole suit' for priests to wear on the appropriate occasions; six chalices and five pyxes (caskets containing the Consecrated Host, that is to say, the bread which, when blessed by the priest during the Mass, was believed to have been transformed into the flesh of Christ – incidentally in the view of Protestants a thoroughly superstitious and erroneous belief). On Corpus Christi Day a pyx containing the Sacrament would be paraded round the streets of Poole accompanied by lighted torches, whilst the church bells were rung. Again too on the Anniversary Day, the names of all the benefactors of the Church would be recited and the Great Dirige or dirge would be celebrated by prayers for the souls of the dead benefactors and their families, to secure for them, so it was believed, a reduction in the period of suffering in Purgatory. In 1530 6s. 4d. was paid out for the Church Dirige on 26 February, and it was noted that John Ellis had bequeathed the Church his feather-bed so that prayers might be said for his soul. Such ceremonial was regarded by Protestants as erroneous and superstitious and was intended to enrich the Church. As early as 1516 one Michael Gamare, a surviving Lollard or pioneering Protestant, from Wimborne St Giles, poured scorn on the women there who came and set their candles before a piece of wood, the image of St Giles. 'They might just as well', he said, 'put their candles in their pew seats or upon a chimney, for all the good it would do, for the saint is in Heaven, or wherever it pleaseth God, and the image of St Giles is but a stone and if the said image fell down it would break their heads'.

Reformers regarded such practices as idolatrous and superstitious and held that the priests were hoodwinking the laity with mock miracles, when they should be teaching their parishioners the basic Christian truths set out in the Bible. Henry VIII was in fact much troubled by the activities of one English priest and scholar, William Tyndale, who, without permission of the bishops, was busy translating the New Testament into English, following the example of Martin Luther who had translated the Bible into German. Tyndale, like Luther, took the strong Protestant view that every man and woman had a right to read the Bible or to have it read in his or her own language. Despite the fact that Tyndale in his *Obedience of a Christian Man* insisted on obedience to a monarch even if tyrannical, Henry VIII condemned his activities lest readers of the Bible should form their own opinions which might clash with those of the king. Tyndale had fled to the continent, carried on his work of translation and smuggled printed copies of the gospels into England concealed in bales of wool. Henry appealed to the Emperor Charles V, ruler of Belgium, to hunt Tyndale down as a dangerous heretic. A certain Henry Phelips, third son of Richard Phelips, of Charborough, who had been M.P. for Poole in 1511 and was Collector of Customs at Poole, 1522-6, had been sent up to London with a sum of money to settle a debt owed by his father, but there 'chanced to fall into play' and gambled the money away. The angry father disinherited young Phelips, who in dire need of money let himself be recruited as a secret agent with the task of tracking down Tyndale and betraying him. He found Tyndale living in the 'English House' at Antwerp, a safe house where English merchants could lodge without fear of interference. Henry Phelips enrolled as a student at Louvain University and contrived to be introduced to Tyndale, who showed him his books and explained the nature of his work. Phelips duly reported this to the Emperor's officials and carefully planned to betray the scholar into their hands. Leaving the secret police outside the 'English House', Phelips invited Tyndale out for a meal, though Tyndale responded, 'No, I go forth this day to dinner and you shall go with me and be *my* guest'. The entrance to the house consisted of a narrow passage along which two men could not walk abreast. Accordingly as it is related in Foxe's *Book of Martyrs*, 'Master Tyndale, being a man of no great stature, went before, and Phillips, a tall comely person, followed behind him, who had set officers on either side of the door upon two seats, which being there, might see who came into the entry; and coming through the same entry, Phillips pointed with his finger over Master Tyndale's head to indicate that he was the man to be arrested'. The soldiers duly pounced on Tyndale and led him away to prison, 'saying of him that they pitied his simplicity when they took him'. Tyndale was cross-examined in Vilvorde Castle, declared to be an heretic and duly executed – strangled and then burnt at the stake in October 1536. Before he died, Tyndale prayed aloud, 'Lord, open then the King of England's eyes'. Ironically, that same year Henry VIII had ordered that a translation of the Bible into English – by Miles Coverdale, an earlier associate of Tyndale – should be placed in each parish. This was, perhaps, Henry VIII's main concession to Protestantism.

Henry Phelips gained very little from his act of treachery and, dissatisfied, he began to rail against Henry VIII as 'the tyrant of England' and in 1539 his name was included in a list of English traitors abroad. Penniless and desperate he wrote six letters home to England pleading for help and forgiveness – to his father and mother, two brothers and two brothers-in-law, one of the latter being John Stocker, a merchant of Poole, probably son of the man of the same name who was mayor of Poole in 1518. There is no evidence that Henry Phelips' father responded to the appeal. He was very busy at this time arranging the purchase of the manors of Corfe Mullen and Corfe Hubert. Henry Phelips was reported to be in prison in Vienna in 1542, but nothing is known of his ultimate fate. His nephew, John Phelips, served as M.P. for Poole in 1555 and his elder brother, Thomas, as Poole's M.P. in 1557.

In 1547 Henry VIII was succeeded by his nine-year-old son, Edward VI, who under the guidance of his uncle, the Duke of Somerset (who incidentally became lord of the manor of Canford), set to work to make England a Protestant country. Parliament repealed all the laws against Lollards and by an Act of 1547 ordered the dissolution of all chantries and gild chapels and the confiscation of their endowments on the grounds that prayers for the dead were no longer needed since the existence of Purgatory was now rejected. Consequently in Poole the Guild of St George was dissolved, although its property was purchased from the Crown on behalf of the town for £21 14s. 2d. and was taken over by five trustees to be administered on behalf of the burgesses of Poole. Ultimately in 1586 the two remaining trustees, Thomas White junior and Christopher Havilland, handed over all the premises to the mayor and burgesses of Poole. These arrangements had ensured the continuance of the Almshouses. In Wimborne the 1547 Act had meant that Lady Margaret's Chantry was dissolved and there were loud protests at the closure of the school which it had provided. It was argued that a school was 'very requisite and necessary' to a 'great market town' like Wimborne and that there was no other grammar school within 12 miles to which the townsfolk could send their children. The Churchwardens' Accounts show that interim steps were taken to provide some sort of education and money was found to employ a schoolmaster, but it was only in 1563 that the problem was resolved when Queen Elizabeth granted a Charter setting up a corporation to run the town of Wimborne and also to provide a free grammar school.

Meanwhile under Edward VI elaborate clerical vestments and surplus church plate were confiscated, the clergy were allowed to marry and Archbishop Cranmer in 1549 produced an English-language Prayer Book, incorporating many Protestant doctrines, which all clergy were required to use. Protector Somerset was essentially a moderate, hoping that, by bringing in changes a few at a time, he could carry public opinion with him, but there were extreme Protestants, like the Rev. Thomas Hancock, Rector of Poole, who wanted to eliminate all Roman Catholic error at once and would not compromise with what they regarded as truth. Certainly the forthright and tactless Thomas Hancock stirred up trouble wherever he went, as he showed only too clearly in his autobiography. In this he related how he was allowed to preach at Christchurch, where he was born, by the vicar, Mr. Smith. The priest then being at Mass, Hancock told the congregation that what the priest held over his head (that is, the consecrated bread), they saw with their bodily eyes, but Christ had said 'plainly that we shal se him no more; then you that doo knele unto hytt, pray unto hytt, and honor hytt as God, doo make an idol of hytt and yourselves doo commyte most horrible idolatry'. The vicar then interrupted Hancock and told him that up to that point he had done well, but then he had played the part of a bad cow, which, having given a good bucket of milk, then kicked it over with her foot, so that all was lost. Hancock was then called, as he put it, 'to be minister of God's word at the town of Pole', whose people were 'the first thatt in thatt parte of England were called Protestantes'. One Sunday in July 1547 he inveighed against idolatry and covetousness and denounced the Catholic mass and doctrine of transubstantiation (the belief that when the priest blessed the bread and wine, it actually turned into the flesh and blood of Christ). This was too much for 'olde Thomas Whyghtt a greate rych marchant and ringleader of the Papistes' who 'rose owtt off hys seate and wentt outt of the church, saying "Come from hym, good people; he came from the divell, and teacheth unto you develish doctrine"'.

Then on All Saints Day Thomas White, John Northerell and William Havilland – all former mayors – told the curate to say Dirige for all souls, whereupon Hancock forbade him to do so and they threatened to make Hancock say the 'Dirige', too. Then, said Hancock,

did they all as hytt wer with on mouth call me Knav and my wyff strompett, som of them threatning me thatt they wold make me draw my gutts after me. The vicar, being an honest good man, Morgan Reade by name, thrust me into the qwier, and pulled the qwyer dorse fast too, commanding them to kepe the King's peace, but they spared nott to call the maior Knave; the maior had much worke too stopp thys horly burly, untyll he had gotten the chef of them owtt of the churche.

Hancock also related how the wife of a man named Woodcock went into Wimborne saying that there was a voice following her saying that he whom the king trusted best would work treason against him. Hancock reported this to Protector Somerset, who was in fact soon afterwards accused of treason, overthrown and executed by his ruthless rival, the Duke of Northumberland, who then, as Protector, carried the Reformation still further and ordered the destruction of all images and altars.

As young Edward VI was dying of tuberculosis and the designated heir was his Catholic sister, Mary Tudor, Northumberland persuaded the king to nominate his young Protestant cousin, Lady Jane Grey, daughter of the Marquess of Dorset, as his successor. Northumberland had married her off to his own son, clearly hoping to keep himself in power. Fearing just that outcome, a majority of influential people declared in favour of Mary, who on becoming queen declared that she intended to remain in the Roman Catholic faith and hoped that her people would wish to embrace it. Hancock preached a sermon saying that God had sent three plagues to punish the people for their sins: (1) a sweating sickness which spared no one, so that people who were dancing in the court at nine o'clock were dead by eleven; (2) the death of the virtuous King Edward VI; (3) 'to be robbed and spoyled of the jewel and treasure of God's holy word'. Understandably Hancock was excluded from the general pardon granted by Queen Mary and he thought it wise to flee the country with his wife and son, finally making his way to Geneva, the headquarters of John Calvin, the radical Protestant theologian.

44. Poole coat of arms (1554), now in Scaplen's Court.

Mary I restored the Roman ritual and her cousin, Cardinal Reginald Pole, became Archbishop of Canterbury and secured a reconciliation with the Pope. She launched a policy of persecuting Protestants and was supported in this by the Bishop of Exeter, James Turberville, a member of the Bere Regis family. Public opinion was alienated when 300 Protestants were burnt at the stake as heretics. When Mary died childless in 1558, a majority of the people accepted a moderately Protestant settlement worked out by the new queen, Mary's half-sister, Elizabeth I and Parliament, by which she was proclaimed 'Supreme Governor of the Church', and the English prayer book was restored. Roman Catholics who would not attend the new services were merely fined, and even Bishop Turberville, who refused to accept her as 'Supreme Governor', suffered only a short term of imprisonment. Simon Berwyke, a former monk of Cerne, who had been rector of St James's 1557-9 and whose neat handwriting in the Poole parish register is such a delight to read, was one of the 200 clergy who gave up his living rather than accept the new Protestant settlement. One later rector, Matthew Havilland (1566-70), seems to have been unpopular with his Protestant parishioners, so that he too was forced to resign.

Meanwhile the nephew of Gertrude, Marchioness of Exeter, James Blount, Lord Mountjoy had succeeded her as Lord of Canford manor. He was soon busy excavating alum-bearing shales and clays from Durley Cliff near Alum Chines, to obtain alum and copperas, both used in dyeing, in his two factories in Parkstone. Soon he was persuaded, in return for a

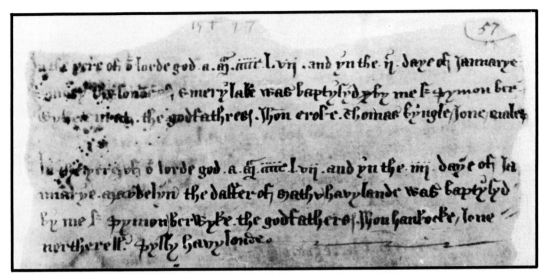

45. Extract from the 1557 baptismal entries in the parish register of St James's, Poole. Note the reference to Matthew Havilland.

present of the huge sum of £100 from the burgesses of Poole, to drop any objections to Queen Elizabeth granting to Poole the Charter of 1568, which so greatly increased the powers and the independence of the Borough of Poole. The Great Charter of Elizabeth contained the following provisions:

(1) The town of Poole was given corporate status, the right to sue and to be sued in the courts and the power to purchase and hold land and other property. (This was to make it possible for the borough to own the former property of the Guild of St George.)

(2) The Mayor and two Bailiffs were to be elected by the Burgesses each year on the Friday before the Feast of St Matthew (21 September) and were to be sworn in before the burgesses (not before the steward of the Lord of the Manor).

(3) Poole continued to be a port of the Staple and its burgesses were to elect the Mayor and two Constables of the Staple.

(4) Poole was created a county of itself and styled 'THE COUNTY OF THE TOWN OF POOLE, distinct and separate from the County of Dorset'.

(5) Poole was to have its own Sheriff, the monarch's representative, elected annually by the Burgesses. He was to hold a monthly court, to carry out all writs from the Crown, to act as Returning Officer in parliamentary elections, to be responsible for prisoners in the Town Gaol and to superintend executions.

(6) A court was to be held in the Guildhall every Thursday.

(7) The mayor was to be in control of checking the price, weight and measure of bread, ale, wine and other foodstuffs.

(8) The Mayor, together with 'one skilled in the law' (that is, the Recorder, or local judge) and four burgesses were to act as Justices of the Peace in the town of Poole. This meant that Poole had its own Quarter Sessions before which more serious offences could be tried.

(9) All fines imposed in the Borough should go to the Mayor, Bailiffs, Burgesses and Commonalty of Poole – and not to the Crown or to the lord of the manor.

(10) The people of Poole were to be exempted from all tolls or quayage (duties on imports or exports) in other parts of England.

There was a special need for an adequate meeting-place for the town council and a safe building to hold criminals. A new building in Fish (now Castle) Street provided for a new guildhall on the first floor, with a prison beneath. When the Poole people petitioned for this charter, they suggested that a free grammar school should be set up, but that amenity seems not to have come until 1628.

The extensive privileges contained in the Great 1568 Charter undoubtedly reflect the growing importance of the town and port. The nature of its population and shipping resources were set out in a 36-page book containing the findings of a census conducted on 5 May 1574. This showed that Poole had a total of 1,373 inhabitants, of whom 165 were householders and sub-tenants and 296 were listed as 'able-bodied men'. Typical entries:

> James Lambert & his wife & 4 sons & 2 daughters & a Jersey
> lad upon assay [that is, on trial] & a man servant   10
> Peter Gaydon, his wife and 4 children, and a maid-servant
> called Ann Colers & a man-servant called James Gilford
> [N.B. Peter Gaydon was Mayor in 1574]   8
> Matthew Runner & his wife & one child; & Nicholas Curry &
> his wife & sister which have been in the town but a month
> or thereabouts   6

46. (*left*) The Tudor gable behind No. 14 High Street, Poole.

47. (*above*) A Canadian stamp portraying Sir Humphrey Gilbert.

The average in each household was probably about eight. Thirteen poor people were living in the Almshouses of St George in Pillory Street and another eight paupers in an almshouse in West Street. Nineteen ships were listed. Among these was the *Falcon*, jointly owned by Dennis House (one of the two Constables who conducted the census), Christopher Farewell, John Bramble and John Rogers, all three of whom served as mayors.

Brewing beer was one of the new industries in Poole and many casks of Poole beer were exported to the Channel Islands. When the corporation imposed a tax of one penny per cask, the brewers loudly protested, especially Nicholas Curry, the newcomer featured above in the 1574 census. Poole men also began to mount expeditions across the Atlantic to fish for cod off Newfoundland, which John Cabot had discovered and claimed for England in 1497. As early as 1551 the town accounts record the payment of 6s. 6d. by 'two men which brought herrings and laded awey certain Newlonds fyshe'. In 1583, when Sir Humphrey Gilbert landed in Newfoundland and took possession in the name of Queen Elizabeth, the captain of one of the fishing vessels with him was Christopher Farewell, of Poole. The powers that be in Poole were not amused by Farewell's pioneering voyage, for he had been elected Senior Bailiff for the year. Accordingly he was removed from office and fined the huge sum of £30 for 'absentinge himself from his Office . . . this present yere in goying in a long voyage towardes the Newfound Land without the consent of the Maior, Justices, Brethren & the rest of the Burgesses'.

Threats of foreign invasion and concern for the safety of Poole shipping made the Poole community anxious to establish some fortifications on Brownsea Island as a first line of defence. During the Middle Ages the island had belonged to Cerne Abbey which held 'the right of wreck of the sea' and 'the right of free warren', i.e. to kill any rabbits and other wild life there. On the Dissolution it reverted to the Crown, and was subsequently granted to a succession of individuals. Henry VIII called upon Poole to help him construct a blockhouse or castle as part of a chain of coastal defences extending from Southsea to Portland. Thus in 1545 Mayor Thomas White paid out £10 for 'stone and chalk for the Castle at Brownsea'. A report in 1551 noted that the great tower was 44 feet square, but that the walls needed to be eight feet higher and that the wall of the barbican must be similarly raised since otherwise defenders would be exposed to the fire of enemies if they occupied the hill behind the castle. Ten years later the mayor and burgesses complained to the Privy Council that the castle was in a dilapidated state and that the guns were not in good order. The Crown therefore provided new cannon and Poole agreed to continue to pay the wages of six men to man the blockhouse. The 1574 Poole census may have been concerned with the need to provide men 'to attend & serve at the castle of Brownsea'. Then in 1576 Queen Elizabeth granted the castles of both Corfe and Brownsea to her favourite, Christopher Hatton, later to be Lord Chancellor, and gave him the title of 'Admiral of Purbeck'. The Poole Corporation protested, but in vain and were forced to hand over the castle. In fact 50 years earlier Poole had been granted exempt admiralty jurisdiction and the Poole Admiralty Court, presided over by the Mayor of Poole as Admiral, had authority within the waters traditionally controlled by Poole to enquire and take action regarding piracy, theft, assault, manslaughter or murder on board any vessels, breach of fishing regulations – concerning the size of nets, the season for dragging oysters, the organisation of amenities such as mooring-posts, the dredging of the channel between Poole quay and Hamworthy, and the repair of landing-stages or 'piles', such as 'Barber's Piles'.

Hatton was soon in dispute with the men of Poole, particularly when his new gunner on Brownsea violently interfered with Poole men operating the ferry between South and North Haven Points. When the government tried to confine larger ships to harbour in case they were needed for defence against the Spaniards, the Vice-Admiral of Dorset insisted that only small vessels should be allowed to leave Poole and then only if they had documents relating to the cargo and destination. The master and owner of the bark, *Bountiful Gift*, Walter Meryatt, wanted to take a cargo of copperas – green copper sulphate, used in dyeing, tanning and the manufacture of ink – and obtain a warrant from the Poole Comptroller of Customs. However, the gunner at Brownsea, Walter Partridge, refused to accept the warrant and ordered Meryatt to turn back. When Meryatt tried to proceed, Partridge fired two shots at the *Bountiful Gift* so severely wounding Meryatt and one of his mariners, William Drake, that they both died later the same day. At an inquest held at Poole a verdict of wilful murder was returned against Walter Partridge and in the Poole Parish Register there are these entries, 22 February 1589 (i.e. 1590):

> Walter Merrit was buryd. Master and owner of the *Bountiful Gift* was killed by a shot from
> Brounckesey Castle as was Wm. Drake, his man.
> The inquest of the Jury in the Town Chest
> Febr. 22, 1589. Will'm Drake was buried

Partridge, however, secured a pardon.

The cod-fishermen and indeed all sea-captains venturing from Poole faced not only storms but also attacks by pirates. In 1578 a small Poole barque returning from Guernsey was boarded by French pirates a mile off Swanage. Studland seems to have been the favourite lair of pirates who lay in wait for shipping coming in or out of Poole Harbour or sailing along the south coast. In 1581 the Privy Council was told of the capture at Studland Bay of 'John Piers (Pierce), a very notorious pirate, born in Cornwalle, who hath an old mother dwelling at Padstowe, noted to be a Wytche, to whom by reporte the said Piers hath conveyed all such goodes and spoiles as he hath wickedlie gotten at the seas'. Piers was described as 'a tall sklender man havinge longe black heare on his hed hanginge almoast downe to his shoulders, his visage beinge of a pale sikelye color, and sumwhat more heavye in the upper part of his bearde towardes his eares then on his chinn, beinge of the age of 28 or 30 yeares or sumwhat more'. He and his accomplice were locked up in Dorchester gaol, but bribed the gaoler to allow them to escape. They were, however, recaptured, tried and sentenced to death at Corfe Castle. Piers was duly hanged at Studland, 'to the terrifying of others for that the same place hathe bene much frequented and the inhabitants molested with pirates'.

It is on record that at least forty vessels were piratically seized and brought into Studland Bay in the space of three years. The captured cargoes were spirited away and exchanged for powder, shot and matches as well as beef and beer. The searcher at Poole is alleged to have supplied powder and matches to two notorious pirates in exchange for wine. Hawley, the vice-admiral of Purbeck, and his associates were said to have accepted bribes to permit the open sale of stolen goods. At Studland rowdy scenes took place in several inns frequented by the pirates offering for sale their ill-gotten gains. The most notable inn-keepers at Studland in league with the pirates were Joan Chaddock, Roger Munday, 'a common receiver', William Munday of whom a leading pirate, Clinton Atkinson, said that 'his house is the hell of the worlde, and he the divell'.

Understandably the burgesses of Poole petitioned the Privy Council for protection against the bands of pirates infesting Studland Bay and preying upon the shipping using Poole harbour 'to the utter undoing' of the trade of Poole merchants, but it was some time before they received any effective aid.

Meanwhile the pirates continued to prey on shipping, both English and foreign. One of the most successful, Stephen Heynes, captured the *Esperance of Dieppe*, laden in Brazil with 405 tons of brazil wood, 12 puncheons (casks) of pepper, a great quantity of cotton wool, 360 parrots and '54 munkeys, apes and other beastes', and brought the ship and its cargo into Studland. Mr. Phillips, 'captain of Bronckseye castle', had a parrot and a monkey from Heynes to whom he sold beer, though most of the monkeys were put on sale in

Devonshire. Heynes then seized the *Desperance of Humflytt* laden with '35,000 Newland fish' and 10 casks of train oil. Later Heynes captured a Scottish vessel, the *Salomon*, with a cargo of herrings, salmon and cloth and also the *Anne of Plymouth*, laden with hops, dye and raisins, and both of these ships were brought to Studland. With the connivance of the captain at Brownsea, Heynes was able to store three tons of brazil wood in the chapel on Brownsea and 112 hogsheads of Scottish herrings in the castle itself.

However, in the summer of 1583 the Admiralty sent two armed ships with 100 men on each to round up the pirates. Nine of the leading pirate captains of Studland Bay were arrested, taken up to London and hanged. Heynes was not one of them. He seems to have slipped through the net. Studland appears not to have been entirely cleaned up, for documents of 1585 and 1586 in the Poole archives refer to two French vessels with cargoes of salt having been taken by pirates to 'a certain roadstead on the coast of the realm about four miles from Poole' (presumably Studland Bay). The mayor of Poole took active steps to recover one of these ships and its cargo.

Pirates were not the only threat to Poole at this time, for invasion by the Spaniards was an imminent threat. Many clashes had occurred between English sea-captains like Francis Drake, who defied the Spanish King Philip II's ban on foreigners trading with the Spanish colonies in the West Indies and Central America, and Drake's circumnavigation of the world (1577-80), in the course of which he plundered many Spanish ships and ports on the Pacific coast, had further enraged the Spanish king. As the champion of the Catholic Counter-Reformation, he had been involved in several plots to depose Elizabeth, the chief Protestant monarch, and replace her by the Catholic ex-queen of Scotland, Mary Stuart. When Elizabeth allowed Mary to be executed in 1587, Philip planned to send a great fleet, the Armada, carrying a large invasion force up the Channel to occupy England. Antagonism towards Spain had been stirred by the story of the sufferings of a certain Miles Phillips who returned to Poole in 1582. He had been captured in Mexico whilst on one of Hawkins' trading expeditions; he was condemned as an heretic by the Inquisition and confined to a monastery; eventually after many adventures he was able to make his way back to England and Poole. At the end of 1586 a report was circulated in Poole that 600 French and Spanish ships with a huge army would soon attack England to avenge Drake's latest raid on the West Indies.

Poole seems to have been wide open to attack, for in 1577 it was reported to the Privy Council that Poole's trained band was 'a weak and simple company', since the best men were engaged in navigation, and that it had refused to pay a tax for mustering 30 soldiers. In 1586 the mayor wrote to the Privy Council begging that, in the event of invasion, Poole's small force should not be moved elsewhere, since the enemy might 'plant' himself in Poole and be difficult to eject. Yet there was only one corselet among all the inhabitants of Poole!

In 1587 a letter from Sir Henry Ashley, of Wimborne St Giles, one of the Deputy Lieutenants of Dorset, urged the mayor of Poole to strengthen the defences of the town and expressed his astonishment that when James Reade, captain of the trained bands in Poole, 'did of late call his band together and set up a maypole with a parrot upon the top thereof, so that his men could put in some archery practice, the Mayor had prohibited it'. However, the warning beacons in the area were duly manned in order to signal the arrival of the Spanish Armada in the Channel. In April 1588 Poole was called upon to contribute one ship and one pinnace to the naval defence force, but the mayor replied that Poole 'had only one ship above 60 tons in port and she was about to sail for Newfoundland', and lamented 'the great decay and disability of this poor town', due particularly to the activities of the pirates of Studland Bay. Poole did, however, make some contribution to the running battle with the Spaniards up the Channel by sending small vessels to replenish the royal warship *Anne Royal* with additional supplies of gunpowder during the battle fought against the

48. (*above*) Court House, Corfe Mullen (late 16th
century). This is now a private residence.

49. (*right*) The first-floor ceiling with ornamentation
including the Tudor rose and foliage at the Court House,
Corfe Mullen.

Armada off the Isle of Purbeck. One captured Spanish flagship, the *San Salvador*, after being stripped of its powder, sank later in the year in Studland Bay. The Armada was badly battered by the broadsides of the new-style English warships off the Flemish coast and the plan to land a large invasion force proved to be a fiasco.

Despite the defeat of the Armada, it was widely believed that Philip II would send another force to invade England. Roman Catholics had naturally been regarded as potential traitors since 1570, when the Pope had excommunicated and deposed Elizabeth, and absolved her subjects from their duty to obey her. Fines for non-attendance at church were greatly increased. Jesuits, members of the missionary society pledged to spread Roman Catholicism, were banned and it was made treason to convert any of the queen's subjects to Rome. The mayor of Poole received a copy of instructions that any persons, especially young men, coming into England or embarking on a ship to go abroad, should be cross-examined and that any suspected of being Jesuits or priests, or intending to travel to a Catholic seminary, should be detained. One such school had been set up in St Omer, northern France, and in 1602 it was said that 'above 160 English children of good families had been sent there secretly by their Catholic parents to be educated by a Jesuit, so that later they might be infiltrated into England to spread the Catholic faith'. William Pike, a carpenter of West Parley, was hanged, drawn and quartered in 1598 in particularly horrible circumstances for denying the Royal Supremacy. He was beatified in 1987. William Warmington, of Wimborne, who trained at the Catholic seminary at Rheims, became secretary to Cardinal Allen, whose manifesto justified the invasion of England and called upon all English Catholics to assist it on peril of their souls. However, they did not revolt when the Armada arrived and the shock of its defeat caused most English Catholics to be disillusioned. Warmington was one of these and in the reign of James I he returned from exile and readily took the Oath of Allegiance to the king, and declared that the Pope had no power to dethrone the monarch. Warmington then settled down at Hampreston, although in 1624 he was in trouble for keeping a school and teaching the Rhenish Testament, and was 'vehemently suspected of immorality by common fame'. The most prominent Catholic landowner in the Poole area was Henry Carew, of Hamworthy, who had paid the master of a Poole ship £10 not to fight against the Armada.

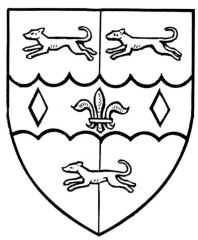

Arms of the White family.

Chapter Six

Strife Under the Stuarts

On the death of Queen Elizabeth (1603) her Scottish Protestant cousin, James VI of the House of Stuart, became James I of England. James prided himself on his wisdom and tolerance, but he quickly decided to maintain the Elizabethan religious settlement and to require all his subjects to conform. A group of disappointed extremist Catholics planned to blow up both the king and his Parliament and thus in one fell swoop to eliminate the Protestant Establishment. The discovery of the Gunpowder Plot was to be commemorated as a day of deliverance and henceforth in the public eye Catholicism was more than ever equated with treason. In 1728 the Churchwardens' Accounts at Corfe Mullen show: 'Pd ye Ringers Gunpowder Treason day 0–4–0'.

During the reign of James I there were repeated clashes between the king, a convinced believer in the Divine Right of Kings, and the House of Commons in which the merchants, country gentry and lawyers were dominant and which increasingly thought of itself as speaking on behalf of the people. Hence there were clashes between king and parliament – on foreign policy, on taxation and on religion. Very sensibly James negotiated peace with Catholic Spain, but this move was very unpopular. Because of inflation, the Crown's existing revenue was no longer sufficient to finance the administration and so James increased customs duties, but these new 'Impositions', which had never received the consent of Parliament, were deeply resented by the merchants of Poole. The radical Protestants, who came to be known as Puritans, wished to purify the Church from 'the dregs of Popery' – crucifixes, altars, vestments and bishops appointed by the king. James agreed to organise an improved translation of the Bible – what became the Authorised Version – but told the Puritans that he was not going to have the Church reorganised on Presbyterian (Calvinist) lines with control in the hands of local congregations electing representatives to a General Assembly or church parliament.

Puritans who would not toe the line could expect to be harried out of the land. It was reported in the Wimborne Royal Peculiar Court in 1610 that 'our preacher master Norman dothe not read divine service nor minister the sacraments of the Lordes supper nor baptism according to the Canon, nor wear such ornaments as spesified in the booke of Canons'. Despite further admonishments he was still defying the authorities in 1616. Some Puritans thought the best solution was to follow the example of the 'Pilgrim Fathers', who had emigrated and founded a settlement in 'New England', where the king was willing to let them – at a distance of some three thousand miles – worship as they pleased. A prime mover in an enterprise to plant Puritan colonies on the other side of the Atlantic – in conjunction with the Rev. John White, of Dorchester – was Sir Walter Erle, of Charborough. Under his governorship the 'Dorchester Company' was set up in 1624. Erle thought that it would be beneficial to 'Western' merchants who had continued a trade of 'fishing for Cod and bartering for Furres in those parts' to have a base where corn could be planted and fish, fowl and venison provided. In 1623, 14 Dorset men had been left in the area of Cape Ann and in 1625 the Dorchester Company sent out another small vessel with cattle.

When in 1625 Charles I came to the throne, the confrontation between king and Parliament intensified. The leader of the Opposition was Sir Edward Coke, who had married the shrewish widow of Christopher Hatton and had become co-owner with her of Corfe Castle and Studland. As Chief Justice of the Common Pleas, until dismissed by James I, he had clearly declared that the king was not above the Law and that a Royal Proclamation could not establish a new law, since any new law required the consent of Parliament. After quarrelling with and dissolving three parliaments, Charles ruled arbitrarily for 11 years without summoning a parliament. Despite guarantees to the contrary in the Petition of Right (1628), he levied taxes without Parliament's consent, arrested critical subjects without laying any charge of breaking the law and gave full backing to Archbishop Laud of Canterbury, who ordered the clergy to use a variety of vestments and to rail off the altar at the east end of the church as a sacred zone – clear indications to Puritans that he was planning to lead England back into the Roman Catholic fold. Poole was already staunchly Puritan and would have greatly resented such 'Popish' trends.

James I had tried hard to extract money from Poole. In 1614 Poole received a demand for a 'forced loan' – a loan of 'plate or money' and in 1619 another letter from the Privy Council requested a sum of £100 as Poole's contribution to the fitting out of a fleet to suppress piracy. The mayor replied that Poole could contribute only £50, since the town was poor, having lately sustained great losses by casualties at sea, and there was only one merchant adventurer in port, since Poole's trade was not in any staple, but in 'fishing voyages for the New Found Land and so home'. During the wars with Spain and France (1625-30) privateers from Dunkirk waylaid many Poole vessels in Studland Bay and off the Purbeck cliffs, and letters of marque were issued to the owners of several of these Poole ships, including Thomas Robartes (mayor in 1627 and 1628), authorising them to recoup their losses by seizing enemy ships and cargoes. Thomas Robartes still found the time and money in 1628 to establish a free grammar school for Poole. Charles I decided that it was necessary to build a bigger and better navy to protect English shipping from pirates and also south coast villages from raids by Barbary Corsairs from North Africa. In 1634 and again in 1635 he demanded that Poole should provide £60 as 'Ship Money'. As usual the town pleaded poverty and, perhaps because of this, the demands in 1636 and 1637 were reduced to £30 and £24 respectively. The Sheriff of Dorset, however, reported the distress caused by the demands for Ship Money. 'Some sell their only cow, which should feed their children, and some come to the parish' (i.e. for relief). In 1639 Poole's mayor, Aaron Durell, made two journeys – to Dorchester and Blandford – 'about the Writ that came to us concerning Ship Money'. Resistance came to a head in 1640. When goods were distrained because people had not paid, and offered publicly for sale, the few people who came to the sale refused to bid or else offered absurdly low amounts, such as sevenpence or ninepence for an ox worth £8.

Meanwhile Charles had ordered inland counties to pay 'Ship Money', which hitherto had been collected only from coastal counties. John Hampden, a Buckinghamshire squire, refused to pay on the grounds that any extension of the tax to inland counties required the consent of Parliament. It fell to the Attorney-General, Sir John Bankes, the new owner of Corfe Castle, to prosecute Hampden. The judges by seven votes to five found that Hampden should pay up and imposed a heavy fine upon him, but he emerged from this case as a national hero, as a champion of the rights of Parliament against a tyrannical monarch. Sir Edward Coke had died in 1634, and his widow, the fiery-tempered former Lady Hatton, had then sold Corfe Castle to Bankes. Later she became an enthusiastic supporter of Parliament in the forthcoming Civil War, so that ironically, had she retained possession of Corfe Castle, it would have been a great Parliamentary stronghold during the war instead of being a Royalist outpost successfully defended by Lady Bankes, wife of the new owner! Bankes was also called upon to prosecute in the Court of Star Chamber William Prynne, a leading Puritan lawyer, for denouncing the bishops. Prynne was sentenced to be mutilated and imprisoned for life.

50.   Sir John Bankes.

At last in 1640 after ruling without a parliament for 11 years, the king summoned Parliament in the hope of securing a vote of more money. Parliament did in fact grant him some money, but only after 'Ship Money', Impositions and any other levies without parliamentary consent had been declared illegal. Charles also had to agree to meet Parliament at least once every three years, and not to dissolve the present Parliament without its own consent. He also had to agree to the ending of torture and to the abolition of prerogative courts like Star Chamber which operated without a jury. So far nine-tenths of the M.P.s supported these measures reducing the king's power, but a reaction in the king's favour set in, when Puritan M.P.s introduced the Root and Branch Bill to end the system by which the Church was controlled by bishops. Many moderate men, who did not want the king to wield tyrannical powers, then came over to his side because they did not want to see the Church Puritanised. Encouraged by this reaction, Charles then prepared to collect together an army for the purpose of coercing Parliament. Sir John Bankes, now Chief Justice of the Common Pleas, wrote to the leaders of Parliament urging compromise and an 'accommodation' foreseeing that 'if we should have civil war, it would make us a miserable people'. His efforts were unsuccessful, but Parliament seems to have appreciated his attempt to avert disaster and urged that he should continue as Chief Justice.

It was in 1639, when no one foresaw that civil war was imminent, that Sir Anthony Ashley-Cooper, of Wimborne St Giles, wrote, when he was only 18, an interesting survey of the characters and outlooks of a number of country gentlemen, living in the area just to the north of Poole, who used to meet once a week at a bowling green at Sixpenny Handley. Ashley-Cooper had many close links with Poole. His father, Sir John Cooper, had been M.P. for Poole in 1625 and he himself was to serve as M.P. for Poole in 1654. He described Sir Thomas Trenchard, Sheriff of Dorset in 1534, as 'a very honest, well-natured, worthy man, a favourer of the Puritans', yet his son-in-law, Mr. Chaffin, was 'an enemy of the Puritan party'. Sir Walter Erle, of Charborough, M.P. for Poole four times from 1613 to 1624, 'had been a Low Country soldier [one of the volunteers who went to fight for the Protestants in the Thirty Years' War], valued himself upon the sieges and service he had been in; his garden was cut into redoubts and works representing these places, his house hung with the maps of those sieges and fights'. He and Mr. Hanham, of Wimborne, 'were both inclined to the Puritan', Mr. John Tregonwell, of Milton Abbas, 'enjoyed his nightcap, his poached eggs, his chamber pleasures and thought no further of the world '. The most vivid description was of Henry Hastings, squire of Woodlands, whose grandfather, father and nephew, the earl of Huntingdon, had been lords of Canford manor from 1581 to 1611:

> He was, peradventure . . . an original in our age, or rather the copy of our nobility in ancient days in hunting and not warlike times; he was low, very strong, and very active, of a reddish flaxen hair, his clothes always green cloth, and never all worth when new five pounds. His house was perfectly of the old fashion, in the midst of a large park well-stocked with deer, and near the house rabbits to serve his kitchen . . . He kept all manner of sport-hounds that ran buck, fox, hare, otter and

badger, and hawks long and short-winged, he had all sorts of nets for fishing; he had a walk in the New Forest and the manor of Christchurch. The last supplied him with red deer, sea and river fish; and indeed all his neighbours' grounds . . . were free to him who bestowed all his time in such sports, but what he borrowed to caress his neighbours' wives and daughters, there being not a woman in all his walks of the degree of yeoman's wife or under, and under the age of forty, but it was extremely her fault if he were not intimately acquainted with her. This made him very popular, always speaking kindly to the husband, brother or father, who was to boot very welcome in his house whenever he came . . . There he found beef pudding and small beer in great plenty, a house not so neatly kept as to shame him or his dirty shoes, the great hall strewed with marrow bones, full of hawks perches, hounds, spaniels and terriers, the upper side of the hall hung with foxskins . . . here and there a polecat intermixed, guns and keepers' and huntsmen's poles in abundance. The parlour was a large long room . . . on a great hearth . . . lay some terriers and the choicest hounds and spaniels; seldom but two of the great chairs had litters of young cats in them, which were not to be disturbed, he having always three or four attending him at dinner, and a little

51. Henry Hastings, squire of Woodlands and patron of Poole oysters.

white stick of fourteen inches long lying by his trencher, that he might defend such meat as he had no mind to part with to them. . . . *An oyster-table, at the lower end, which was of constant use twice a day all the year round, for he never failed to eat oysters before dinner and supper through all seasons: the neighbouring town of Poole supplied him with them.* The upper part of this room had two small tables . . . on the tables were hawks' hoods, bells and such like, two or three old green hats with their crowns thrust in so as to hold ten or a dozen eggs . . . tables, dice, cards and boxes were not wanting. In the hole of the desk were store of tobacco-pipes that had been used. On one side of this end of the room was the door of a closet wherein stood the strong beer or wine, which never came thence, but in single glasses, that being the rule of the house exactly observed, for he never exceeded in drink or permitted it . . . He was well natured, but soon angry, called his servants bastard and cuckoldy knaves, in one of which he often spoke truth to his certain knowledge and sometimes in both, though of the same man. He lived to be a hundred and never lost his eyesight, but always writ and read without spectacles, and got to horse without help. Until past fourscore he rode to the death of a stag as well as any.

Then from 1642 to 1646 this rural routine, however rumbustious at Woodlands, was interrupted by civil war, although it is likely that for months on end when Dorset was not in the front line there was little to indicate that the country was torn by war. However, there must have been several weeks when the Royalist squire Hastings was unable to have his two daily meals of oysters from Parliamentarian Poole. Gentry, merchants, clergy and lawyers had to decide whether to support king or Parliament, often an agonising choice, or whether to stay on the side-lines and maintain a low profile. Poole was overwhelmingly

52. The Old Rectory: the Carews' mid-17th-century manor house in Hamworthy, with its unusual carved brickwork.

Puritan and Parliamentarian. Its rector in 1642 was the Rev. Josiah White, a Puritan like his uncle, the influential Rev. John White, of Dorchester. The Recorder – the chief magistrate – of Poole, William Constantine, of Merley, who had also been elected one of Poole's M.P.s in 1640, declared in favour of the king and was removed from both offices. He was replaced as M.P. for Poole by George Skutt. Henry Harbin, mayor of Poole in 1642, was arrested on suspicion of planning to hand Poole over to the king and was sent up to London, Parliament's headquarters, for cross-examination. He was released after paying a large sum of money as a guarantee of his loyalty. However, when the Marquess of Hertford sent a drummer to Poole calling upon it to allow him to fortify it for the king, the mayor and townsfolk refused. Two of the local gentry were staunch Roman Catholics and Royalists – George Carew, of Hamworthy, and Sir John Webb, lord of the manor of Canford. The latter served the king as a major-general, and both had their estates sequestered for delinquency by Parliament, which meant that two-thirds of their estates were farmed out and the rents were paid to Parliament. Colonel John Bingham was appointed Governor of Poole, Brownsea was fortified and a Parliamentarian warship usually rode at anchor in the Brownsea Roads. As Colonel Bingham noted in a letter, 'Towards the sea Pool is not fortified, we there trusting to our ships'. Throughout the war Poole successfully held out against all Royalist attempts to seize it. Wimborne favoured the king; Wareham declared for Parliament, but was to change hands several times during the war. Sir John Bankes joined the king at his Oxford headquarters and died there in 1644, but his wife, Mary, resolutely defended Corfe Castle until 1646.

In the summer of 1643 a Parliamentarian army from Poole, numbering nearly 600 men under the command of that old professional soldier, Sir Walter Erle, embarked on the siege of Corfe Castle. Lady Bankes, initially having only five armed men to assist her, was reinforced by 80 soldiers commanded by Captain Lawrence from Creech Grange. During the six weeks' siege the defendants 'sallied out and brought in eight cows and a bull into the castle without the loss of a man, or man wounded. At another time five boys bought in four cows' to build up food stocks. Most of our 'information' about the siege comes from a partisan but vivid account from Mercurius Rusticus. Two siege-craft – the *Sow* and the *Boar* – were brought up to try to make some impression on the massive

53. Mary, Lady Bankes

masonry of the castle. The 'sow' was a kind of battering ram in a covered shed, but Lady Bankes's musketeers shot at the legs of the men in this contraption, so that nine out of eleven ran away and one was killed. The village church provided an excellent vantage point for the attackers, and Mercurius Rusticus said: 'of the surplice they made two shirts for two soldiers; they broke down the organ and made the pipes serve for cases to hold their powder and shot; . . . and they cut off the lead of the church and rolled up and shot it without ever casting a mould'. The same account, poking fun at Sir Walter Erle, alleged that he 'never willingly exposed himself to any hazard, for being by chance endangered with a bullet shot through his coat, afterwards he put on a bear's skin; and . . . he was seen to creep on all fours on the sides of the hill to keep himself from danger' when he was reconnoitring. Success for the besiegers seemed more likely when 150 mariners from the Parliamentarian fleet together with scaling ladders and some cartloads of grenades and other explosives arrived on the scene. Erle promised £20 to the first man to scale the castle walls and similar rewards down to £1 for the twentieth man to go over the top. He also dosed them with strong liquor to reinforce their courage. Despite these stimulants the Parliamentarians were repulsed and the assault on the upper ward was beaten off by Lady Bankes, her daughters, women and five soldiers who dropped stones and hot embers on the attackers attempting to climb the ladders. Interesting confirmation of the account given in the Royalist pamphlet comes from Parliamentarian accounts featuring:

7 July	For boards, hair and wool for making a Sow against the Castle	£2 3s. 4d.
12 July	For the truckle-boards for the Sow	£0 6s. 0d.
2 August	For a firkin of hot water for the soldiers when they scaled the Castle	£1 12s. 3d.

News, however, now reached Erle that Prince Maurice and the Royalists had captured Dorchester and were advancing eastwards. Erle therefore abandoned the siege, leaving Captain William Sydenham to 'bring off the ordnance, ammunition and the remainder of the army'. In the event the proximity of the enemy forces caused Sydenham to make a hurried departure, leaving behind a good supper laid out in the church, artillery, ammunition and 100 horses in order 'to take boat for Poole', probably from Ower. Thus the intrepid Lady Bankes was left in control of an undamaged Corfe Castle.

The tide seemed to have turned and before long the Royalists were in control of all Dorset except Lyme Regis and Poole. William Constantine, Poole's deposed M.P., wrote from Merley to the Poole authorities urging them to surrender the town to the king. Indeed the Royalists tried to take over Poole by a stratagem. In a pamphlet 'A True Relation of A PLOT to betray the Towne of Poole' it was stated that a Poole woman visiting Wimborne 'a malignant towne – foure miles distant' got into conversation with a Captain Thomas Phillips who dwelt not far off [Thomas Phelips of Corfe Mullen] and mentioned that she

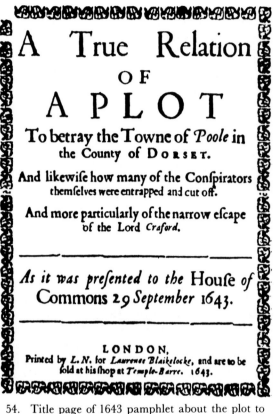

A True Relation

OF

A PLOT

To betray the Towne of *Poole* in the County of DORSET.

And likewife how many of the Confpirators themfelves were entrapped and cut off.

And more particularly of the narrow efcape of the Lord *Craford*.

As it was prefented to the Houfe *of* Commons 29 September 1643.

LONDON,
Printed by *L.N.* for *Laurence Blaikelocke*, and are to be fold at his fhop at *Temple-Barre*. 1643.

54. Title page of 1643 pamphlet about the plot to seize Poole.

had a Captain Francis Sydenham, brother of William Sydenham, billeted on her. Phelips indicated that he would like to get in touch with young Sydenham, who was apparently disgruntled at the turn of events. Sydenham did in fact meet Phelips, who tried to persuade him to defect to the king and to help the Royalists to seize Poole. Sydenham, having informed Colonel Bingham, Governor of Poole, pretended to fall in with Phelips' suggestions. Thus in return for £40, a promise of more money and a pardon, Francis Sydenham undertook when he was Captain of the Guard on an agreed night to leave the Town Gate open so that a Royalist contingent could infiltrate into Poole and carry out a surprise takeover. Before reaching the Town Gate it was necessary to cross a semi-circular area called a half-moon. The pamphlet explained, 'before the gate the garrison had raised a half-moon – at the entrance to which were chains to be drawn up at pleasure'. At the agreed time (2 a.m.), Sydenham lured the Royalist cavalry contingent under the Earl of Crawford into a trap. When Crawford and his troopers were inside the half-moon, 'the chains were suddenly drawn up; and the muskets and great guns loaded with small shot . . . gave fire upon those who came on'. The slaughter would have been greater 'had not the great Gunns been mounted too high above the ground where many of them were'. Nevertheless, the defenders captured 300 Royalist weapons, 50 horses and 20 of their riders and Lord Crawford himself only narrowly escaped. The Royalists admitted to 10 men killed; the Poole defenders said 'there were divers Cart-loades'. The Royalists, however, made no further attempt to take Poole either by direct assault or by stratagem.

It was at this stage, when the outlook for Parliament looked very bleak, that Anthony Ashley-Cooper, having initially supported the king but having failed to persuade him to agree to a truce, 'plainly seeing the King's aim destructive to religion and the state', resigned his commissions at the beginning of 1644 and 'privately came away to the Parliament, leaving all his estate in the King's quarters . . . and two houses well furnished at the mercy of the enemy, resolving to cast himself on God and to follow the dictates of a good conscience'. The Parliamentarians then appointed Ashley-Cooper (still only 23) 'Field Marshall General' in command of a force which went on to retake Wareham, and to capture Abbotsbury later in 1644.

In October 1644 the Poole garrison attacked the 'Queen's Regiment' between Poole and Blandford, killed 16 Royalists and took 60 prisoners. Lord Goring's Royalist cavalry twice attacked Christchurch, 'a little unfortified fisher town', as it was described, in January 1645 but, despite a temporary withdrawal to Hurst Castle, the Parliamentarians retained it.

Early in 1645 there was a new and unexpected development – the emergence of a neutralist movement, a backlash on the part of ordinary farmers and yeomen against the constant to-ing and fro-ing of first one army and then another across their land and the seizure of food and stock that these incursions involved. 'The Clubmen', as these neutralists called themselves, from Dorset and Wiltshire met and agreed to organise bodies of watchmen to seize plunderers and carry them for punishment to the nearest garrison of whichever side the offenders were attached. Early in June 1645 wearing white cockades, some four thousand Clubmen 'armed with clubs, swords, Bills, Pitchforks and other severall weapons' met at Badbury Rings, where a lawyer from Manston, Thomas Young, read out their grievances and intentions:

> We miserable inhabitants of the said Counties being too too [sic] deeply touched with the apprehension of our past and present sufferings occasioned only by these Civil and unnatural Wars within this Kingdom . . . are unanimously resolved . . . to join in petitioning His Majesty and the two Houses of Parliament for a happy Peace and accommodation of the present differences without further effusion of Christian blood . . .
>
> And we do hereby declare that we really intend
> (i) To maintain and defend the true reformed Protestant Religion, and the inheritance of the Crown;
> (ii) To join with and assist one another in the mutual defence of our Liberties and Properties against all Plunders and all unlawful violence.

One of the banners of the Clubmen was inscribed: 'If you offer to plunder or take our cattel, Be assured we will bid you battel'.

However, in June 1645, the well-disciplined Parliamentarian 'New Model Army' under Fairfax and Cromwell had defeated King Charles decisively at the Battle of Naseby and Parliament was in no mood to parley with these 'Clubmen'. Fairfax and Cromwell were sent to Dorset and in August a confrontation occurred between Cromwell's forces and 2,000 Clubmen encamped on Hambledon Hill, north of Blandford. However, a cavalry charge by Cromwell's brother-in-law, Major John Desborough, 'beat them from the work', as Cromwell wrote to Fairfax, 'killed not twelve of them, but cut very many "and put them all to flight"'. And so the Clubmen movement collapsed.

In Dorset at the beginning of 1646 only Corfe Castle and Portland still held out for the king. A Royalist, Colonel Cromwell, a cousin of Oliver Cromwell, the Parliamentarian general, suddenly turned up at Wareham and pressed on to Corfe Castle with the intention of rescuing Lady Bankes. She refused to leave the castle, even when another force from Poole laid siege to it again. By this time most people accepted that the king's cause was lost and that was the view of Colonel Pittman, a member of the Corfe garrison. Further resistance in his view would mean needless slaughter and, on the pretext of bringing reinforcements into the castle, he planned to infiltrate a party of 100 Parliamentarians in disguise. Anketell, governor of the castle, becoming suspicious, would admit only half of them, but they were able to seize part of the castle, and then, faced with an assault by Colonel Bingham's force from Poole, Lady Bankes finally agreed to surrender – on 27 February 1646. The following month Parliament voted that Corfe Castle should be 'slighted', that is, rendered unfit for defence. The same fate also later befell Christchurch Castle. Lady Bankes's property was sequestered, but later she was able to recover it on payment of a fine of £1,400.

Despite the military successes of the local Parliamentarians in 1645-6, Poole suffered severely from food shortages and another outbreak of bubonic plague. Four pest-houses had to be built and the windmill on the remote Baiter peninsula was turned into an isolation hospital. The Mayor's Account listed such items as: 'For pitch & tar for the sick people to burn in their houses – 4s. 9d.; Paid William Young for a load of turfs and for his horse to draw dead corpses – 6s. For fetching in Shutler's wife and Barnes' wife to the windmill – 1s 6d.; For digging of graves to the gunner and Andrew's boy – 2s.'

CORFE CASTLE IN 1643.

55. An engraving showing Corfe Castle from the south in 1643 at the time of the first siege during the Civil War.

Three years of confusion and dissension between Parliament, the Army (predominantly Independent, that is Congregationalist in religion) and the Presbyterian Scots culminated in the trial of Charles I on a charge of High Treason and his execution in January 1649. A republic or 'Commonwealth' was then proclaimed. Meanwhile Parliament's military victory had not brought peace and harmony to Poole, for the popular Colonel Bingham was replaced in 1647 by a Lieutenant-Colonel John Rede, who soon stirred up protests by favouring various extremists, such as Dippers (Anabaptists believing in total immersion) and Levellers, who stood for social equality. There was a storm when Rede tried to foist an extremist preacher named Gardiner on the town as minister. Eventually in 1651 the Council of State removed Rede, who seems to have belonged to the Republican 'loony Left'.

In 1651 a Captain Tattersall brought his brig, the *Surprise*, into Poole with its usual cargo of coal from Shoreham, but no one suspected that, taking advantage of fine weather, he had *en route* taken across to France Charles, Prince of Wales, son of Charles I, on the run after his defeat by Cromwell at the battle of Worcester, the end of his attempt to claim his father's throne. From 1653 to 1658 Oliver Cromwell ruled virtually as a monarch though his title was that of Lord Protector, and Anthony Ashley-Cooper, M.P. for Poole (1654), soon headed the Opposition to him. After Cromwell's death in 1658, his son, Richard, soon resigned the office of Lord Protector, and then, to avert the threat of civil war between rival factions in the Army, moderates like Ashley-Cooper joined together with level-headed army leaders like Monck to bring back Charles II.

Chapter Seven

From Restoration to Revolution

The Convention Parliament, which invited Charles to return in 1660, passed in a spirit of clemency and conciliation the Act of Indemnity and Oblivion pardoning all offences, confiscations and thefts committed in the name of Parliament during the period of civil war and revolution, apart from the actions of a very small number of people. Royalists were able to recover sequestered estates where two-thirds of the rent had gone to Parliament, but they had little hope of recovering property that had been sold off or just looted. Thus many Royalists felt that this Act meant indemnity for the king's enemies and oblivion for his friends. Mary, Lady Bankes, the courageous defender of Corfe Castle, lived on to see the restoration of Charles II, and her son, Sir Ralph Bankes, was heir to the family estates. Sir Walter Erle and John Bingham, Parliamentarian commanders respectively at the first and second sieges of Corfe Castle, were M.P.s for Dorset in the 1659-60 Parliament in which Ralph Bankes was M.P. for Corfe Castle. It was, however, not practicable for Ralph Bankes to re-establish a family home in the ruined castle at Corfe and so, whilst living temporarily at Chettle, he decided to build a brand new home, designed for comfort, on the Bankes estates near Wimborne. The result was Kingston Lacy House. Sir Ralph Bankes employed Roger Pratt as his architect (from 1663 to 1665) and the new Kingston Hall was built in the currently popular classical style with such Greco-Roman features as an impressive triangular pediment in the centre of the north front as well as some round-headed archways and rectangular windows. It had brick walls with Chilmark stone dressings, although Charles Barry's alterations after 1835 masked the original brickwork with ashlar. Bankes had hoped to use much of the stone and timber from Corfe Castle, but he had no success in regaining any of this building material, which had been carted off by such people as Erle and Bingham. From them and others Bankes had little more success in getting back furniture, tapestries and other fittings which these Parliamentarians had confiscated. An old servant of the Bankes family provided Sir Ralph with a long list of former Bankes property which his sharp eyes had spotted in the homes of Erle and Bingham. Bankes wrote a very polite letter to Erle saying that he assumed that he would want to 'make restitution or some recompense' and that Sir Walter's failure to do so he explained as 'want of memory' and 'rather the defect of your age [Old Watt was 75] than of your will'. 'The Scripture which you profess (and we all ought) . . . cannot justify you in such proceedings [using Bankes' stone and timber in his house at Charborough], nor can you bring any text from them which allows you to build with my timber'. Erle denied that he had ever instructed any one to transport the stone and timber in question to Charborough, though he did admit that he later found some stone and timber alongside the ruins of his own house, but he maintained that the 'five or six load of timber' were 'in point of value no great matter'. So Sir Ralph did not recover his stone for incorporation in his new house at Kingston Lacy. The old servant had noticed in John Bingham's house some attractive items of loot from Corfe Castle, such as 'Two pieces of Fine Tapestry for ye Gallery, one piece to hang behind my La: bed . . . Two large satin wrought window cushions; one cushion of crimson velvett for a window . . . A Rich ebony Cabbinett wth gilded fixtures; two mantles in red silk damaske, a white silke damaske, with 2 silver bindings'. Bankes sent Colonel Bingham a list of his missing treasures and from him he had a more favourable response.

Nobel S^r – My being in phisicke made me not to send an answer to y^r servant's let^r last Saturday. I beseech you let it plead my excuse. S^r, I have a large bed, a singel velvit red chair, and a sute of fine damaske [actually a set of damask table linen]; had not ye horse plague swept away my horses, I would have sent these to you; . . . I beg that you'll please to command one of y^r servants to come to Blandford next friday morning by 10 o'clock, there these things shall be ready for him at ye Crowne.

That yet a continued gale of happiness may ev^r blow on you here below the stars, and ye may yet enjoy heaven heareafter, is ye real wish of, S^r,

y^r very hearty servant,

Jo. Byngham.

It seems that the rents from his ample estates enabled Sir Ralph to complete the building of his new house and to stock it with fine furniture and paintings. Some, such as the Van Dyck portraits of members of the Royal Family as well as portraits of Sir John and Lady Bankes, seem to have been salvaged from Corfe Castle, but he also invited the fashionable Court artist Peter Lely to stay at Kingston Lacy, where he painted portraits of Sir Ralph and three of his sisters.

Meanwhile at Corfe Mullen Thomas Phelips, who had organised the unsuccessful stratagem for the seizure of Poole in 1643 was spending his last years quietly in the fine manor house which had probably been built towards the end of Elizabeth's reign. The incorporation of the device of the Tudor Rose in the design of one bedroom plaster ceiling suggests that it dates from the late Tudor rather than the early Jacobean period. The present Court House is one wing of this Tudor manor-house, most of which was demolished in the mid-19th century. Phelips' estates had been sequestered but, whatever losses he had sustained, when he died in

56. Table tomb of Thomas Phelips (1593-1663) in Corfe Mullen churchyard, showing the Phelips coat of arms.

1663, he bequeathed £500 and some houses in Blandford for the benefit of 'the people of Corfe Mullen. A third of the interest on this endowment was to provide a curate for Corfe Mullen, a third to clothe and apprentice poor children living in Corfe, Lytchett Matravers and Sturminster Marshall and a third for the benefit of 10 poor children of Corfe Mullen, who were to be given bread and cheese every Sunday and beef at Christmas – to be distributed at the big stone or cross 'in the churchyard'. Thomas Phelips was buried in the churchyard in a large altar tomb which has on it the family coat of arms – a chevron between three roses – which appears so frequently in Montacute House, built by another branch of the Phelips family. An Act of Parliament designed to help the woollen industry required that the shroud of any corpse must be woollen, unless a fine was paid. The burial entries in the Corfe Mullen parish register contain the statement: 'Mr. Thomas Phelipps was buried in linnen, and we have received £5 of his wife, whereof £2 10s. 0d. to the poor, and £2 10s. 0d. to the informer according to the statute'.

Under pressure from the king and his advisers or voluntarily in order to win favour with them, the authorities in Poole elected as burgesses several prominent Royalists not resident in the Borough, such as Charles, Duke of Richmond; Giles Strangways; Captain Winston Churchill (1660); Sir Ralph Bankes (1662). These outside burgesses could vote in the borough's parliamentary elections. In a declaration just before his restoration, Charles had promised that 'no man shall be disquieted or called to question for differences of opinion in matters of religion'. Yet although he and his chief adviser, Lord Clarendon, wanted toleration, the strongly Anglican majority in the 'Cavalier Parliament' of 1661-79 insisted on passing a set of four laws, inappropriately called the 'Clarendon Code', designed to make life as difficult as possible for Puritans. The Corporation Act, particularly intended to remove the Puritan domination of old Parliamentarian strongholds like Poole, required the members of each borough council and all its officers to take the Sacrament according to the rules of the Church of England at least once a year and to make a declaration that it was wrong to take up arms against the king in any circumstances. In Poole some Puritans refused to conform, believing that the Anglican ceremonial still contained too many Romish errors, 20 burgesses were removed and surprisingly the Recorder, William Constantine, who had been removed in 1643 as a Royalist sympathiser and had only just been reinstated, was also removed. The Act of Uniformity (1662) required all parish clergy to use the Anglican Prayer Book and to declare publicly that they agreed with 'all and every thing contained and prescribed in and by the Book'. Two thousand ministers, a fifth of the total, in England dissented and these 'Nonconformists' or 'Dissenters' were ejected from their livings. Poole's Presbyterian Rector, Thomas Thackham, toed the line, but the ministers of Wareham (Thomas Chaplyn), Wimborne (Baldwin Deacon), Bere Regis (Philip Lamb), and Lytchett Matravers (Thomas Rowe) declined to give the required undertaking and were ejected. The Conventicle Act (1664) made it an offence to hold or attend a service not in accordance with the Prayer Book if more than five people over and above a family were present. The ejected Thomas Rowe would have been breaking this law no doubt when he preached in the yard of a Wimborne hosier or in Ashley Wood for greater security. Under the Five-Mile Act (1665) any Nonconformist minister was prohibited from living within a corporate town or any place where he had been a minister. Thomas Rowe complied with this regulation when he settled down at Little Canford, just over five miles from Poole and six miles from his old parish, Lytchett Matravers. However, John Wesley, who had been deprived of his post as minister at Winterborne Whitchurch, where he had been 'diabolically railing against the late king and his posterity, and praising Cromwell', was certainly breaking the law when he persistently preached to a group of Independents (Congregationalists) in Poole. For this offence, as a plaque testifies, he 'suffered six months' imprisonment for conscience sake in the reign of Charles II . . . in the Guildhall Prison'. One of his sons, Samuel, born in Winterborne Whitchurch, grew up to become a minister himself and the father of John and Charles Wesley, the pioneers of Methodism. When the rector of Poole, Thomas Thackham, died in 1667, he was replaced by Rev. Samuel Hardy who, since Poole was a Royal Peculiar not under the direct control of the bishop, managed to conduct services which were basically Puritan, though he tried to keep out of trouble by occasionally reading the Creed and the Prayer for the king. He seems to have been very popular with most of the Poole people and many Dissenters from far and wide flocked into Poole to hear him. Hardy 'took great delight in doing good' and among his good deeds was the collection of '£500 to free some captives from the bond of slavery'. However, at last a group of Anglicans headed by a former mayor, Allen Skutt, complained to the king that Hardy 'did not wear the surplice, omitted the sign of the cross in baptism and did divers other things contrary to the rules of the Church of England'. Accordingly in 1682 Hardy was expelled.

Charles II himself had certainly been very popular when, on 15 September 1665, he paid a visit to Poole at the time when he and the Court had moved out of London whilst the Great Plague was raging there. He was accompanied by the Duke of Monmouth, his 16-year-old illegitimate son and several of his chief ministers including Anthony Ashley-Cooper, now created Baron Ashley and Chancellor of the Exchequer, who, as a free burgess and former M.P. for Poole, probably arranged the visit. The king was entertained to dinner at the house of Peter Hiley, a former mayor. Then, to quote the account in the Corporation Record Book:

> After dinner it pleased His Majesty with the said Duke and Lord Ashley, etc. to take Colonel William Skutt's boat to Brownsea, steered by the said Colonel, and now by six masters of ships, where His Majesty took an exact view of the said island, castle, bay and the harbour, to his great contentment, etc., and returned in the said boat unto the quay of Poole, where the said Mayor had the honour to hand His Majesty on shore, from whence he went on foot to the house of the said Colonel Skutt, the said Sheriff going before, and the said Mayor and Edward Mann, Senior Bailiff, bearing their maces before him.

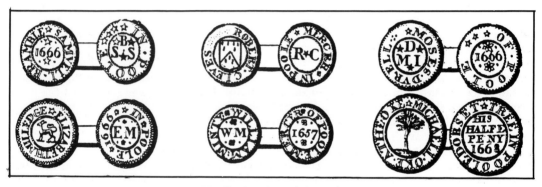

57. Poole tokens (1657-68).

The king then had a second 'stately banquet provided for him [at Skutt's house], the which he was pleased right graciously to accept of'. This was indeed the high point of reconciliation in Poole, for Colonel William Skutt, Mayor in 1646 and 1657, had taken a leading part in the first siege of Corfe Castle, in the account of which the Royalist pamphlet had described him as 'that arch-traitor Skutt of Poole'. The king even nominated Skutt as mayor for the coming year, although in fact the burgesses independently held the customary election and chose someone else.

Maybe Skutt and the king exchanged personal reminiscences about their respective activities in the Civil War. It could well be that the merchants at the banquet may have discussed with Charles the acute problem they found in providing small change to their customers, in consequence of which several tradesmen had for some years past been issuing their own farthings. In 1667 in fact Moses Durell was to arrange for the issue of nearly 20,000 farthings inscribed 'FOR THE MAYOR OF YE TOWN AND COUNTY OF POOLE'. These had to be withdrawn when in 1672 the king issued his own farthings and halfpennies.

Another royal proclamation in 1672 announced a Declaration of Indulgence, suspending the laws against Roman Catholics and Protestant dissenters. Catholics were to be allowed to celebrate Mass privately and Nonconformists could hold public services provided that they obtained a licence. William Minty, a mercer, one of those tradesmen who had issued his own token, applied for a licence as an Independent preacher 'in the malthouse of a Mr. Aire, In Poole'. Lord Ashley, now Lord Chancellor and Earl of Shatfesbury, favoured a

policy of religious toleration, but Parliament, suspecting that this might promote the spread
of Catholicism, persuaded the king to cancel the Declaration of Indulgence in 1673.
Shaftesbury then gave his support to the Test Act of that year requiring all holders of state
office – including officers in the army and navy – to take the Anglican Sacrament and to
make a declaration against the key Roman Catholic doctrine, transubstantiation. Shaftesbury would have liked to see Protestant dissenters exempted, but the High Church majority
penalised them, too. One of the victims of the fresh wave of persecution was a Poole Baptist
preacher, William Bayly, who had joined the Quaker movement, which believed that a
regular religious service or ordained ministers were unnecessary. Bayly was sentenced to
be transported to the West Indies and died at sea in 1675.

Shaftesbury was deprived of his position as Lord Chancellor for helping to pass the Test
Act, which had forced the king's brother and heir, James, Duke of
York, to resign his office of Lord High Admiral and to admit publicly
that he had become a Roman Catholic. Shaftesbury then detached
himself from Court circles and formed the Country Party – later to
be known as the Whigs – to uphold the rights of Parliament and
press for toleration for Protestant Nonconformists. Next Shaftesbury
suggested the exclusion of the Catholic Duke of York from the throne
and in consequence was arbitrarily imprisoned for a year. One
consequence was that Shaftesbury, when he was released, persuaded
Parliament to pass the momentous *Habeas Corpus Act* (1679), which
gave all arrested persons the right to be told which law they were
accused of breaking and to be tried at the next Quarter Sessions on
a charge of breaking that law. In so far as this law stopped a
government from shutting up any critics of its policy just because
they were a nuisance, the Habeas Corpus Act was to become a vital ingredient in modern

58. Anthony Ashley-
Cooper, first Earl of
Shaftesbury.

democracy. Charles II refused to consider the Exclusion Bill of 1680 which would have
deprived the Duke of York of the right to succeed to the throne because he was a Catholic,
especially because Shaftesbury, instead of nominating either of the duke's staunchly Protestant daughters as next in line of succession, proposed the Duke of Monmouth, eldest of
Charles II's illegitimate children, also a firm Protestant, as heir to the throne. Shaftesbury
was tried for treason and acquitted, but, despite the Habeas Corpus Act, thought it wise to
flee to Protestant Holland, where he died in 1683. His body was brought back to Poole,
which he had served as M.P., and was brought ashore in the presence of many of the leading
men of the area. Many Poole men followed the cortège out to Wimborne St Giles where
the body was buried in the family vault.

The young Duke of Monmouth had also gone into exile in Holland and on the death of
Charles II (1685) the Duke of York duly succeeded as King James II. Most Englishmen
accepted him in the hope that he would not interfere with the Protestant Church of England
and that a few years later he would be followed on the throne by one of his Protestant
daughters, Mary and Anne. In June 1685 Monmouth decided to make a bid to raise a
Protestant rebellion in the West Country. Landing at Lyme Regis, a Protestant stronghold
in the Civil War, he allowed himself to be proclaimed king, but was defeated at the battle
of Sedgemoor in Somerset. One of the officers commanding a troop of horse against the
rebels at Sedgemoor was Thomas Chafin, of Chettle, M.P. for Poole at the time. Monmouth
fled southwards disguised as a shepherd, apparently making for Poole, where he had been
so well received when he visited the town with his father in 1665 and which was known to
be solidly Protestant. There he hoped to secure a safe passage to Holland. Monmouth
entered an area of growing crops, called the 'Island' on Horton Heath, north of Wimborne.
Unluckily for him, a woman in a nearby cottage, Amy Farant, knowing that there was a

large reward for the apprehension of the rebels on the run, told the militiamen searching the area that she had seen two strange men climbing over a hedge. Early on the morning of 8 July Monmouth's companion, a German officer named Buyse, was captured and admitted that he had been with Monmouth a few hours earlier. He may have helped the militiamen to locate Monmouth for he himself was later pardoned. One of the militiamen, Parkin, pulled at a piece of leather which proved to be part of the jacket of a hungry dishevelled man, lying in a ditch among the bracken under an ash-tree. A search of his pockets revealed some unlikely possessions for a Dorset yokel, for apart from some raw peas there were several gold guineas, four notebooks, including notes on fortifications and cosmetics and, what really betrayed his identity, the badge of a Knight of the Garter. Monmouth was taken before the nearest magistrate, Anthony Ettrick, of Holt Lodge, who had been Recorder of Poole from 1662 to 1682. Later Amy Farant received a reward of £50 and the contempt of her neighbours. Lord Lumley was given £5,000 to distribute among the militiamen of his search party. Monmouth himself, despite a letter to the king, expressing his remorse for 'the wrong I have done you' and pleading that he had been led astray by 'some horrid people that made me believe things of your Majesty', James II showed no mercy and, when Monmouth was sent pinioned up to London, he was condemned to be hanged, drawn and quartered. He conducted himself with extraordinary courage on the scaffold. A friend testified to his charm and bravery, but admitted his 'most poor understanding as to politics'.

At the Bloody Assizes at Dorchester later in 1685 Judge Jeffreys inflicted a terrible revenge on those who had taken up arms on behalf of Monmouth in the belief that they were striking a blow against a Roman Catholic dictator. Allen Skutt, mayor of Poole, addressed the following instructions to the Constable of Lytchett Matravers – by order of Judge Jeffreys:

> I doe hereby will and require you to take into your care and custody two quarters of severall persons this day executed within this towne and county [i.e. Poole], and herewith send you by Charles Barfoot, of Sturminster Marshall, husbandman, and to affix them on poles or spykes in the most notable places in Upper Lytchett – and thereof fail you not at your perills. The officer to pay 5d. carridge.

Lytchett Matravers was probably singled out to receive these gruesome remains, since the family of the lords of the manor, the Trenchards, were Puritan and had supported Parliament in the Civil War. John Trenchard, brother of Thomas Trenchard, M.P. for Poole 1670-4, had hidden in the lodge of one of his keepers at Lytchett, and fully expected to be charged with aiding Monmouth.

Various moves by James II in the next three years, including his appointment of Roman Catholics as his advisers, seemed to be aimed at establishing a royal dictatorship and at restoring Catholicism – and the growing alarm became acute when James's second wife, a Catholic, gave birth to a healthy son, who would obviously be brought up as a Catholic and would succeed his father. The prospect of an absolutist Catholic dynasty for the foreseeable future caused seven leading Protestants, including Lord Lumley, whose troops had captured Monmouth on Horton Heath, to send an invitation to William of Orange, the Protestant ruler of Holland and his wife Mary, elder daughter of James II, to bring an army across to England to help them depose James II. William and Mary landed at Tor Bay, advanced to Sherborne, where a proclamation announced that they came as liberators not conquerors.

Despite the recent display of the heads and quarters of those executed for rising in support of Monmouth, some Poole people had the courage actively to help William of Orange in his enterprise. Thomas Hyde of Poole had carried vital messages for William at the time of his invasion, and his wife Elizabeth had also played her part by taking some letters concealed in her petticoats. The Hyde family was rewarded with a pension of £50 a year.

59. Two playing cards illustrating the Monmouth Rebellion, from the collection of Lady Charlotte Schreiber, formerly Lady Charlotte Guest. The three of spades shows the capture of the Duke of Monmouth on Horton Heath, and the nine of clubs shows the flogging of one rebel, Pitts from Christchurch.

60. 'The man in the wall': the sarcophagus of Anthony Ettrick, Recorder of Poole (1662-82), in Wimborne Minster. The altered date is said to be due to his belief several years earlier that his death was imminent.

The Hydes were to play a prominent role in the later municipal history of Poole. Thomas Hyde himself served as mayor in 1696, as did his son George in 1737 and his grandson Thomas in 1764.

James II had hoped to use Poole Harbour as a base from which to resist William of Orange, but the only ship in James II's navy which put into Poole, the *Speedwell*, was 'seized for the Prince of Orange', as its commander, Captain Edward Poulson, related when 'on the morning of the 11th [December 1688] he was inveigled into the *Antelope* tavern at Poole and there seized as a prisoner'. The Poole authorities put 'one Robinson' in command of the ship and Robinson offered Poulson the command back if he would take the ship to the Prince's fleet at Plymouth, but Poulson refused. Most members of his crew had already deserted.

Support for James II melted away (December 1688), and he fled to France. The 'Glorious Revolution' of 1688-9 ensured that all future monarchs (William III and his wife, Mary II, were confirmed as joint successors to James II in 1689) must be Protestants, that the consent of Parliament was required for all new laws and taxes, and that the Church of England remained the state church, though Nonconfomists were henceforth to have freedom of worship. An inscription over an ice-house in Charborough Park claims that 'Under this roof in the year 1686 a set of patriotic gentlemen of this neighbourhood concerted the great plan of THE GLORIOUS REVOLUTION with the immortal King William, to whom we owe our deliverance from Popery and Slavery'.

61. Cottage at Hillbutts (1697).

This was quite a bold claim, but the Poole area could well have been a major centre of the movement to overthrow James II. Walter Erle, of Charborough Park, grandson of the old soldier who had besieged Corfe Castle, would certainly have strongly upheld the Protestant cause; John Trenchard, of Lytchett and Bloxworth, brother-in-law of Walter Erle, had made several journeys to Holland and became a confidential friend of William of Orange; whilst his uncle, Henry Trenchard, four times M.P. for Poole, would also have wanted to get rid of James II. After the Glorious Revolution, John Trenchard was knighted, served as M.P. for Poole and became one of King William's principal secretaries of state. When he died in 1695, Lord Ashley, grandson of Lord Shaftesbury, followed him as M.P. for Poole; and Sir John's son, George Trenchard, was to represent Poole in Parliament from 1713 to 1745 and 1747 to 1754.

A manuscript quoted by the historian of Poole, John Sydenham, contained this entry: '1689. April 13. News of the coronation of King William and Queen Mary: great rejoicing at Poole'. Very few in the Poole area would not have rejoiced, but among those would have been the Catholic lord of the manor of Canford, Sir John Webb. Towards the end of his reign Charles II had withdrawn from Poole the many privileges of self-government conferred by its numerous charters including that of 1667 granted by himself, just as he cancelled the privileges of London and many other boroughs critical of his policies. When the Catholic James II was reigning it was widely feared that Sir John Webb might try to re-establish his control over Poole as lord of the manor. Indeed, he did claim the right to choose the mayor. James II had granted a new charter which, however, gave the monarch the right to remove any borough officers to whom he objected – much to the alarm of the burgesses of Poole. James II, anxious to regain his popularity, had hastily issued a new charter to Poole (8 December 1688) restoring all its old privileges. The man primarily responsible for securing this charter restoring self-government to Poole was the Whig, Sir Nathaniel Napier, of More Crichel. Both he and Henry Trenchard, another Whig, were elected members for Poole in the 1689 Convention Parliament which declared James II to have vacated the throne when he fled to France, and which offered the throne jointly to William and Mary.

The Jolliffe Gold Medal showing William and Mary.

Chapter Eight

The Social Scene

The recurrent problems of each parish, human frailty, economic disaster, poverty and disease are all mirrored in the local records of the Poole area, extending from the 15th to the 19th centuries. Few of the manorial court rolls of Canford have survived, but the records of the court which met there on 19 November 1472, in the middle of the reign of Edward IV, throw light on local problems. Inn-keepers regularly gave short measure and so Stephen Coppe and John Kepe were each fined sixpence for having 'broken the assize of beer' and having 'sold beer by cups and other measures'. Thomas Mascall, of Little Canford, husbandman, was charged with breaking into the park of the lord of the manor (George, Duke of Clarence, the king's brother), and killing a buck, and on another occasion having with a 'hokenet' poached divers fish, including salmon, from the lord's waters at Mochel (Great) Canford. John Cole (of Hamworthy) pleaded guilty to having with William Kypping, a wheeler, who was not present, killed a 'hyne-calf' with a dog, whilst John Rogers was fined sixpence for fishing in the lord's waters without a licence. William Peynet and John Mabely were fined one penny each for failing to clean out their section of a ditch, 'as they have many times been ordered', but warned that they would have to pay 12d. each if the work was not completed by the time the next court met. Likewise John Hayward paid a fine of 3d. for not repairing his cottage on the pain of paying 3s. 4d. at the next court, if he had not toed the line by then. More serious was the case of Matthew, former servant of a Poole merchant, Dennis Mesurer. This Matthew was charged with murder, in that he lay in wait to wound and kill John Tarde and . . . with a stick made assault upon the same John . . . and gave the said John a mortal wound with the said stick in his head, by which he died. Matthew was arrested pending a trial by a higher court.

On 2 January 1472/3 another Matthew – or the same Matthew? – was before the Poole court on a charge of assault. Matthew Turtell was charged with assaulting John Tartyffe with a staff, and was fined 3d. for striking the blow and a further 6d. for drawing blood, whilst John Tartyffe was found guilty of assaulting Matthew Turtell with a sword and refusing to hand over a sword to the borough bailiff, and was consequently fined 3d. on each charge. A Poole couple were arrested on a charge of arson. They were William and Wilhelmina Tutyn, accused of having 'burnt down the hous of John Worsfede, of Poole, to the great terror of this town'. One John Hall, of Salisbury, was also charged with allowing a ship to lie in the channel by the quay for a long time, 'to the injury of the Lord and the annoyance of the mariners of the town'. He was ordered to move the ship by the Feast of the Annunciation on pain of having the ship confiscated, half of it to go to the Lord of the Manor, the other half to the town.

Consumer protection was well to the fore in the activities of the Hundred Court at Christchurch in the reign of Henry VIII. In 1519 three 'common fishermen', John Frayle, William Petyte and Thomas Hancock (perhaps a relative of the radical preacher who stirred up so much trouble in Poole during the next reign), were fined for taking 'excessive profit'. In 1543 James Trym and Richard Genge, 'candle makers', were found guilty of taking 'excessive profit', Trym was fined 3d., but Genge was let off as he was poor. John Frayle and Leonard Holender, shoemakers, John Crocker and Thomas Smart, millers, Robert Kayne, a butcher, were also found guilty of taking 'excessive profit'. George Clement and Nicholas Crepyn, brewers of ale, were each fined 3d. for giving short measure, whilst Henry

Whyte, another brewer of ale, was likewise fined 3d. for refusing 'to give the ale-taster his taste'. In 1544 Joan Penyll, widow, was fined 4d. for allowing her pigs to go at large through the street against the ordinance of the Court. A heavier fine of 9d. was imposed on Brian Pryor, who had attacked and intimidated Richard Blake and struck him with a stick so that blood was drawn. Vincent Toker had to pay a fine of 6d., for failing to repair the king's road in front of his door, as he was ordered to do in the previous court, and was told that he would have to pay a further 3s. 4d. if he had not done so by the time the next court met.

Throughout the centuries there were those who could not support themselves and in the Middle Ages the relief of the poor was especially the concern of the Church. At Wimborne from the 13th century onwards a hospital, dedicated to St Margaret and St Anthony, maintained entirely by alms, helped the sick and the poor, and in 1547 still maintained eight poor men. Among the outstanding private benefactors in the area was the mother of Henry VII, Lady Margaret Beaufort, who held the manor of Canford from 1485 until her death (1509). The Fraternity or Guild of St George in Poole had provided almshouses for the poor since 1429, if not earlier. Each monastery had its almoner to dispense food and other essentials to the local poor. Indeed the last prior of Christchurch, John Draper, in his forlorn plea that the priory should not be dissolved in 1539, stressed its generous help to the poor. The confiscation of the monasteries by Henry VIII and of the chantries and fraternities under Edward VI aggravated the problems of poor relief. In Poole, however, the property of the Guild of St George was purchased from the king for the town for £21 14s. 2d., and with the proceeds of the yearly rent the good charitable work was continued. In the 1574 census of Poole it was recorded that 13 'poor Pepull' were living in the Almshouses of St George in Pillory Street, and a further eight in an almshouse in West Street. Under the will of Robert Rogers, a prosperous leather merchant of London (dated 11 September 1601), £10 was bequeathed to the poor of Poole and Rogers went on to make an even more generous bequest in these words: 'Item: I give to the town of Poole, in Dorsetshire, where I was born, 500 marks (£333 6s. 8d.) to build an almshouse and to place therein six poor couples, householders, married or unmarried, of the most aged or decayed, by sea, if any such be, or to such others as shall most need of relief; and the governors of the town to purchase so much land as shall amount to £15 12s. yearly, with the said money, and to allow each couple twelve pence per week, during their natural lives, and after their decease, to place others in the same houses, with the like allowance'. The almshouses were duly constructed in Purbeck stone in West Street. By the beginning of the 19th century the six cottages had been turned into 12 one-room tenements, each inmate being allowed 6d. per week and an allocation of coal at Christmas time.

In the reign of Elizabeth I many manorial lords, attracted by the high price of wool, enclosed open fields and common, converting labour-intensive arable land into sheep-runs managed by a few shepherds. The resulting distress and depopulation was denounced by the Rev. Thomas Bastard, vicar of Bloxworth, in his *Epigrams* (1598).

> Sheepe have eate up our medows and our downes,
> Our corn, our wood, whole villages and townes.
> Yea, they have eate up many wealthy man
> Besides widows and Orphane childeren . . .
> Till now I thought the proverbe did but jest,
> Which said a black sheepe was a biting beast.
>
> I knowe where is a thiefe and long hath beene,
> Which spoyleth every place where he resortes;
> He steales away both subiectes from the Queene,
> And men from his owne country of all sortes.
> Houses by three, and seaven, and ten he raseth,

To make the common gleabe, his private land;
Our country Cities cruell he defaceth,
The grasse grows greene where little Troy did stand,
The forlorn father hanging downe his head,
His outcast company drawn up and downe,
The pining labourer doth begge his bread,
The plowswayne seaks his dinner from the towne.
O Prince, the wrong is thine, for vnderstand,
Many such robbries will vndoe thy land.

The Queen and Parliament had in fact taken some steps to help the poor. The Poor Law of 1572, whilst prescribing harsh treatment of 'Roges, Vacabondes and Sturdye Beggers', laid down that 'aged, ympotent and poore People should have convenient Habitacions and Abydinge Places . . . to settle themselves uppon'. 'Justices of the Peace, Maiors, Sheryffes, Baylyffes and other Officers of all and every Cytye Borough . . . within this Realme' were to assess all the inhabitants for the payment of poor rates and should appoint Overseers of the Poor to organise the relief. Accordingly a page from the Poole Relief Book of 1585 compiled by one of the overseers listed the names of 41 paupers in addition to inmates of the Almshouses to whom he had distributed bread and also noted that 2s. 6d. had been spent on a yard and a quarter of a material called russet to make a jerkin for a poor man named Stare, together with 6d. for lining, 1d. for buttons and 6d. for labour.

Several other statutes were enacted – all to be consolidated in the Elizabethan Poor Law of 1601, which was to be the basis of the poor relief system until 1834. It made the parish with its elected 'Overseers of the Poor' the unit for poor law finance and administration. It distinguished between the 'deserving poor' and the idle rogues and vagabonds, and also between the 'able-bodied on the one hand and young children, the old and the disabled, incapable of supporting themselves. Pauper children were to be apprenticed to a trade to enable them later to support themselves. Housing was to be found for the aged and disabled. Each parish was to provide 'a convenyent Stocke of Flaxe Hempe Wool Thread Iron and other necessary Ware and Stuffe to sett the Poore on worke' – more easily said than done. Those who refused work were to be sent to the House of Correction.

In 1790 we find the overseers at Canford putting out and binding as an apprentice to John Redman, of Great Canford, yeoman, 'John Lodder, a poor child of this parish till he shall com of ye age of one and Twenty years . . . he shall faithfully serve . . . and shall not frequent Taverns, Inns or Alehouses except it is doing his master's business . . . and shall not play at Cards, Dice or other unlawful Games'. For his part, in the standard wording of the apprenticeship indenture, the master undertook to provide 'sufficient, wholesome and competent meat, Drink, Lodging, Washing, apparel and all other necessaries meet for such an apprentice, i.e. two coats, two waistcoats, two pairs of breeches, two pairs of stockings, two pair of shoes, three shirts, one Hatt and all other necessaries'. In 1748 a poor girl of Lytchett Minster was apprenticed to a Mantua-(dress) maker. In 1804 the Lytchett Minster overseers were paying two shillings a week to 'the Factory' (probably a twine factory at Organford) and in 1805 occurs the entry, 'Paid for Canvas Buttons and Thread to make Frocks and Trousers for the Factory Boys 6s. 9d.'

An Act of 1662 made the parish, where a person was born and had a legal settlement, responsible for that person if he or she became a pauper. This led to frantic and often cruel efforts to prevent a pauper woman giving birth to a child in the parish. Thus the Churchwardens' Accounts of Hampreston have these entries for 1715:

Paid and gave to a Travelling Woman big with child to
    get her out of the Parish   2–6

> Paid and gave to another Travelling Woman and to the
> Officers to convey her away so that she might not
> trouble the Parish   9–6

Even more callous was an entry for 1716:

> Paid for conveying a Dying Soldier away out of the
> parish   1–6

– so that Hampreston would not be put to the expense of burying him.

Most parish records contain Removal Orders under which paupers were deported back to their parish of settlement, such as one dated 16 June 1783 in Poole ordering the removal of 'Elizabeth Russell, the wife of John Russell, who has lately left the said Town and County of Poole, and Mary almost 4 and Hannah almost 2, children by the said John', to Cranbrook in Kent, and on 14 August the same year the Poole magistrates ordered 'Susannah Elford, widow of George Elford deceased' with her children, George (12), Benjamin (5), James (4), and Susannah (11 months) to be carted off to Sherborne.

There were admittedly a number of ne'er-do-wells who constituted a continuing problem. On 8 February 1821 Jane and Matilda Grant were convicted of 'wandering abroad and begging' and were committed to the House of Correction in Poole 'to be kept in hard labour for 7 days'. Again on 23 November 1822 Joseph Davis, joiner, was convicted in that he 'being able to work hath long time past by drunkenness and other disorderly conduct, wilfully neglected to maintain his Family. Whereby it is likely they will become chargeable to the Parish'. He was convicted of being 'an idle and disorderly person', but no sentence is mentioned. Perhaps he posed as difficult a problem to the magistrates of 1822 as some inadequate individuals do to the J.P.s of the 1980s.

Parish officials could, however, be compassionate, if perhaps occasionally gullible, when strangers turned up with tales of woe, as when Charlton Marshall Churchwardens recorded:

| 1663. | To Mr. Garrat sustained great losses in the Isle of Kelegary by Pirats. | 6d. |
| 1664. | Paid to two gentlewoman and ther Children wch ther husbands were tooke in to Turkey ther houses burnt | 1/6d. |

The Kinson Churchwardens recorded these payments under 1735:

| Pd. | four frenchmen Castaway | 00.02.06 |
| Pd. | Six men that was taken into turkey and had redemption | 00.02.06 |

The Lytchett Minster Overseers entered up the following in their accounts:

1783.	To make Jane Fancys Maids Shift and gown	1s. 2d.
1783.	Gave to Skinner when fell down Chimney	2s.
1796.	Releved three sailors came out of Fench Presen.	1s.

In Poole in 1811 it was recommended that Parish Officers should:

Not to exceed the following Allowances to Paupers that is to say –

To Grown Persons	£0. 2. 6 pr week
To Children under 10 years of age	£0. 1. 6 pr week
To Children from 10 to 12 years of Age	£0. 1. 0 pr week

At this time a widespread method of calculating allowances under the so-called Speenhamland System was to relate them to the price of bread and the size of a labourer's family. Unfortunately this seemingly sensible and caring system had harmful side effects since, though it prevented starvation, the supplementing of the wages of the lowpaid up to what was reckoned to be subsistence level discouraged employers from paying a living wage. The situation caused labourers not to work hard for an employer who manifestly paid only part of their weekly income. Eventually in 1834 a new harsh Poor Law Amendment Act was passed to restore, so it was argued, the working man's spirit of independence. In future able-bodied persons were to receive relief only if they were completely destitute and went to a workhouse where conditions were to be 'less eligible' than the worst conditions prevailing among independent labourers. A workhouse had been built for the town in West Street as long ago as 1739 by Thomas Missing, who later served as M.P. for Poole. Because the 1834 Act required a number of adjacent parishes to join together as a Union and to share a workhouse, a new building was required. The new Union Workhouse was duly built on a new site at the southern end of St Mary's Road, Longfleet, in 1839. The Poole authorities went ahead with great energy to fit out the new Union Workhouse properly. They placed orders for, among many other things, '3 dozen bolsters, 50 large knives and forks and 50 small knives and forks and 50 iron spoons. They also placed contracts, with James Boyt, for bread of best seconds at 7½d. per 4 lb loaf, with John Frampton for Beef at 4d per lb by the Quarter, Mutton and suet 5½d. per lb, Legs and Shins of Beef at 2/6 each; with Benjamin Moore for sugar at 5¼d. per lb, Pepper 10½d. per lb, Bohea Tea, 3s. 1d. per lb, Starch 5½d. per lb, with G. G. Roe for Treacle at 5¾d. per lb and oatmeal at 24/- per hundred weight, with A. Lawrence for Green Bacon at 58s. per side per cwt.; with B. Vines for candles at 6/3 a dozen, with John Whittle for Best Eden main coals at 20/9 per ton; with John Hatcher for Blue Potatoes £2-15-0 per ton and White do. at £2-12-0; and with John Goff for Men's shoes at 4/6, Boys over 12 3/9, Under 12 3/-, Girls over 12 3/-, under 12 2/6 per pair'.

The lord of the manor, Lord de Mauley, after visiting the workhouse, called for improvements. He was disturbed that the children were sleeping three in a bed in many instances. He thought the Day Room for Women was small and required more seats and also a shelf, and he insisted that in the Day Room for Old Women 'backs to the benches were wanted and more of them'. He also noted that 'they complain of the Stone floor'. The Poole Board of Guardians also resolved 'That it is the opinion of this Board that the quality of the Water obtained from the Well of this Establishment is such as to render it unfit for the permanent use of the inmates and that it is necessary to take steps for procuring a supply of better quality'.

These observations show a creditable concern for the inmates of the Poole Workhouse, but on 11 December 1837 the Wimborne Board of Guardians addressed a letter to the Poole Board of Guardians complaining of the 'improper removal of William Gilpine', who in the opinion of Mr. Johns, the Medical Officer, was too ill to be removed and who died two or three days after his removal from Poole. In January 1837 the Wimborne relieving officers had been directed to visit the parishes and 'during the prevalence of Influenza to afford relief in cases of necessity according to their discretion'. In February the Wimborne Guardians had persuaded Nathaniel West of More Crichel to pay two shillings per week towards the support of his father and mother belonging to the parish of Witchampton. In November 1837 they resolved that 'Elizabeth Noble, wife of George Noble, having refused work and having been guilty of other misbehaviour in the Workhouse, be taken before a Magistrate for committal to the House of Correction'. A year later the Wimborne Guardians resolved, 'That all unmarried Females admitted into the Workhouse pregnant or having a bastard Child shall be distinguished by a particular dress, that is, for the first time to wear a small plain mob Cap and the second time to wear a yellow serge Dress and Mob Cap. These dresses to be immediately prepared'. The next week the Wimborne Guardians compassionately agreed 'That the quantity of Snuff and Tobacco given to the Old inmates of the Workhouse be doubled'.

The condemnation of moral delinquency echoed the strictures recorded in the records of the Royal Peculiar Court of Wimborne two hundred years or so earlier. After the Reformation the parishes of Canford and Poole, whose churches had formerly belonged to Bradenstoke Priory, were exempted from the authority of the Bishop and came directly under the king

himself in ecclesiastical matters. The early records of the Great Canford and Poole Royal
Peculiar Court seem not to have survived, but they would have doubtless contained cases
of immorality, sabbath-breaking and misbehaviour in church such as are found in the
neighbouring Royal Peculiar Court of Wimborne. Some of the accusations of immoral
behaviour may well have arisen from malicious gossip on the part of some people with a
grudge against their neighbours. A certain William Jubber, accused (in 1579) three women
from Kingston of adultery, but he in turn was accused of being seen in bed with a widow.
The new organist at the Minster, Robert Durman, was seen in Redcotts Field making love
to Elizabeth May but, when seen, 'he did take to his heels'. In 1635 Agnes Randall alias
Barter, wife of Stephen Barter, admitted that, before she got married, when returning from
Blandford Fair she had had intercourse with Allen Lodge at Spetisbury and again at
Whitsuntide at the setting up of the Maypole there. In 1613 a certain Simon Parker was
accused of offering a married woman a pair of shoes 'to have the use of her body'. In 1640
John Purchas, accused of living with Grace Spruce, accepted the punishment pronounced
by the Court:

> He is enjoyned some Sunday betwixt this and the next Courte to repaire to the Church of Wimborne
> Minster at the time of the reading of the second lesson in morning prayer . . . and there apparelled
> in a white sheet with a white rod in his hand, stand upon a penitential stool appointed for that
> purpose, confesse and say after the minister before the whole congregation as followeth – 'Good
> people, I acknowledge and confess that for suspicion of incontinent life with one Grace Spruce of
> this parish . . . I was worthily punished . . . and I am heartily sorry that by my loose life and
> behaviour I have given cause of this offence and scandall, and I do desire God to forgive me'.

Likewise Luce Brewer wearing a white sheet and holding a white rod in her hand had to
declare before the whole congregation that

> at the instigation of the Devill I have soe much misdemeaned myself in my life and Conversation
> by committing the damnable Sin of Fornication with one John Merritt yje younger, of Blandford . . .
> and haveing a male bastard child lately borne of my body, of which Childe he is the Father, that I
> am of all Creatures most miserable, unless Allmighty God out of his infinite mercy and goodness
> be pleased to forgive me.

John Barnes, of Holt, accused (in 1602) of living with another man's wife, had defied the
Court, declaring he would continue to do so, 'do what thou canst'. What the Court could
do in such circumstances was to excommunicate the offender and this would mean an order
that no one was 'to eat or drink with him, or to buy from him or sell to him, or to be in his
society' under penalty themselves of being excommunicated. Several cases before the Royal
Peculiar Court involved non-attendance at church, Sabbath-breaking and lack of respect
for the church and its officials. The sidesmen were sent round the town to track down
absentees from divine service. Christopher Syler (in 1595) was reported 'for sitting by the
fire in the sermon time and saying he would go to church when he listeth'. John Keynell
(1602) was declared to be 'a common drunkard', and Arthur Mylles was reported for
'keepinge card-playinge in his house, the 2nd of Maye being Sunday'. Simon Smith was
condemned for 'sitting in the quier at prayer time and keeping the quier men out of their
places'. Thomas Frip was admonished 'for playinge of tables, le backgammon, and keeping
of company of Whit Monday last in the church house in service and sermon tyme'. In 1665
Philip Faury, Henry Faury, John Percy and Richard Debben were reported to have been
'playing unlawful games as Coytes or the like upon the Saboth day at the tyme of divyne
service'. George Long was rebuked for 'playing bowls with his servant during matins',
whilst the even more irreverent John Jay played 'at the game of fives' (probably in the
churchyard against the church wall) on Sundays as well as throughout the week 'to the
hurt and grief of the minister'. John Dale was admonished for fighting and brawling in the
churchyard, whilst Michael Dike and John Stronge were reported as 'talkinge in the church

in the sermon tyme'. Parents were often rebuked for not keeping their children quiet during the service. Edward Lovell, gentleman, let his pigs feed in the churchyard and in 1691 John Ansty was denounced for making dunghills in the churchyard. Jane Clarke stayed away from Divine Service to keep her shop open to sell food and drink. Edward Anketill was caught selling candles on a Sunday, William Forrist kept his shop open and John Birde went on mending shoes on the Sabbath at the time of prayer. John Budden was presented for 'killinge of two Bullockes upon the Saboth Day'. It was not surprising that an efficient or officious sidesman engaged in snooping expeditions should report 'Henry Locke for abusing me in my office and calling me an asse and sayinge that if I did use this kind of means I woulde drawe all people uppon my eares'. Likewise when Richard Alim was discovered sitting in Cook Row he refused to accompany the sidesmen to the minister and abused them as 'knaves and baggage fellows'.

In the early 19th century Poole constables had to be vigilant to prevent licensed taverns from opening their doors during the time of Divine Service and in 1827 Poole publicans were fined for allowing tippling during the hours of divine service.

62. The stocks outside the church at Charlton Marshall.

Parish records refer to many of the routine repairs to maintain church and village amenities. In 1584 the churchwardens at Charlton Marshall 'layed out (20d) for mending the stockes'. The stocks, doubtless many times repaired or replaced, are still outside the church – and Wimborne stocks are preserved in the garden of the Priest's House Museum, whilst at Lytchett Minster the parish laid out money 'for a wraping Clamp and Iron work about the Stocks' in 1752. At Hampreston in 1724 Churchwardens spent a shilling 'for mending and fine drawing [the parson's] surplice where mice had eaten it'. Nine years later they devoted twopence 'for Brass Screws to hang the minister's Hat Upon'. At Lytchett Minster in 1810 the sum of 6s. was paid for 'the strings of the Base Viol'. At Hampreston in 1705 5s. 9d. was spent on 'Glazing the Church windows'.

When the ringers put on a special performance to celebrate festive occasions, they had to be rewarded adequately with beer. Thus in 1728 at Corfe Mullen 2s. 6d. was spent on 'Liquor for the Ringers the 29th of May' (the anniversary of the restoration of Charles II). Pest extermination seems to have been a preoccupation of many villages. Thus in Corfe Mullen Churchwardens' Accounts we have these entries in 1728:

Pd. for three fox heads		3	0
Pd. Robt Haywerd for polecats head	0	0	4
Pd. for six dozen of Sparrows heads	0	1	0
Pd. for a Stoates Head	0	0	2
Pd. Robt Roggers for a Notters head	0	1	0

These rates seem to have been generally standard in local parishes, for at Hampreston in 1711 J. Barry and Thomas Sparks were paid 3s. 10d. for 23 dozen sparrows, Charles Edwards 6s. 0d. for 'six Otters Heads last winter' and in 1707 Hampreston 'Pd. Smith Froud for a Badgers Head 1s. 0d.' In that parish, however, Robert Gillingham and Thomas Sparks collected 3s. 8d. for 11 stoats' heads at the rate of 4d. per head. The poor otter was not then a protected species. Keeping the churchyard in good order was a major task and in 1737 Corfe Mullen spent 6d. for 'bancking ye Churchyard' and a further 5s. 6d. for 'making ye Churchyard hedge and Routing ye thorns and Brambles etc.' In 1759 Corfe Mullen 'paid for caching a want in the Churchyard 0–0–2'. 'Want' was the local name for a mole. Twenty

63. Hampreston Churchwardens' Accounts for 1714.

years earlier Kinson 'Pd. for catching of wants in the churchyard 0–1–0' but in 1747 spent another sixpence 'For catching of mools at church'.

Vice, violence and dishonesty were the regular concern of the Poole magistrates. In 1736 Widow Simmons was accused of 'keeping a disorderly house, being the generall rendezvous for alle Travellers and Vagabonds', and in 1777 the keeper of the Fish Street Gaol was sacked 'for suffering it to be used as a common bawdy house'. In 1793 Mrs. John Easter was prosecuted for keeping in Poole 'a house of ill-fame and a resort for disorderly and idle persons of both sexes'. As was to be expected in a port, prostitutes were a recurrent problem for the magistrates and after a big round-up eight girls, Jane Arney, Rosanna Swetland, Elizabeth Barter, Betsy Pain, Lucy Adams, Elizabeth Bains, Maria Williams and Mary Sims were before them on 2 November 1822. Each was convicted because 'she did wander about in the Public Streets as a common prostitute or Night Walker, not giving a satisfactory account of herself'. Each was convicted of being 'an idle and disorderly person', but the sentence was not mentioned. Poole magistrates sometimes punished beggars or petty thieves with public floggings at the tail of a cart or by a spell in the stocks. Thus 'George Frampton,

POOLE, *April 22.* Friday last the Quarter Sessions for this town and county was held here before Michael Angelo Taylor, Esq. the Recorder, when Michael Dennison, for having broken open a sloop, from which he stole various articles, was sentenced to be transported for seven years.

Monday morning last some villains broke open the stable of Mr. Whettel, at the Old Antelope Inn, and stole two horses, with which they have escaped hitherto undiscovered. They went through the turnpike gate between two and three o'clock in the morning, and were met about an hour afterwards seven miles from the town, on the Ringwood road.

Yesterday morning the house of Mr. Wm. Caster, at Hamworthy, near this place, was discovered to be on fire, but timely assistance being procured, it was happily extinguished without doing any material damage.

64. Extract from the *Salisbury and Winchester Journal*, 25 April 1785, concerning the sentencing of Michael Dennison for theft, some horse-stealing in Poole and a fire in Hamworthy.

65. Arrangements for the transportation of Michael Dennison to New South Wales.

Whereas at the General Quarter Sessions of the Peace held at the Guild Hall in and for the Town and County of Poole (by adjournment) on Friday the fifteenth day of April in the year one thousand seven hundred and eighty five Michael Dennison was Convicted of Felony and was by the Court Ordered to be Transported beyond the Seas for the term of Seven Years pursuant to the Statute in that Case lately made And whereas in pursuance of the said Act the same Court did appoint William Spurrier and Samuel Bowden Esquires two of his Majesty's Justices of the Peace for the said Town and County of Poole to contract with any person or persons for the performance of the Transportation of the said Convict and to order sufficient security to be taken for the same pursuant to the said Act Now know all Men by these presents That the said William Spurrier and Samuel Bowden the said two Justices appointed as aforesaid Do in pursuance of the Power given them as aforesaid contract and agree with Duncan Sinclair Commander of the Ship or Vessel Alexander bound to Botany Bay on the Coast of New South Wales and William Richards the Younger of Walworth in the County of Surry Ship Broker for their Transporting the before mentioned Convict to the Eastern Coast of New South Wales or some one or other of the Islands adjacent in pursuance of his Majesty's Order in Council lately made found guilty of stealing a parcel of old rope valued at 10d. belonging to George Ollive of Poole, merchant', was sentenced 'to be publickly whipped at the Carts Tail on Thursday, the fifteenth of February, 1738, between the hours of eleven and twelve of the clock in the forenoon from the Keyhead to the Town Hall'. Mary Phillips of Poole, widow, found guilty of stealing a shoulder of mutton value 10d. from John Strong, was sent to the workhouse, and there whipped and kept in hard labour and to receive the ordinary provisions of poor persons. Women convicted as 'common scolds' were condemned to a dowsing in the ducking stool on the Quay. Those convicted of more serious crimes might be transported. Thus Constance Savage was sent off to Savannah, in Georgia, in 1764 on the Poole ship *Indian Ocean* to serve her sentence of seven years' transportation for a felony. In 1769 George Walters and in 1772 James Towgood were transported to Trinity Bay, Newfoundland and in 1773 Joseph Besant was transported to 'Little Placentre', Newfoundland, at a time when a bitter quarrel was developing between the British government and the New England colonies. After the 13 colonies obtained their independence, another convict settlement was sought. Thus on 25 December 1786 a contract was signed between two Poole J.P.s and Duncan Sinclair, commander of the ship *Alexander*, for the transportation of Michael Dennison 'to the Eastern Coast of New South Wales or some or other of the Islands adjacent'. The *Alexander* was one of the convict transport ships in the 'First Fleet', which duly arrived in Australia in January 1788. Although 28 convicts on board the *Alexander* died on the voyage, Michael Dennison was not one of them. He arrived safely in New South Wales and further research in Australia should reveal what became of him. Michael Dennison was certainly Poole's first 'Australian'.

The death penalty was rarely imposed. In 1765 Thomas Colpis was sentenced 'to be burnt on the hand' for the manslaughter of a child after he had struck it on the head. A sailor named John Thresher was likewise 'burnt on the hand' in 1781 for the manslaughter of his wife whom he had beaten to death in blind fury when she tried to persuade him to come home from a tavern. Yet William Hardyman 'attainted of uttering a Bill of Exchange, knowing it to be forged' was sent to the gallows. 'Let him be hanged by the neck until he be dead. Let this prisoner be executed on Friday, the 8th day of April next' (1786) was the sentence. Two particularly unpleasant cases of murder led to two executions. In 1740 the owner of a saltworks at Parkstone, Henry Smith, was tried and found guilty at Dorchester Assizes of the murder of a young pregnant woman from Witchampton who was found on the heath at Parkstone lying with a knife beside her with 'her head almost off'. Smith was sentenced to be hanged in chains on the spot where the murder had been committed. In 1752 Anthony Colpis and his wife were tried for the murder of 'Widow Buckler' by throwing her from a third-storey window. Mrs. Colpis was acquitted, but her husband was executed at Windmill Point on the Baiter peninsula.

The duties of modern Trading Standards officers were carried out each September by the Sheriff, who with a jury on the appointed day of the 'Sheriff's Tourn' set off at 8 a.m. to inspect the weights and measures of each shop in Poole. By 6 p.m. he had usually detected a number of incorrect scales and the offending shopkeepers – bakers were frequent offenders – were normally fined 5s. 0d. and might have the defective scales confiscated. In 1820 Charlotte Langdon, shopkeeper, was fined 6s. 8d. for using deficient weights.

Complaints about neglect and decay in the state of public services and buildings were frequent. In 1770 John Osmond, the man who kept the Passage House in Hamworthy and who was supposed to be in charge of the ferry service, was reported to the magistrates since 'notwithstanding he has frequently been presented for not appointing a proper person for plying the Passage Boat, many complaints have been made of his neglect, and this day the said Boat was adrift and several people waiting to go over, being a great nuisance'. In 1784 it was said that the ferry boat was 'in a leaky condition and not fit for passengers to go over in her'. Yet still eight years later the magistrates were told that 'some passengers have complained they have nearly lost their lives in crossing the water'.

66. The Georgian Guildhall (Market House), built in 1761.

In 1767 complaints were lodged against the mayor for allowing 'the well of the Town Pump in Thames Street to remain open and uncovered, it being very dangerous for children to fall therein, being a great nuisance'. At various times public buildings such as the Old Guildhall in East Street, the Fish Shambles and the Salisbury Prison were reported to be in such a ruinous state that they were liable to collapse. In 1761 the two Poole M.P.s, John Gulston and Colonel Thomas Calcraft, built a new Guildhall for the town in Market Street. The ground floor, now enclosed, was originally open at the south-western end and served as a market, whilst the upper floor was a large council chamber, now housing a large part of the Guildhall Museum. Among the natural disasters which struck this area was the Great Storm of Friday/Saturday 26-27 November 1703 – 'the most terrible hurricane that has ever visited this island', at least until October 1987. Many houses, barns and trees were blown down in the Christchurch area and there was 'a prodigious tide'. The Christchurch churchwardens collected the large sum of £6 10s. 'for the widows and orphans of seamen who perished in the Great Storm'.

Perhaps because of the disastrous fires which had occurred in other Dorset towns, Blandford (1731), Wareham (1762) and Bere Regis (1717 and 1788), the authorities in Poole seem to have been particularly alert to the hazards of fire, and they were considerable where several industries involved the use of furnaces. One mayor, Timothy Spurrier, ordered the town crier to 'cry for people to put water at their doors and not to smoak tobacco in ye streets or ye key'. In 1749 the magistrates were told that Dinah Sims often kept a large number of heath faggots in the Fish Shambles 'to the great hazard of setting the town on fire'. Mrs. Ursula Skinner was reported in 1782 to be a fire hazard because her 'fowel house' was right up against a bakehouse chimney. Great alarm was caused in 1775 when the schooner *Industry* arrived with six tons of gunpowder aboard, 'the whole town being in danger of being demolished, and a very great nuisance'. The *Industry* was ordered to move down to the lower harbour, farther away from the town. Nevertheless, there was another scare a month later when a fire broke out in John Hooper's wash-house which was adjacent to a warehouse within which was stored half a ton of gunpowder. This incident finally led to the building of a Powder House for the storage of gunpowder on the more remote Baiter peninsula. The foundations of this can still be seen. The Guildhall Museum houses a Newsham-type fire engine in use in Poole from about 1770 to 1850.

There were frequent complaints about obstruction of the streets and quays. In 1752 Messrs. Bowden and Turner were accused of 'leaving empty pitch casks and staves behind ye Towne Cellars and obstructing Salesbury Street'. It was also reported that 'a large flat stone has remained on the Quay for near three years, it belonging to James Keats, of Corfe Castle'. One Richard Fabian of Wimborne was also said to have allowed four 'hogsheads of bones to continue on the Great Quay for a year or more'. On another occasion some unknown individual dumped a large mill stone in Thames Street. As late as 1822 it was

67. Royal Insurance plaque.

68. Newsham-type fire-engine in use in Poole
c.1770-1850 and now in Poole Guildhall Museum.

To the Inhabitants

OF THE

TOWN AND COUNTY OF POOLE.

The Surveyors of the Highways, anxious at all times to perform the duties which devolve upon them, according to the best of their abilities and the means placed at their disposal, feel, at the present Juncture, a peculiar solicitude that nothing should be omitted on their part, that can keep the Town in a state of cleanliness and thereby preserve the health of the people; They therefore take the liberty to call the attention of the inhabitants to *the condition of the gutters,* which in consequence of the level state of the Streets, can only be kept clean and wholesome by a plentiful supply of water. *They therefore respectfully, but earnestly request that every householder will cause six buckets of water (at the least) to be thrown into the gutter opposite his house, every morning AT NINE O'CLOCK.*

JAMES SALTER,
TITO D. HODGES. } *Surveyors:*

POOLE, July 24th, 1832.

69. Cleansing notice, 1832.

reported that John Manlawes had left 'a number of cannons which carry an accumulation of dirt and filth at the entrance to Durnford's Lane', leading off the Quay. The following year Widow Wharton, who seems to have run a chimney sweeping business, was in trouble 'for putting soot near the road in Hill Street, for loading the same in the street and suffering her boys to beat out their soot bags against the walls'. Even more unpleasant obstructions had frequently been deposited in the streets, as in 1744, when a man named Frampton and others dumped so much rubbish at the upper end of the High Street that 'carriages are obliged to break into the footway with great inconvenience in wet time to passengers on the road walking that way'. In 1769 William Hillier was charged with keeping pigs in the High Street and on another occasion Widow Culley was ordered to mend her pig sty because the drainings of the sty came through the walls into the lower rooms of her neighbour's dwelling.

Sanitary arrangements were extremely rudimentary. Thomas Strickland was ordered to repair the wall of his lavatory in Town Gate Lane to 'prevent the escape of any noisome smell through that wall'. In 1770 Mr. Willis the schoolmaster was rebuked 'for suffering his Scholars to do their necessary occasion against the Old

70. Benjamin Jesty's tombstone, Worth Matravers churchyard.

Town Hall, being very great nuisances . . .'. The new Guildhall suffered similar contamination for in 1798 there was a complaint against 'a most abominable nuisance, the filth commonly in the Market House [the arched area under the Guildhall], the shameful practice of people frequenting the nitches there causing such indecencies and rendering the place unwholesome'. Town Gate Lane was also a smelly place in 1754 when John Churchill was twice hauled before the magistrates 'for emptying chamber pots' there, and Paddocks Lane must have been a most unsavoury location in 1820 when Deborah Knowles was accused of 'emptying Night soil' there. As late as 1823 the Corporation was rebuked 'for not providing a convenient privy or privies for the use of seafaring persons and fishermen of the Port, for want of which nuisances are frequently committed on the Quays and particularly near the Fish Shambles'. Thus for all the elegance of the beautiful Georgian houses built by the wealthy merchants, Poole in the 18th and 19th centuries had its filthy and unwholesome areas.

All these insanitary practices must have been a substantial threat to good health, and many must have fallen prey to diseases like typhoid, spread by contaminated water supplies. In the 18th century the major killing and disfiguring disease was smallpox. How much it was feared may be gauged by the entry in the Lytchett Minster records of 1786. 'Anybody bringing smallpox into the parish to be prosecuted.' The Shapwick burial registers record many deaths from smallpox in January 1725/26, whilst in the space of five weeks in early 1729/30 eight were carried off in the small village of Shapwick by 'an uncommon malignant fever'. One method of countering smallpox was inoculation; that is, inducing what it was hoped would be a mild attack of actual smallpox by introducing into the blood-stream matter from a smallpox pustule. The Poole authorities favoured this practice but the Wimborne Vestry in 1767, evidently thinking that this might well spread the disease and spark off an epidemic, announced through an advertisement in the *Salisbury and Sherborne Journal* that it was banning 'all persons from opening a House or Houses for Inoculation in this Parish'. Towards the end of the 18th century news spread of a better and safer method of providing immunity through vaccination – inducing a mild attack of cowpox – a practice for which Farmer Benjamin Jesty, of Worth Matravers in Purbeck, became justly famous. In 1835 Parliament made the vaccination of infants compulsory.

TO THE

INHABITANTS

OF THE

TOWN AND COUNTY OF POOLE.

It is to be feared from the reports contained in the Public Papers, that the Cholera Morbus, which has proved so fatal in Asia and various parts of Europe, has made its appearance in England. It becomes, therefore, the Duty of every one to exert himself to prevent, if possible, the introduction of this direful Disease into his own Family, Town, or Neighbourhood.

By Order of Government, a BOARD OF HEALTH has been formed in this Town, consisting of the Magistrates, the Sheriff, the Parochial Minister, the Collector and Comptroller of the Customs, and the Gentlemen of the Medical Profession; who will at all times be ready to afford any information, or receive any communication that may tend to promote the Health of the Inhabitants.

The Board of Health have endeavoured to obtain the best information as to the most effectual means of Preventing the Introduction or Spread of this Disease, and they beg to call the attention of their fellow Townsmen to a few suggestions which they earnestly beseech them to adopt, believing that if they do so, they will prove efficacious (under the divine blessing) in preventing the introduction or spread of the Cholera Morbus in Poole.

First. The Board recommend constant attention to EXTERNAL CLEANLINESS. That the Streets, Lanes, and other Highways of the Town, be kept free from Dirt, Filth, or Stagnant Water; and they hope that every Householder will cheerfully co-operate with the Scavengers in endeavoring to accomplish this important object; and as there are but few public Pumps, that they will cause a few Buckets of Water to be daily thrown into the Gutter opposite their respective Dwellings, in order to prevent Noxious Exhalations arising therefrom, which are at all times very prejudicial to health.

Second. The Board recommend INTERNAL CLEANLINESS. That no accumulation of Dirt, or Decayed Vegetables or Fruit, be allowed to remain in or about their Habitations, but that every care be taken to keep their Houses Clean and well Ventilated. A free circulation of Air is of much importance, the Windows should therefore be opened as often as Weather will permit.

Third. PERSONAL CLEANLINESS. It is very important that Parents should pay particular attention to their Children being kept clean, and sufficiently Clothed to protect them from the Effects of Cold and Damp Weather, and those who from extreme Poverty are unable to do so, should make known their situation to their Wealthier Neighbours, whose liberality they may be assured will be manifested as on all former occasions.

Fourth. The Board earnestly recommend a strict regard to Habits of Temperance and Sobriety, as nothing tends to predispose the human frame to disease, more than intemperance. *All immoderate use of Spirituous Liquors should especially be avoided.*

Lastly. While the Board have felt it their duty to place these Remarks before the Inhabitants by way of Caution and Guidance, they feel pleasure in encouraging them to hope and believe that such is the Climate of England, that if general attention be paid to Cleanliness, Ventilation, and Sobriety, together with timely application for Medical advice and assistance, the continuance of this Disease in England will not be long, but that our Country will speedily, by the blessing of God, be freed from its direful consequences. All unnecessary Fear and Anxiety should therefore, be avoided, under the full assurance that if we invoke the Protection of an invisible but Almighty Guardian, and diligently use the appointed means of safety, he will crown our endeavours with his blessing.

ON BEHALF OF THE BOARD.

G. W. LEDGARD, *Mayor,*
CHAIRMAN.

11th November, 1831.

Chapter Nine

Poole's Golden Age

The period from the 'Glorious Revolution' until the Battle of Waterloo (1815) was preeminently Poole's Golden Age. The replacement of the Catholic James II by the Protestant William and Mary brought great relief to the radically Protestant people of Poole and, although it involved war with Louis XIV, the autocratic king of France who continued to uphold the Catholic Stuarts, the conflict with him resulted in the recognition of Newfoundland as British territory. This cleared the way for a massive development of Poole's involvement in the cod fisheries of that island and this in turn brought unprecedented prosperity to the Poole merchants involved in the Newfoundland trade – and indeed to the town itself and to the whole surrounding area. The lasting memorial to this prosperity is still to be seen in the magnificent Georgian houses and public buildings built by these 'merchant princes'.

James II in a 'declaration of indulgence' had suspended the laws against both Catholics and Dissenters, but most of the latter believed this concession to be just a stop on the road to the restoration of Catholicism and so declined to support James. The Protestant Nonconformists were rewarded by the Toleration Act (1689) which permitted most of them to set up their own places of worship and to hold their own services provided that they took an oath of loyalty and declared against the Roman doctrine of transubstantiation. Thus in the reign of the Presbyterian William III 'The Congregational Fund Board', a society founded to help the poorer Independent churches and ministers, granted in 1695 a sum of £5 'to the people of the congregation in Poole'. Grants of £10 were made in 1696 and 1697, though the following year this was made conditional on the congregation paying at least £20 to the pastor. In 1705 it seems that a Congregational chapel was built in Hill Street, for a record in the Borough's Session Book dated 14 January 1705/6 stated that 'The Meeting House, lately built in the garden of Richard Burkman . . . near Hill Street in the said towne and county . . . is licensed for an assembly for religious worship . . . according to the act of parliament in that case made and provided'. In 1704 a Rev. William Madgwick was appointed pastor of the new church, and won a large following in Poole during the 30 years of his ministry until his death in 1734. Among the members of the church were the veteran preacher, William Minty, and some leading Presbyterians – all merchants – Moses Durell, John Carter and Thomas Young, who left St James's and joined the Congregational church. Nonconformists were still debarred from office, unless they were willing to take the Anglican sacrament at least once a year. Many in fact did just that and compromised in order to exercise influence as members of the town council or as mayor.

Despite the breakaway of a number of Presbyterians like Moses Durell and John Carter and despite the rift between the 'Arians' or Unitarians, who took over that chapel in 1753, and the Congregationalists who were excluded and who eventually established the Skinner Street church, relations between the various Protestant groups in Poole were usually harmonious, perhaps because of the Low Church tradition at St James's. Certainly there was general admiration for its parish clerk for 29 years from 1739 to 1768, William Knapp, who attained nationwide fame as a composer of hymn tunes. Knapp was probably born in 1698 in Wareham, where he may have been a glove-maker. He moved to Poole, where he had property in the High Street and in Fish (now Castle) Street. He may have played an instrument in St James's church, as he was certainly passionately fond of music. In 1738 he published 'A Sett of New Psalm Tunes and Anthems', which proved to be so popular that it went into seven editions, and then in 1753 he produced his second book 'New Church Melody' which contained a large number of hymn tunes which he had composed. He named these after various Dorset towns and villages with which he was familiar, such as Blandford (now called 'Wareham' in modern hymn-books), Poole, Wimborne, Lichet, Spetisbury, Longfleet, Hamworthy, Kinson, Canford, Creekmore, Longham and Corfe Mullen. 'Wareham' is the melody most frequently played nowadays to the words of 'Rejoice, O land, in God thy might', 'Jesus, where'er thy people meet', and 'O Father, by whose sovereign sway'. The words he assigned appropriately to what he called his 'Poole New Tune', based on Psalm 107, Verse 23 onwards were:

> They that in Ships with Courage bold
> O'er swelling Waves their Trade pursue,
> Do God's amazing Works Behold
> And in the Deep his Wonders view.

Also featured in 'New Church Melody' is the Christmas carol, 'While Shepherds watch'd their Flocks by night, All seated on the Ground . . .'.

The high regard in which Knapp was held may be gauged by the fact that, although a 'foreigner' from Wareham, he was elected a Burgess of Poole. Knapp died in Poole in 1768 and was buried on 26 September 'somewhere near the old town wall'.

The burial of one of Knapp's friends and contemporaries had been recorded in the Poole

71. Skinner Street Congregational chapel, built 1777.

2. (*above*) Portrait of William Knapp.

3. (*right*) The Blandford Tune, now called 'Wareham', from Knapp's *New Church Melody*.

burial register thus: 'Feb. 2nd, 1750/1 Henry Price, a Poet'. Price was the son of a Poole brewer who kept *The George* in what is now Scaplen's Court. He was educated at Oxford and became a land-waiter in the Customs Service, but seems not to have been able to hold that job, perhaps because of his artistic temperament or alcoholic tendencies, and he seems to have been a teacher at the Free School just before his death. One sample of his verse, possibly occasioned by Knapp rebuking him for being overcome with hiccoughs in Divine Service, is as follows:

> Save me, O Lord, I pray . . .
> From doctor's bills and lawyer's fees
> From ague, gout and trap
> And what is ten time worse than these
> George Savage [the sexton] and Will Knapp.

However his genuine admiration for Knapp the hymn-tune composer may be gauged from these lines which he wrote on the publication of Knapp's first book:

Long as the Sun's enliv'ning Glories shine
So long shall last this deathless Work of thine
And future Worlds with one Consent agree
Where'er they sing of GOD, to mention thee.

The Glorious Revolution involved England in war with France, for Louis XIV in the 'War of the English Succession' (or 'King William's War') strove to restore his cousin, James II, whilst England, Holland, Austria and other allies strove to check French ambitions, for example, to seize Belgium and take over the whole of Newfoundland. In June 1690 Poole town council took emergency action 'for the better securing of the towne against the dangers threatened . . . by the French . . . now having a very great fleet in sight of this place'. In fact the formidable Admiral Tourville had arrived in Poole Harbour with 17 men-of-war and 122 fire-ships. Consequently, all owners of 'muskets, fowling-pieces, blunderbusses, pistols, powder, bullets or other arms . . . more than what is for their, or their friends' use', were required to hand them in at the Guildhall so that they could be 'cleaned and made fit for use', whilst all physically fit men were to be available for watch duty at night, and four great guns were to be mounted at the Town Gates and guards were

74. Monument to Peter Jolliffe in St James's church.

to be posted at Brownsea Castle. In fact Tourville did not attempt a landing, but sailed eastwards to win a great naval victory off Beachy Head. During the next few years English ships were frequently attacked and seized, even after Tourville's defeat off Cape La Hogue in 1692 by Admiral Russell.

Two Poole sea-captains won fame by their courageous action in the face of overwhelming odds. A report by the mayor, Thomas Smith, related that

On May 20, 1694, Peter Jolliff, of the said town and county [Poole] mariner, master of the *Sea Adventure*, a small hoy about 25 tons . . . saw a French privateer . . . (though of three times his strength) make a prize of a Weymouth fishing vessel. He gave chase to the privateer and her prize, retook the prize and forced the privateer ashore near Lulworth, where she was broken in pieces; the men, 24 in number, were secured by Jolliff, who landed six of them at Weymouth and brought the other 18 to Poole.

In recognition of this exploit **Peter Jolliffe** was presented with a gold chain and medal bearing the portraits of King William and Queen Mary and an account of his courageous action. The gold medal is preserved in Poole's Maritime Museum and a memorial to Peter Jolliffe in St James's church recounted how in 'the late wars . . . against the French . . . [he] frequently revenged their insolencies against the English by captivity and death'.

A year later William Thompson, another Poole man, master of a small fishing vessel, when 'out fishing having with him only one man and a boy' off the Isle of Purbeck,

perceived a privateer of Cherbourg bearing down on him. He had two small guns mounted and some small arms and made ready to defend himself, which he did with such good success that . . . he wounded the captain, the lieutenant and six men and put the privateer to flight . . . But Thompson in his turn, encouraged by his success, gave chase to the privateer, fired upon her incessantly for two hours and at length compelled the enemy to surrender. He took possession of the sloop and with 14 prisoners . . . brought her into Poole harbour.

Like Jolliffe, Thompson was presented by the Admiralty with an inscribed gold medal and chain of the value of £50.

During the war Poole merchants continued to engage in the Newfoundland cod trade but, because of the danger of attack by their French rivals, they petitioned the government in 1696 to send eight men-of-war to Newfoundland 'with a competent number of land forces for the recapture of the harbours lately taken by the French, for their better preservation in the future'. They also wanted St John's and Ferryland – as well as Cabonear and Bonavista – to be fortified, 'being the principal places of fishing and security of ships'. The Poole merchants went on to ask that 'A convoy should be ready in January next to sail with the ships bound for Ireland to take in provisions for the inhabitants of Newfoundland, and another convoy for the ships that sail to Spain and Portugal for salt, the want of which

would overthrow the fishing ships and planters' voyages'. Again, they said that 'Sufficient convoys should be appointed for the ships homeward bound with train-oil, wet fish, and passengers'. In 1697 peace with France was negotiated and Louis XIV recognised William III as rightful king of England. Nevertheless in 1699 Sir William Phippard, one of Poole's leading merchants and M.P. for Poole, reported that his ship the *William and Elizabeth*, laden with a cargo of tobacco bound for London, had been captured the previous autumn near the banks of Newfoundland by a French pirate.

The conflict with France continued in the War of the Spanish Succession, during the reign of Queen Anne (1702-14), a staunch Protestant and younger daughter of James II. He had died in 1701 and Louis XIV had recognised as king of England his 12-year-old son, James Edward, who was being reared as a Catholic, and Louis XIV had also agreed that his own grandson should become king of Spain and its vast empire. In Germany and the Low Countries the victories of John Churchill, Duke of Marlborough, shattered the reputation of the French army for invincibility. Marlborough's father, Winston Churchill, was a burgess of the borough of Poole. In Newfoundland there was heavy fighting between Poole fishermen and the French.

During this war Woodes Rogers, who was probably born in Poole in 1679, sailed

75. Woodes Rogers depicted on a stamp of the Bahamas.

round the world in command of the same ship – only the third English captain to do so. His father and namesake – members of an old Dorset family – had engaged in the tough Newfoundland trade from Poole but had later moved to Bristol, where Woodes Rogers junior soon came to be recognised as one of the most enterprising sea-captains. Spain had been brought into the war on the side of France and, since the English had suffered many losses at the hands of the Spaniards, Woodes Rogers received authority to lead a privateering expedition intended to surprise the Spaniards on the Pacific coasts of their American colonies – an imitation of Francis Drake's great voyage. Woodes Rogers (only 29 years of age), taking as one of his officers, William Dampier, an experienced navigator of the South Seas, set out on his expedition in 1708 in command of the *Duke* (320 tons, 30 guns and 117 men) and the *Dutchess* (260 tons, 26 guns and 108 men). He sailed round the Horn into the Pacific early in 1709, and decided to stop at the remote island of Juan Fernandez to take on board fresh water, fruit and goat-meat. It was here that the most famous incident on his voyage occurred. Seeing a light ashore Woodes Rogers sent some men to investigate. As Rogers himself related in *A Cruising Voyage Round the World*, 'Our pinnace returned from the shore, and brought a man cloth'd in Goat Skins who looked wilder than the first Owners of them'. The stranger was in fact Alexander Selkirk, a Scotsman, who had been marooned there over four years earlier after a dispute when he was a member of Dampier's expedition. Woodes Rogers made him a mate on board the *Duke*. After his return to England Rogers wrote and published his account of the voyage, possibly with the help of Daniel Defoe, with whom he probably had many discussions on the subject of trading in the Pacific area. The extraordinary adventures of Alexander Selkirk provided Defoe with much of the material for his *Robinson Crusoe*, published in 1719. Sailing northwards after picking up Selkirk, Rogers captured several Spanish ships collecting considerable loot, but being careful to make a detailed record of what was captured and to allocate the plunder fairly. Deciding like Drake on his 1577-80 voyage that the Spaniards would be waiting for him if he returned to England by the same route, he decided to cross the Pacific to the East Indies and to return to England via the Cape of Good Hope. He reached England in 1711, having circumnavigated the world. In his later years as Governor of the Bahamas, Woodes Rogers waged a successful campaign against piracy in the West Indies, dying in the Bahamas in 1732.

The Treaty of Utrecht (1713) at the end of the War of the Spanish Succession confirmed as British territory not only Gibraltar, captured in 1704, but also the whole of Newfoundland, hitherto in dispute with the French. Louis XIV also recognised the Protestant succession, that is, that Anne was legally queen and that she should be succeeded by her Protestant German cousin, Sophia of Hanover or, if she died before Anne, then by Sophia's son, George. In the event he duly succeeded in 1714 as King George I and this meant that England was spared a second experience of a Catholic autocrat on the throne.

It was therefore understandable that people in the Poole area should wish to celebrate the Protestant succession. Thus at Hampreston the sum of three shillings was paid for 'Prayers upon his Majesties Accession to ye Crown' and that in 1716 the Wimborne churchwardens paid 14s. 5d. 'to the Ringers 28th May at being King George's birth day'. The continuing fear of Catholic take-over is indicated by the payment by the Corfe Mullen churchwardens on 5 November 1728 of four shillings to 'ye Ringers Gunpowder Treasons day'. The Catholic lord of Canford manor, Sir Thomas Webb, was the object of suspicion in 1745, when the one serious threat to the Protestant House of Hanover occurred in the 'Forty-Five' Jacobite rebellion, launched in Scotland by 'Bonnie Prince Charlie' on behalf of his father the exiled 'Old Pretender' (James III), the ageing son of James II. One Jacobite sympathiser, 'Gerard Lewis, late of Poole, yeoman' (perhaps the Christian name, Gerard, indicated that he was a Catholic), according to the jurors 'on 3 November [when Prince

Charles Edward Stuart and his army were advancing southwards into England] . . . in a certain discourse with diverse liege subjects of our said lord the King . . . concerning . . . the then unnatural rebellion carrying on in Scotland . . . having in his hand a mug with liquor therein then and there drank the health of King James!' and said 'He [meaning the person then in Scotland] is of the Royal blood of England', Lewis pleaded guilty, but seems to have been fined only a shilling. The Young Pretender got no further south than Derby and in 1746 was decisively defeated at Culloden. Under that year in the Corfe Mullen accounts is this entry: 'Pd. for a Prayer at time of Rebellion – 1s. 0d.'

During the period of almost uninterrupted peace from 1714 to 1739 Poole merchants were able to take full advantage of their opportunities in Newfoundland, and local industries flourished. Daniel Defoe was favourably impressed, as too had been another intrepid traveller, Celia Fiennes, some forty years earlier. This prim but remarkably tough Nonconformist spinster, daughter of a Cromwellian colonel, made extensive journeys all over Britain on horseback, alone but for two or three servants, along roads that were hazardous to say the least. About 1682 or earlier she visited Poole and Poole Harbour. Her account in her *Journal* is as follows:

> I went to Blandford in Dorsetshire through a hare warren and a forest of the Kings [Cranborne Chase]. Blandford is a pretty neate country town [even before the rebuilding after the 1731 fire] – thence to Merly by Wimborne over a great river called the Stour (a large arched bridge) to a relations house Sir William Constantines house – thence to Poole a little sea-port town where was a very good Minister in the publick Church, Mr. Hardy [who was expelled in 1682].
>
> From thence by boate we went to a little isle called Brownsea 3 or 4 leagues off, where there is much Copperise [copperas] made, the stones being found about the Isle on the shore in great quantetyes, there is only one house there which is the Governors, beside little fishermens houses, they being all taken up about the Copperice workes; they gather the stones and place them on the ground raised like the beds in gardens, rows one above the other, and are all shelving so that the raine disolves the stones and it draines down into trenches and pipes made to receive and convey it to the house; that is fitted with iron panns foursquare and of a pretty depth at least 12 yards over, they place iron spikes in the panns full of branches and so as the liquor boyles to a candy it hangs on these branches. I saw some taken up; it look't like a vast bunch of grapes, the coullour of the Copperace not being much differing, it lookes cleare like sugar-candy, so when the water is boyled to a candy, they take it out and replenish the panns with more liquor; I do not remember they added anything to it only the stones of Copperice dissolved by the raine into liquor; there are great furnaces under, that keepes all the panns boyling; it was a large room or building with severall of these large panns; they do add old iron and nailes to the Copperas Stones. This is a noted place for lobsters and crabs and shrimps, there I eate some very good.
>
> From Merly we went to the Isle of Purbeck. At Warrum [Wareham] we passed over a bridge where the sea flowed in and came by the ruines of Corffe Castle . . . The shores are very rocky all about the Island, we went to Sonidge [Swanage] a sea faire place not very big; there is a flatt sand by the sea a little way; they take up stones by the shore that are so oyly as the poor burn it for fire, and its so light a fire it serves for candle too, but it has a strong offensive smell [Kimmeridge shale; early clues to the East Dorset oilfield]. At a place called Sea Cume [Seacombe] the rockes are so craggy and the creekes of land so many that the sea is very turbulent . . . and it being a spring-tide I saw the sea beat upon the rockes at least 20 yards with such a foame or froth . . .

Another account of the Poole area is contained in Daniel Defoe's survey, *A Tour through the whole island of Britain*, published 1724-6. Defoe referred to Christchurch as 'a very inconsiderable poor place, scarce worth seeing [he seems to have missed the Priory!], and less worth mentioning . . . only that it sends two members to Parliament, which many poor towns in this part of England do'. At Wimborne he 'found nothing remarkable, but the church', in which he noted the brass of Ethelred I.

> South of this town [wrote Defoe], over a sandy, wild and barren country, we came to Pool, a considerable sea-port, and indeed the most considerable in this part of England; for there I found

some ships, some merchants and some trade; especially there were a good number of ships fitted out every year to the Newfoundland fishing, in which the Pool men were said to have been particularly successful for many years past.

The town sits in the bottom of a great bay or inlet of the sea, which entering at one narrow mouth opens to a very great breadth within the entrance, and comes up to the very shore of this town. The place is famous for the best, and biggest oysters in all this part of England, which the people of Pool pretend [i.e. claim] to be famous for pickling, and they are barrelled up here, and sent not only to London, but to the West Indies, and to Spain, and Italy, and other parts. 'Tis observed more pearl are found in the Pool oysters, and larger than in any other oysters in England.

Later in the century Hutchins was to write in his *History of Dorset*:

Without the bar, and in the boundaries of Poole, is an extensive bed of oysters from which there are several sloops loaded every year, and carried to the creeks in the mouth of the Thames, where they are laid to fatten, to supply the London markets; and in the catching of which upwards of forty sloops and boats are employed for two months every spring, which season is the fisherman's harvest; during which time they receive between 6 and £7,000. The last day's catching is, by a prescriptive regulation, thrown back into the channels within the harbour, where they fatten, and supply the town and country during the winter with excellent oysters . . . The harbour Plaice are most excellent. Herrings have been caught in such plenty as to be sold for a penny a dozen.

Aubrey, in the 17th century, commenting that the Thursday market in Devizes was the best in Wiltshire, had noted that 'they bring fish from Poole hither, which is sent from hence to Oxford'.

The 18th century saw a great expansion of English overseas trade, the establishment of many overseas trading outposts and the consolidation of many colonies which laid the foundations of the British Empire. Traders of the East India Company opened up trade with India and one of these merchants who especially prospered was Thomas Pitt (1653-1726), son of the Rev. John Pitt, rector of Blandford St Mary, whose great-grandmother was Helena de Havilland of Poole. Thomas Pitt amassed enough money to enable him to buy an estate at Old Sarum and to enter Parliament as M.P. for this rotten borough, thereby establishing for his family a firm foothold in Parliament. Whilst he was away in India, where he became Governor of Madras, he became alarmed at the extravagance of his wife, whom he had left in charge of the money he sent home, and in a letter he rebuked her for 'spending my estate faster than I can get it'. Despite this 'Governor' Pitt continued to be a rich man for he bought for some £20,000 a huge diamond, weighing 127 carats, as large as a pullet's egg, which he got his son, Robert, to bring back to England concealed in a hole constructed in the heel of his shoe. Eventually 'Diamond' Pitt sold the gem to the Regent of France for £135,000 and it became the chief ornament in the French crown. 'Diamond' Pitt used some of his wealth to repair and beautify the church at Blandford St Mary.

His grandson, William Pitt the Elder, was the effective head of the government (1757-61) and 'the organiser of victory' during the Seven Years' War (1756-63) in the climax of the struggle with France for mastery in India and North America. By maintaining British supremacy on the high seas, by subsidising our brilliant Prussian ally, Frederick the Great, who kept the French busy in Europe, and by encouraging and promoting keen young generals, Pitt wrested both India and Canada from French control. Thirty-one-year-old Eyre Coote, commander of the 39th Regiment of Foot, the first king's regiment to be sent to India (later to be combined with the 54th to form the Dorsetshire Regiment with the appropriate motto *Primus in Indis* – 'first into India'), played a major part in Clive's victory in the Battle of Plassey (1757) over the pro-French ruler of Bengal. Later Eyre Coote's decisive victory over the French in the Battle of Wandewash (1760) ensured British supremacy in the sub-continent. General Sir Eyre Coote was M.P. for Poole (1774-80). Meanwhile the 32-year-old General Wolfe, who exercised his troops on Blandford Downs before taking them to Canada, had been victorious on the Heights of Abraham and ensured the British capture of Quebec.

Britain was again involved in war with France during the American War of Independence (1775-83), when the French intervened on the side of the 13 rebel colonies. Britain temporarily lost command of the seas, and Poole merchants trading with Newfoundland lost many ships at the hands of French and Spanish privateers. At the end of the war Newfoundland remained British, but the 13 colonies obtained their independence as the United States of America.

Five years later Britain was drawn into the war with the French Revolutionaries, which was to last nine years, during which Poole mariners suffered greatly at the hands of the press-gangs seizing recruits for the Royal Navy, and many Poole vessels engaged in the Newfoundland trade were seized by French privateers. After a one-year truce the continuing ambitions and aggressions of Napoleon Bonaparte involved Britain in the Napoleonic Wars, 1803-15. There was considerable local resentment at the activities of the press-gangs, but substantial support for the war effort. In 1798 the Corporation voted £500 towards the defence of the realm, and £1,300 was raised by voluntary contributions the next day. Armed volunteer associations were formed, whilst Poole became a general rendezvous for militia regiments. A visitor in 1795 found it difficult to find accommodation in Poole because 'the town was full of military, the 112th and the 124th regiments being in quarters there'. When in 1803-5 Napoleon prepared to invade Britain plans

76. General Sir Eyre Coote, M.P. for Poole (1774-80).

were revived for establishing a system of warning beacons. The Lord Lieutenant of the county in October 1803 warned Henry Bankes that the French might try to seize the Isle of Wight and asked him to 'give directions for an assemblage of faggots, furze and other fuel, also of straw to be stacked and piled on the summit of Badbury Rings, so as the whole may take fire instantly, and the fire maintained for two hours . . . this beacon may be fired whenever the beacon of St Catherine's (Christ Church) is fired to the eastward, or whenever the beacons on Lytchett Heath or Woodbury Hill are fired to the westward'.

Nelson's victorious Trafalgar campaign (1805) meant that the invasion never came and also gave Britain overwhelming naval supremacy, which enabled Poole merchants to make huge fortunes during the next 10 years as a result of the almost complete monopoly enjoyed by Britain in trade between Britain, Europe and the rest of the world.

Although the war with Napoleon was on a larger scale than Britain had been involved in to date, it was far from being a total war. Very few men in the Poole area would have served abroad in the British army, but one of these was Sergeant William Lawrence (1791-1869), who left behind an autobiography containing vivid accounts of his experiences. He was a ploughboy from Bryant's Piddle, whose father apprenticed him to a builder in Studland, who kept him short of food and thrashed him with a horsewhip. Young Lawrence then ran away and, in the company of another runaway apprentice, made his way to Poole and, as he wrote later, he planned to contract with a merchant named Slade to serve for two summers and a winter in Newfoundland 'myself for £20 and my companion for £18 for the whole time, and our food and lodging till the ship left harbour' on board the Newfoundland packets. However his companion's master caught him, and young Lawrence set off for Dorchester. 'On the road' he wrote, 'I met two boys who were going to Poole to try to get a ship bound for Newfoundland . . . I told them not to go to Poole, as the press-gang was about and, when I had been there a few days before, had fired a blunderbuss at me, but I happened to go round a corner and so had escaped'. Eventually Lawrence enlisted in the

40th Regiment. He fought under Wellington throughout the Peninsular War and throughout all the hardships and horrors he preserved his sense of fair-play and compassionate nature.

Sergeant Lawrence survived the Battle of Waterloo (1815), where he was put in charge of the regimental colours after 14 other sergeants had been wounded or killed in charge of them. After the war he stayed on in the army of occupation in Paris, fell in love with a French girl, Clotilde, and obtained his colonel's consent to marry her. He brought her back to England and, after he retired from the army on a pension of ninepence a day, he and his wife settled down in Studland and ran a little inn for some years. They are buried alongside each other in Studland churchyard.

The extraordinary importance and prosperity of Poole between the 'Glorious Revolution' and Waterloo was based primarily on the Newfoundland trade, but also upon other important longstanding economic factors. Poole acted as an entrepot for a large hinterland – Dorset and parts of Wiltshire and Somerset. We have seen how locally-caught fish was taken inland and in return agricultural produce (pigs, calves, sheep, cheese, butter, barley, flour, potatoes, rabbits and leather) was brought in by road and exported to London and elsewhere. Wool from the Dorset Downs was stored in the town cellars and then exported, usually to Hull. Purbeck stone for building and paving was exported through Poole to London. Clay from the shores of Poole Harbour was 'in great repute with the Staffordshire and Yorkshire potters from its peculiar excellency' and formed 'the principal ingredient in Staffordshire ware'.

Among the local industries associated with the port were shipbuilding, sail-making, rope-making, salt-making and net manufacturing (though Bridport continued to be the main producer of nets). Shipbuilding was largely centred on Hamworthy, and in 1804 there were five shipbuilding yards using timber imported from North America and the Baltic and employing 23 men and 43 apprentices. There were three rope-walks, one near the landward entrance to the town (the later Ladies' Walking Field, now occupied by the bus station), one on the eastern side of the town near Baiter Green and another

77. Tombstone of Sergeant William Lawrence, Studland.

near the extremity of the Hamworthy peninsula. These rope-walks produced cordage for local shipping, but also carried out government contracts.

One of the earliest Poole seafaring and merchant families to gain fame and fortune was the Thompson family. Mention has already been made of Captain William Thompson, who was awarded a gold medal for his courage in defying a French privateer in 1695. His two brothers, James and Thomas, traded with Newfoundland and with the Carolinas on the east coast of North America, importing from the latter pitch, tar, indigo, rice and mahogany. The son of Thomas, James Thompson, moved to London and set up an import-export business with Hamburg in North Germany, and was joined by his brother, Peter, who ultimately inherited the Hamburg business as well as the Poole property of his uncle, James. Peter Thompson lived in Bermondsey, where he became a J.P. and then High Sheriff of Surrey and later M.P. for St Albans. George II bestowed a knighthood upon him, perhaps in recognition of his outspoken loyalty at the time of the 1745 Jacobite rebellion. Sir Peter Thompson (1698-1770) was a man of culture and learning, who became a Fellow of the Royal Society and a member of the Society of Antiquaries. Despite his absence in London, he had always maintained strong ties with his home-town of Poole, which indeed owes him a great debt of gratitude for his energy and dedication in acquiring a collection of books and documents relating to the history of Poole. He gave the Rev. John Hutchins a great deal of help in writing his *History of Dorset*, especially the section dealing with Poole, and had a map of Poole drawn. It was fitting that in 1774 Peter Thompson was elected a Burgess of Poole. As Hutchins wrote, Sir Peter 'made it his choice in 1763 to withdraw from . . . commercial affairs, that he might enjoy the pleasures of studious retirement and reflection, and the conversation of his friends, in the place of his birth, where he lived respected by all ranks

78.   Sir Peter Thompson.

of people for his affability and benevolence; and where in an agreeable situation in Market-street, he had, in 1746, built a handsome house in which he generally resided till his death, and at great expense he formed a capital collection of books'. Sir Peter had purchased two acres of land alongside Pillory Street (now the northern extension of Market Street) and had engaged the Bastard brothers, the architects of Georgian Blandford, when it was rebuilt after the great fire of 1731, to build him a fine mansion. Sir Peter protested at the speed with which John Bastard presented his bill on the completion of the building. In his reply (July 1752) John Bastard defended the quality of the structure, saying: 'the house stands bleak, and much exposed. And I think there never was a house beter defended against storms nor more care taken in Rooffing, and lead work. I never saw nor hard of a drop that came in aney whar'. Whatever the defects of Bastard's spelling, there was nothing amiss with his skill as a builder. 'The Poole Mansion', as Sir Peter's house was to be called, is as impressive an example of Georgian architecture today as it was when it was completed 236 years ago. It would have looked even more impressive when Sir Peter had the garden laid out with paths and lawns around a small ornamental lake and surrounded the grounds with fine decorative wrought-iron railings – right in the heart of the old town. Sir Peter never married, but lived in his mansion with his widowed sister acting as his housekeeper during his last years. Both of them died in 1770 and were buried, like Sir Peter's brother,

79. The Poole Mansion, Sir Peter Thompson's house.

80. 'West End House', West Street, built *c*.1740.

James, in St James's churchyard. A memorial inside the church commemorates all three. The Poole Mansion was bought in 1788 and occupied by George Kemp, a member of a merchant family originating in Christchurch and engaged in the Newfoundland trade. The Mansion remained in the hands of the Kemp family until 1890, when it was bought by Sir Ivor Guest, of Canford, and his wife, Lady Cornelia, who turned it into a hospital in 1897. When, 10 years later, the 'Cornelia Hospital' was transferred to a new site in Longfleet, Poole Corporation bought the Mansion House and used it as the Poole Municipal Offices until the new Municipal Buildings at Park Gates East were opened in 1932.

By building his Poole Mansion Sir Peter Thompson helped to set a fashion, which was to be followed by many of the 'merchant princes' of Poole, who invested part of the fortunes made in the Newfoundland trade in elegant Georgian mansions, some of which still survive, as in Thames Street and West Street. Many others were built in the High Street but, when in the 19th century the High Street became the main shopping centre, many of these fine houses had their ground floors gutted or were pulled down to accommodate shops.

Poole's connection with Newfoundland goes back at least 400, if not 450, years. John Cabot after his return to Bristol from Newfoundland in 1497 had asserted that the codfish were so plentiful in the fishing grounds that they sometimes hampered the passage of ships. It was not long before merchants in West Country ports, especially Poole and Dartmouth, were sending out ships to scoop this wealth out of the seas. An entry in the 1551 town accounts would seem to indicate that Poole men were already bringing back dry salted cod from the rich fishing grounds off Newfoundland: 'The 4th May of two men which brought herrings and laded away certain Newlonde fyshe – 6s. 6d.'

A table of quayage rates, quoting one of 1528, listed among other items 'Fyshe of Newfoundland drye'. In 1583, as we have seen, Christopher Farewell, merchant and former mayor of Poole, was absenting himself from his duties as Senior Bailiff by accompanying Sir Humphrey Gilbert to Newfoundland, when he formally took possession of the island in the name of Queen Elizabeth. Despite the hazards of the voyage across the Atlantic in small ships – the mountainous seas, icebergs and pirates – Poole merchants and sea-captains increasingly concentrated on cod-fishing expeditions to Newfoundland, so that in 1619, when the Privy Council asked Poole to contribute £100 towards the suppression of piracy, the mayor protested that 'Our town is poor . . . for our trade is not in any staple, but in fishing voyages for the New Found Land and so home'. From time to time certainly blinding fogs, sudden squalls, great storms and pirates and privateers took their toll of the ships, rarely exceeding 250 tons and usually much smaller, going to Newfoundland, but often the profits from these voyages were very great. An attempt to give Bristol and London merchants forming a Newfoundland Company a monopoly of fishing and trade in and around the island broke down and Royal Charters of 1634, 1661 and 1676, the so-called 'Western Charters', gave control of the fishery to the mayors of several western ports, including Poole, in respect of the conservation of timber, the proper disposal of ballast, the protection and use of the fish-drying spaces and other essential rules. These 'Charter' rules were to be enforced in each Newfoundland harbour by an Admiral, appointed from among the masters of the first three ships to arrive each season. The Newfoundland Act of 1699 confirmed these rules and remained in force until 1825. This measure prevented any re-imposition of a monopoly and enabled Dorset ports, above all Poole, to catch the cod on the fishing banks, to process the fish and to supply goods to Newfoundland. George Garland giving evidence in 1817 explained that,

> When this trade was first established [two hundred or more years earlier], the merchants and their immediate servants were the only classes of persons engaged in it. The merchant residing in England made his outfit in the Spring of the year, both as it respected the number of servants he engaged, and the quantity of provisions and tackle he provided . . . the fish was wholly caught, cured and

exported by his own servants, and a very small establishment (if any) was left in the island through the winter. In the process of time, however, a third class of persons sprang up, consisting of servants or sailors, who had chosen to remain on the island after the period of their servitude had elapsed, and of their descendants born in Newfoundland. These persons, denominated Planters, procured supplies of all the necessaries of life, and implements for the fishery, from the merchants, engaging to pay for the same in fish and oil.

In the early 17th century disputes arose between the seasonal visitors and the 'loose and useless' settlers, whom they accused of stealing salt and provisions as well as their gear and small boats left on the shore during the winter, but in the end a *modus vivendi* was worked out.

Under the 'dry' fishery system Poole fishermen unloaded the fish on to wooden stages built out into the water in some safe haven like Trinity Bay, on the east coast of Newfoundland. On the stages were 'disagreeably dark' buildings accommodating the work force processing the fish – the 'Headers', who chopped off the heads and tails, the 'Splitters', who boned the fish and removed the offal and the 'Spreaders' who salted the fish before it was stacked on the 'Flakes', plain brushwood platforms, to dry. Meanwhile the 'livers of the codd fish put into a cask by themselves dissolves most into oyle'. This 'train-oil', as it was called, was a valuable by-product and much in demand for domestic oil lamps back home, despite its penetrating odour. The anonymous author of a *Journal of a Tour from Brighton to Weymouth in 1816*, after describing the journey from Christchurch along 'a barren track' across 'an immense heath', observed that 'the approach to Poole is very good; the streets are clean, the houses well built and the Quay noble. With all this', he added, 'I was never so sick of a place in my life as the two hours we breakfasted there. Everybody knows its trade with Newfoundland' and 'whoever has a gout for Train Oil may have a breakfast of it gratis; indeed he must have his quantum of it' whether 'he will or not, as he cannot enter a house without finding it on the table or go to his chamber without it for a bedfellow.' Train-oil was also used in the manufacture of soap, the curing of leather and in the woollen industry, and Peter Jolliffe of Poole was pleased when he sold train-oil at £22 a tun to 'a person that came here from London'. Among the other goods imported to Poole directly from Newfoundland were cranberries, salmon (one George Skeffington, of Poole, in the 18th century set up the largest salmon fishery in Newfoundland), furs (in the 1724 Christmas quarter Poole imported 2,386 mixed fox, marten, seal and beaver skins), and timber, including staves, essential for making the casks for storage of train-oil, furs, blubber and wine. It is notable that the magnificent pine pillars of the new St James's church, built in 1820, came from Newfoundland. Dried salted cod might be brought back to Poole if storms or privateers prevented a vessel from taking it to another market, but here it was rarely on the menu, since there was plenty of freshly caught 'wet' fish.

Generally the Poole ships involved in the Newfoundland trade followed a triangular route. They might take the salt cod to the West Indies where it was fed to the negro slaves on the sugar plantations. Rum and molasses would then be brought back to Poole. More commonly the Poole vessels took their cargoes of dried fish to the Catholic countries of Southern Europe – Portugal, Spain and the various Italian states – for consumption on Sundays and Holy Days. Having weathered the North Atlantic storms Poole mariners might then fall a prey to the Barbary corsairs. Thus in 1673 the *Charles* of Poole with a cargo of dry fish from Newfoundland bound for Malaga was taken by five Turkish pirate ships and the master, John Edwards, was taken into slavery. The return cargoes from the Mediterranean countries included wine (nearly 10,000 gallons were imported by Poole in 1751-2), oranges and lemons, almonds, figs, currants and raisins. In 1760 William Barfoot entered at Poole Custom House 6,000 baskets of raisins, declared to have been reduced in value 'by salt water and other ways'. Olive oil was another major import from these Mediterranean countries.

The *Thomas and Richard* of Poole in 1737 brought 100 gallons of 'Spanish Oil' into Poole. Sometimes olive oil was taken on the following spring to Newfoundland, where it was in demand for cooking and also to provide a delicacy – bread soaked in olive oil – as a relief from dried fish, oatmeal and 'sea-bird pie'. Above all large quantities of salt were brought back from Lisbon, Cadiz, Alicante and Sicily. Salt was also obtained from France. All this salt was stored in Poole over the winter, ready for export the following spring to Newfoundland where it was absolutely essential for curing the fish.

Since Newfoundland itself produced very little food or other essentials like clothing, non-perishable provisions such as wheat, barley, malt, oatmeal, flour, peas, biscuits, beer, cider and spirits were collected in Poole at the beginning of each season. The main cod-fishing season lasted from May until November and sealing took place after the cod had been caught and processed. Some ships did not return to Poole until November and were ready to set out again at the end of February. More perishable foodstuffs such as butter, cheese, pork and vegetables were taken on board in Southern Ireland on the last leg of the outward voyage. Typical of the manufactured goods taken to Newfoundland was the cargo of the *Willing Mind* of Poole setting out in April 1709 – 'made garments, woollen cloth, blankets, serges and shoes for the workers and settlers' besides nets, lines, cordage, sail-cloth and nails for the fishing vessels. The following year the same Poole vessel had on board a large store of new shoes, '125 suits of wearing apparel' and 227 yards of linen. Other regular exports from Poole to Newfoundland were 'apothecaries' ware', beer, bricks, candles, earthenware, glassware, gloves, grind stones, gunpowder, handkerchiefs, hats, household furniture, leather, musical instruments, soap, stationery, tea and tobacco and tobacco pipes. The Tucker merchant family in Weymouth supplied Poole merchants with large quantities of Virginia tobacco. The Newfoundland trade provided a vast amount of employment in Poole and the Poole hinterland. The ships themselves, of course, gave employment not only to mariners and shipwrights, but also to sailmakers, ropemakers, blacksmiths, whitesmiths, carpenters, blockmakers and pumpmakers. The greater part of West Street was occupied by bootmakers and shoemakers, and to supply them there was a tannery at Tatnam. The merchants set up their own linen factories at Organford and Lytchett, whilst Sturminster Newton and Marnhull specialised in providing soft warm swanskin flannel to help withstand the rigours of the bleak Newfoundland climate.

How was the labour force required by the merchants trading from Poole to Newfoundland recruited? Hutchins observed that 'young, sturdy countrymen indent themselves for two summers and a winter, during which time being constantly employed in boats and ships, they become seasoned to the sea and fit to rank as mariners'. In fact a high proportion of the emigrants to Newfoundland came from Poole and its hinterland. The present premier of Newfoundland, Mr. Brian Peckford, is very proud of his east Dorset ancestry. They needed to be tough to stand up to the Atlantic crossing and the severe climate of Newfoundland. The Sturminster Newton area was very closely linked with Poole's Newfoundland trade and in 1811 Mrs. Jane Dawson of Hinton St Mary, whose son was employed at Carbonear by Messrs. G. & J. Kemp, asked her brother-in-law, a Poole butcher, to purchase and send out to her son a silver watch, four pairs of boots and four pairs of shoes. There were also apprentices of their 'own Voluntary Will and Inclination', perhaps prompted by a spirit of adventure or sheer need of employment. Many pauper children were apprenticed to the Newfoundland trade so that they might 'be not any way a Charge on the said Parish'. On 24 March 1714 the Wimborne overseers 'Paid for Forrist's boy [whose mother had died the previous year] att his going to Newfoundland, 2 neckclothes, a Sea Ring, 2 hatts, a chest, lock, staples, making his bed sack, and blew shirt, and for a comb, and in our Expences in

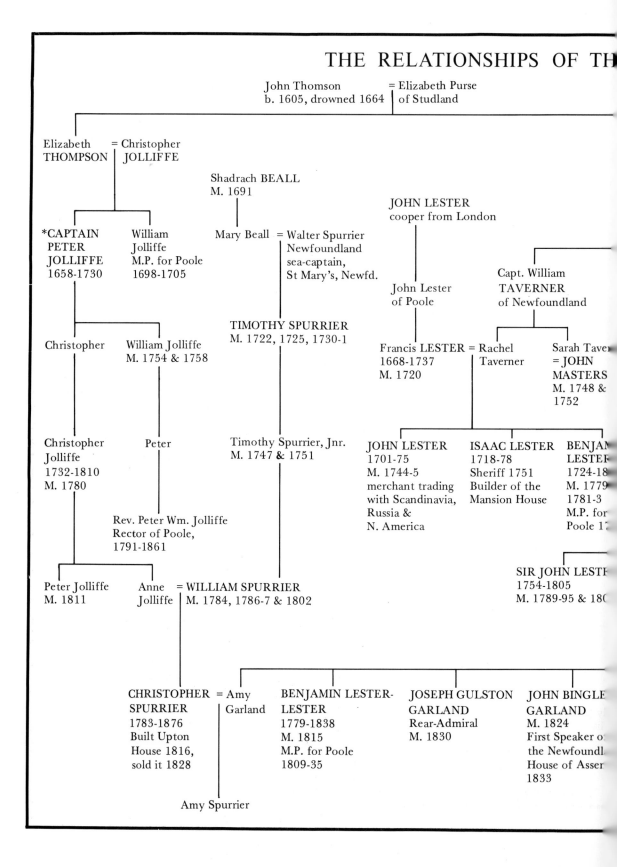

John Thomson = Elizabeth Purse
b. 1605, drowned 1664 | of Studland

Elizabeth = Christopher
THOMPSON | JOLLIFFE

Shadrach BEALL
M. 1691

JOHN LESTER
cooper from London

*CAPTAIN   William   Mary Beall = Walter Spurrier
PETER   Jolliffe   Newfoundland
JOLLIFFE   M.P. for Poole   sea-captain,
1658-1730   1698-1705   St Mary's, Newfd.

John Lester   Capt. William
of Poole   TAVERNER
                           of Newfoundland

Christopher   William Jolliffe
              M. 1754 & 1758

TIMOTHY SPURRIER
M. 1722, 1725, 1730-1

Francis LESTER = Rachel   Sarah Taver
1668-1737 | Taverner   = JOHN
M. 1720   MASTERS
                             M. 1748 &
                             1752

Christopher   Peter   Timothy Spurrier, Jnr.   JOHN LESTER   ISAAC LESTER   BENJAN
Jolliffe   M. 1747 & 1751   1701-75   1718-78   LESTEF
1732-1810   M. 1744-5   Sheriff 1751   1724-18
M. 1780   merchant trading Builder of the M. 1779
                                                      with Scandinavia, Mansion House 1781-3
                                                      Russia &   M.P. for
                                                      N. America   Poole 1

Rev. Peter Wm. Jolliffe
Rector of Poole,
1791-1861

                                                                        SIR JOHN LESTF
                                                                        1754-1805
                                                                        M. 1789-95 & 180

Peter Jolliffe   Anne = WILLIAM SPURRIER
M. 1811   Jolliffe | M. 1784, 1786-7 & 1802

CHRISTOPHER = Amy   BENJAMIN LESTER-   JOSEPH GULSTON   JOHN BINGLE
SPURRIER   Garland LESTER   GARLAND   GARLAND
1783-1876   1779-1838   Rear-Admiral   M. 1824
Built Upton   M. 1815   M. 1830   First Speaker o
House 1816,   M.P. for Poole   the Newfoundl
sold it 1828   1809-35   House of Asser
                                                           1833

Amy Spurrier

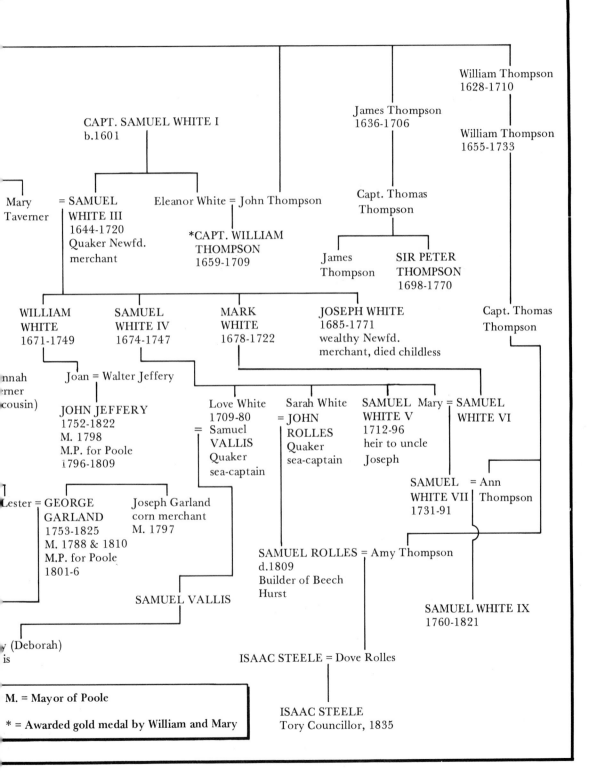

William Thompson
1628-1710

James Thompson
1636-1706

William Thompson
1655-1733

CAPT. SAMUEL WHITE I
b.1601

Mary
Taverner

= SAMUEL
WHITE III
1644-1720
Quaker Newfd.
merchant

Eleanor White = John Thompson

*CAPT. WILLIAM
THOMPSON
1659-1709

Capt. Thomas
Thompson

James
Thompson

SIR PETER
THOMPSON
1698-1770

WILLIAM
WHITE
1671-1749

SAMUEL
WHITE IV
1674-1747

MARK
WHITE
1678-1722

JOSEPH WHITE
1685-1771
wealthy Newfd.
merchant, died childless

Capt. Thomas
Thompson

nnah
rner
cousin)

Joan = Walter Jeffery

JOHN JEFFERY
1752-1822
M. 1798
M.P. for Poole
1796-1809

Love White
1709-80
= Samuel
VALLIS
Quaker
sea-captain

Sarah White
= JOHN
ROLLES
Quaker
sea-captain

SAMUEL
WHITE V
1712-96
heir to uncle
Joseph

Mary = SAMUEL
WHITE VI

SAMUEL
WHITE VII
1731-91

= Ann
Thompson

Lester = GEORGE
GARLAND
1753-1825
M. 1788 & 1810
M.P. for Poole
1801-6

Joseph Garland
corn merchant
M. 1797

SAMUEL ROLLES = Amy Thompson
d.1809
Builder of Beech
Hurst

SAMUEL VALLIS

SAMUEL WHITE IX
1760-1821

(Deborah)
is

ISAAC STEELE = Dove Rolles

M. = Mayor of Poole

* = Awarded gold medal by William and Mary

ISAAC STEELE
Tory Councillor, 1835

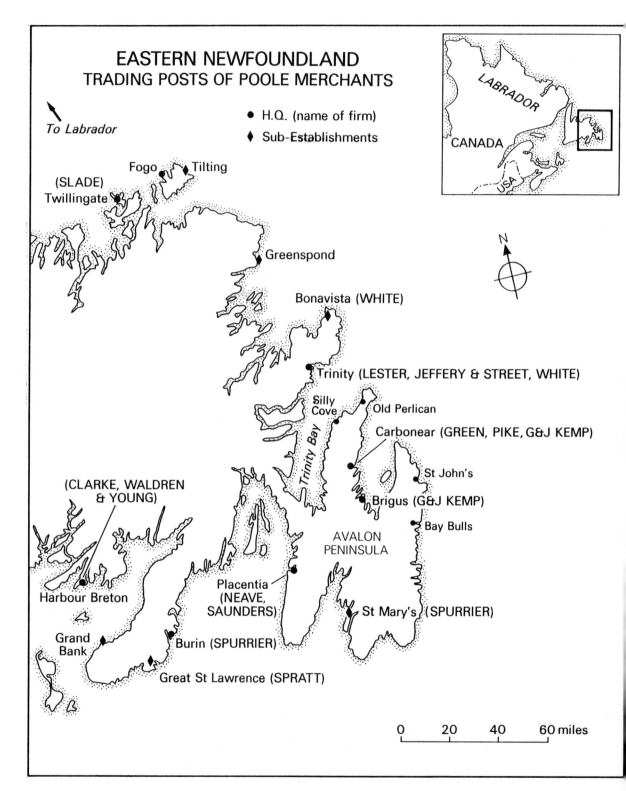

81. Map of Newfoundland, showing Poole merchant bases.

putting him out – 12s.' On a single day (23 March 1774), eight poor boys were bound to Isaac and Benjamin Lester to serve until they were 21 years of age. One of them was 15, four were 12, one was 11 and two were only ten! On 13 March 1786 the Lyme Regis Overseers of the Poor arranged with George Kemp of Poole that William Turner, Samuel Norman, Daniel Norman (each seven years old) and Simon Orchard (only five), should be shipped out to Brigus Bay, near Carbonear, pledged to serve the Interests of the Master for five years. 'In consideration of which service duly performed', the indenture declared, 'each was to have Food and Clothing and at the Expiration of the Term to have Three Guineas, a new suit of Clothes, together with passage out and home.' John Jeffery, M.P. for Poole (1796-1810), who inherited much of the White family's Newfoundland business, admitted that employees were often provided with clothing and other necessaries before leaving Poole, amounting to a third of the wages they could expect to earn. Exploitation undoubtedly occurred and it was claimed that some merchants held back £2 from an employee's wages to pay for the passage home to England. The operation of the Truck System by which workers were paid in vouchers for goods, instead of money, gave them very little freedom. One old fisherman, shipwrecked at Greenspond, said that some of the people among whom he stayed 'never saw money from their birth to their grave and were in debt to the merchants all their lives long'.

Some of the earlier merchants, like some of their employees, took their wives to Newfoundland and raised families there. The Poole parish register for 1781 records the baptism on 29 November of 'Robert, son of James and Mary Brooks, born at Bay Bulls, N-land 11 Aug'st, 1779'.

More than a century earlier a Captain William Taverner from Poole had settled at Trinity in Newfoundland – in the reign of Charles II, and nearby another Poole man, John Masters, senior, established himself with his wife and children at Silly Cove (now Winterton) in Trinity Bay. According to an account set out by Sir Peter Thompson, John Masters was taken out of his bed and had his house ransacked by a French raiding party from Placentia. He then brought his wife, son (John) and four daughters back to Poole and 'bought a low old house at the upper end of the High Street', and installed his family there, whilst he returned to Newfoundland only to be killed in a clash with the Beothic Indians. His widow set up an ale house at the sign of the *Red Cow* to support her family and sent her son, John, who had been born at Silly Cove in 1688, to school at Wimborne. Then at 13 he was apprenticed to Captain William Taverner, worked his way up to be mate, and married his master's daughter, Sarah, and himself became a prosperous merchant. He won the favour of the Poole merchants by prevailing upon the government to fortify Trinity and in appreciation they elected him a burgess in 1744. Sir Peter Thompson described him as 'a fine figure of a man – only wanting polishing'. John Masters was obviously a pushful personality and in 1748 was elected mayor of Poole – the first Newfoundland-born man to hold that office. He was mayor again in 1752, but the following year proposed his friend, Aaron Durell, a shipbuilder, as his successor. Durell secured the votes of a majority of the ordinary burgesses, but the aldermen, who claimed that only they had the right to elect the mayor, chose a rival, George Hyde. On the day when the new mayor was due to be installed, both Durell and Hyde tried to occupy the mayoral chair. A stand-up fight ensued when Masters' partner, an Irishman named Ballard, jumped on to the table and 'with great Fire and Indignation advanced towards Mr. George Tito, the Sheriff, collar'd him and struck him in the face', although Masters claimed that it was the sheriff who first leapt on to the table and started the affray. Masters then used 'persuasive language for peace'. His opponents still protested against Masters referring to them as 'dirty, pitiful Dogs' and gave up their attempt to unseat Aaron Durell. Masters had hoped to get himself elected as M.P. for Poole as a member of an opposition group associated with Frederick, Prince of Wales, who had recently visited Poole, but his plans came to naught when the Prince of Wales died suddenly. Masters himself died in 1754. His widow's claim, inscribed on the memorial in St James's church, that he was held in 'universal esteem' may be a slight exaggeration.

The first aboriginal inhabitant of Newfoundland to come to Poole was John August, a Beothic Indian. Most of these Beothics, who used stone spearheads and arrowheads, had been killed off by the English settlers or driven inland, but in August 1754 a Beothic woman, who had apparently wandered to the coast in search of food, was seen carrying a small boy aged about four. Two fishermen chased her and callously shot her as though she were a wild animal. She crawled away into the woods, probably to die a lingering death, but her child was captured and brought up in Trinity and given the name John August. He learnt English and was employed in fishing by the Poole firm of Jeffrey and Street. Later he was sent to England and exhibited in fairs in Poole and other Dorset towns at a penny a peep as the 'Red Indian from Newfoundland'. He returned to Newfoundland, but contracted tuberculosis, against which he probably had no inherited resistance, and died (aged 38) at Trinity in 1788. He was not the only non-European to have been seen in Poole, for the parish register for 1689 had this entry: 'A Ingen Black Baptized by the name of Margaret'. Again in 1730-1 Poole paid out one shilling 'to a cripl'd black'.

Doubtless racial prejudice was not unknown among the people of Poole in the 18th century, but it seems that the Poole magistrates were ready to hear a complaint of crude anti-Semitism. On 14 April (probably 1786 or 1787) John Horner of Poole, labourer, was accused of abusing and assaulting Moses Abraham of Poole, merchant, 'in a public street by holding his clenched fist against him and saying Damn your Blood, you Jew son of a Bitch. I wish I had some Bacon in my Pockett; I would thrust it down your throat, and choak or suffocate you, and Damn you or words to that effect. Also on or about 17 April and on several occasions John Horner waylaid Moses Abraham in the street and molested him, stopping him going about his lawful business and he now fears for his life'.

One Poole man who befriended John August, the Beothic Indian, was Dr. John Clinch, who went out to Trinity, Newfoundland, as a medical missionary and encouraged John August to contact his tribesmen in the interior and to learn the Beothic language. Dr. Clinch then compiled a vocabulary of the Beothic tongue, now sadly extinct. Clinch was an old friend of the pioneer of vaccination, Dr. Jenner, who sent a supply of cowpox vaccine to Dr. Clinch in Trinity, where he successfully vaccinated his young nephew and popularised vaccination among the Newfoundland colonists. Poole settlers beyond the reach of a qualified doctor in Newfoundland had to resort to a number of dubious remedies, such as 'keeping vinegar in the mouth' for toothache, imbibing 'extract of wild cherries and spirits of turpentine' for a cough, and rubbing into painful joints a fluid obtained from bottling 'the great brown jellyfish' as a cure for rheumatism. The following comment in Dorset-Newfoundland dialect speaks for itself: 'In winter when a man bivers [shivers with cold] he will soon get binicky [ill-tempered] unless his puddock [stomach] is full of hot mush [porridge] and vang [fried salt pork] and he has a bannikin [small tin cup] of switchel [cold tea]'.

Sometimes settlers who were disabled made their way back to Poole in search of medical help or charity, such as the sixpence given in 1730-31 'to a man brought from Newfoundland with no feet' – probably a victim of frostbite. In 1787 the Poole overseers of the poor supported the application of Samuel Harden from Trinity, Newfoundland, for admission to Guy's Hospital, London, whilst in 1799 Richard Routh, Chief Justice for Newfoundland, was certified to be confined to bed 'with gout in his feet, ancles and knees' and accordingly unfit to undertake the return sea-voyage to Newfoundland.

It was said that the Newfoundland trade was operated by 'seven strong firms' of Poole, controlled by seven families – the Whites, Jolliffes, Spurriers, Lesters, Garlands, Jefferys and Slades, and they formed a high proportion of the burgesses of Poole. The Whites, who were Quakers, did not hold office in local government, but the other six families, together with the Westons, also engaged in the Newfoundland trade, in the 127-year period from 1710 to 1836 supplied the mayors in 56 years and, in fact in 36 out of 58 years from 1779 to 1836, several more if relatives with different surnames are included. These families made large fortunes, intermarried and invested their wealth, as did Sir Peter Thompson, in a number of impressive mansions, several of which remain today.

The Quaker White family may have been descended from the staunchly Catholic Whites who were prominent in Poole's affairs in the 16th century. Samuel White (1642-1720) of Lagland Street, married Mary Taverner, a member of the Poole family already settled in Newfoundland, and four of his sons, especially Joseph (1685-1771), were active in the Newfoundland trade with bases in Bonavista and Trinity Bays. The family suffered heavy losses in the Seven Years' War, perhaps because as Quakers they would not use guns to defend themselves, and Joseph White lost all but one of his 14 ships, none of which he had insured. His brother, Samuel, a maltster, was alleged to have been excessively parsimonious and suspicious, and there was a story that, if he had to leave his house in charge of his only servant, he would cut an irregular piece of bacon from a flitch in his

82. Beech Hurst (west front), High Street, Poole.

kitchen and would lock it away in a cupboard and on his return would take it out and fit it into the flitch in order to check that his servant had not purloined any of it during his absence. However, Samuel moved into a fine newly-built mansion in New Street. After this was demolished, and the site was excavated in 1973-4, a fine Chinese porcelain tea-set was unearthed and this has been skilfully reconstructed by Poole Museum. This suggests that though Samuel White was undoubtedly thrifty, his house was not without elegant and costly objects. His brother, Joseph, had an estate in Trinity employing over two hundred people, operated 12 fishing boats and used 10 sailing vessels of over 1,200 tons in all. When Joseph White died in 1771, he left his estate of £150,000 mainly to his nephew, Samuel White, who died in 1796. He in turn left an estate of £200,000, and this fortune he partly bequeathed to his two nephews, Samuel Vallis and Samuel Rolles, who carried on the business at Trinity and Bonavista until 1797. Samuel Rolles used much of his share of the White fortune to build in 1798 Beech Hurst, a fine red-brick mansion with a central doorway at the top of a flight of steps protected by a semi-circular porch of four columns. Surmounting the three storeys of symmetrically arranged windows, round-headed on the ground floor, is a triangular pediment displaying the Rolles coat-of-arms. Standing now in front of the new Sainsbury's food-store, Beech Hurst remains the most impressive Georgian building in the High Street. After Samuel Rolles' death in 1809 the mansion was occupied by his daughter, Dove, and her husband, Isaac Steele, a member like Dove's cousin, John Jeffery (M.P. for Poole 1796-1808) of the firm of Jeffery and Steele, operating in Trinity.

Perhaps the most important, and ultimately the richest, of the Poole families engaged in

83. Map of Poole, with key.

the Newfoundland trade was the Lester family, founded by a John Lester, possibly a Londoner, and a cooper by trade. Early in the 17th century he found his way to Poole, where his craft would have been in great demand in view of the large number of barrels needed to store and transport fish, fruit and wine. His grandson, Francis Lester, became a merchant trading in train-oil, married Rachel Taverner, a member of the Newfoundland family, and owned the *Providence* which in 1731 landed in Poole '9 tuns of oyle, one puncheon of skins and 1,700 deer skins'. He became mayor of Poole in 1720 and the family fortunes were advanced by three energetic sons. The eldest, John, imported timber from North America and Scandinavia and iron from Russia. Isaac Lester (1718-78) looked after the Poole end of the family's trade with Newfoundland from his house in Thames Street and played a leading role in local politics, though he failed to become mayor, possibly because he alienated many burgesses with his sharp tongue. His diaries are full of his condemnatory comments on other townsfolk. He quarrelled with the M.P. Joshua Mauger, whom he called 'that worthless fellow', and was always at loggerheads with his neighbour, John Slade, who used to waylay Isaac's employees, and tried to persuade some of Isaac's best men to work for him instead. Isaac's younger brother, Benjamin Lester (1724-1802), worked for many years in Newfoundland, where he married his cousin, Susannah Taverner. He was at Trinity in 1762 when the French launched a major attack on Newfoundland.

A French fleet under the command of Admiral Charles de Ternay occupied Trinity for a fortnight. Lester as the principal merchant and chief magistrate acted as liaison officer between the English community and the French commander. Helped by a knowledge of French acquired in his schooldays, Lester exercised remarkable tact and ingenuity in his dealings with the French admiral, who at the outset threatened to burn virtually everything, unless his demands for a vast quantity of provisions (on the first day '6 Beefs, 6 Calves, 5 Sheep and 30 fowls') were met instantly. Lester responded with impeccable politeness and sweet reasonableness and soon won over the French admiral to a more considerate attitude. It is true that the fort was destroyed, the guns spiked and thrown into the sea and many

REFERENCES TO THE PLAN ON THE OTHER SIDE.

1 High-street.	28 Crooked-lane.	55 Skinner's-alley.
2 Market-street.	29 Short-way.	56 Old Orchard.
3 Pillory-street.	30 Water-lane.	57 Weston's-lane.
4 Hill-street.	31 Pound-lane.	58 Compton's-alley.
5 Church-street.	32 Deerhay-lane.	59 Levet's-lane
6 Quay-street.	33 Carter's-lane.	60 Great Mount-lane.
7 West-street.	34 Fricker's-alley.	61 Little Mount-lane.
8 Lagland-street.	35 New Orchard.	62 Green-lane.
9 Strand-street.	36 New-street.	63 Baiter-lane.
10 Great-quay.	37 Cinnamon-lane.	64 Hiley's-lane.
11 Little-quay.	38 Quay-lane.	65 Drake's-alley.
12 New-quay.	39 Ditch-lane.	66 Love-lane.
13 Paradise-street.	40 Bennet's-alley.	67 Perry-garden.
14 Salisbury-street.	41 Crabb-lane.	68 Ham-quays.
15 Hancock-alley.	42 Rogers'-lane.	69 Ham-street.
16 Thomas-alley.	43 Rozer's-lane.	70 Horse-island.
17 Barber's-lane.	44 Mud-lane.	71 Oyster-bank.
18 Bay-hog-lane.	45 Button's-lane.	72 Church.
19 Fowler's-lane.	46 Pluddie-lane.	73 Market-house.
20 West-butt-street.	47 Smock-alley.	74 Rope-walks.
21 West-butt-green.	48 Pelly's-lane.	75 Ham-street.
22 West-butt-lane.	49 Petty-lane.	76 Bathing-house.
23 Market-lane.	50 Sutton's Piles.	77 Baptist Meeting-house.
24 Lovel's-lane.	51 Little-lane.	78 Great Meeting-house.
25 Hunger-hill.	52 Toop's-lane.	79 Small Meeting-house.
26 Nightingale-lane.	53 Bell-lane.	80 Quaker's Meeting.
27 Town-gates-lane.	54 Fish-street.	81 Fish-shambles.

84.   Extract from Benjamin Lester's diary concerning the French occupation of Trinity.

vessels, jetties and drying frames were put out of action, but Lester was able to secure an undertaking that his own property should not be destroyed and, when a French officer went round the next day to identify Lester's property, the English guide, well drilled by Lester, asserted that virtually every ship and structure belonged to him. Lester was also able to ensure that some at least of the ships and installations were dismantled rather than burnt. Relatively little damage was done to the business premises and stores of Lester, White and others. Moreover, since Lester had had a few days' warning of the arrival of the French invaders, he and his friends had been able to transfer 18 ships to out-of-the-way coves, where they went undiscovered. The French admiral gallantly returned Mrs. Lester's favourite cow, which his men had seized, and also entertained Benjamin Lester to dinner on board his ship. 'Our dinner', said Lester, 'was a variety of dishes, but not much to my liking'. Lester's comment, like the rest of the other information about the French occupation, is contained in the detailed diary kept by him and now preserved in the Dorset County Record Office. The Treaty of Paris (1763) confirmed Newfoundland as a wholly British possession, and Lester was soon able to repair the damage. In the 1770s Benjamin Lester had a fleet of at least twelve ships and by 1793 he had no fewer than 30 vessels – probably the largest fleet owned by any Poole merchant. In Trinity Lester had built a fine brick house 60 feet by 40 feet with a tiled roof and 15 rooms. Although partially demolished in the 1960s, this 'Lester House' ranks as one of the oldest surviving buildings in Canada.

Back in Thames Street, Poole, brother Isaac Lester arranged to buy the house next door to his 'old hut' (1776) and planned to replace both with a finer dwelling. The result, though Isaac never lived to see this building completed, since he died in 1778, was the magnificent 'Mansion House', which Benjamin occupied during his later years. An appropriate feature in its 'Benjamin Lester Suite' is a marble fireplace with two fillets of cod, carved in white

85. Mansion House, Thames Street, built by the Lesters.

86. Cod fillets in the marble mantelpiece in the Benjamin Lester suite of the Mansion House.

87. The Lesters' Establishment, Trinity,
Newfoundland.

88. Benjamin Lester, M.P.

marble – a reminder of the origins of the wealth of the Lester family. Completed in 1800, this fine Georgian house has recently been skilfully refurbished and now houses the Mansion House Hotel and Club.

Having settled down in Poole, Benjamin Lester played a leading part in local affairs, was four times mayor, and then served as M.P. for Poole 1790-5. He had engaged in national politics as early as 1775 when he gave evidence before Parliament on the views of English merchants towards the 13 rebellious American colonies, who were objecting so strenuously to being taxed by the home government. Lester strongly voiced the opinions of Poole merchants, when he urged that the New Englanders should be banned from trading with Newfoundland and from fishing on its Banks. Like other Poole merchants he suffered losses of ships at the hands of privateers during the wars both with the American colonists and the French Revolutionaries, but equally troublesome were the activities of the Royal Navy's press-gangs. He is said to have sent several of his most skilled mariners into hiding at his house, Post Green in Lytchett Minster, and as a magistrate he would grant exemption passes to skilled pilots. Several sailors returning in the autumn from the triangular voyages would slip ashore at some port or cove before they reached Poole to avoid the press-gangs lying in wait for them. Despite all these hazards Benjamin Lester remained Poole's richest man. His ships alone were reckoned to be worth £100,000; he owned in Newfoundland not only the store-houses and other installations connected with the cod and salmon fisheries, but also many dwelling houses; and in Poole he owned the Mansion House, the *Old Antelope Inn*, several quays, various warehouses, a lumber yard, an iron yard and several dwelling houses – besides two country estates at Stanley Green and Lytchett Minster. Moreover, he had a reputation for fairness and generosity. In his will he bequeathed £400 to the Corporation to pay for an organist at St James's church to receive a salary of £20 per annum. His only son, Sir John Lester who had been eight times mayor, died childless in 1805 and bequeathed some £2,500 to the Rector of St James's to pay for an evening service and improving lecture every Sunday. Benjamin Lester, having no other sons, had bequeathed his business to his daughter, Amy and her husband, George Garland and to their son Benjamin Lester Garland, who in accordance with his grandfather's will 'out of grateful and affectionate respect' for him changed his name to Benjamin Lester-Lester.

George Garland (1753-1825) was the son of a Dorset farmer, who had set up a corn business in Poole and supplied provisions to the Lesters for the Newfoundland settlements. He and his wife, Amy Lester, had eight sons and two daughters and were noted for their happy family life. Although Garland never visited his property in Trinity, he was able to amass a fortune even greater than that of old Benjamin Lester, partly by making improvements such as replacing old ships, but more possibly thanks to the skilful management of two of his sons, John Bingley Garland and George Garland junior, who went out to Newfoundland and carried on the firm there until 1834. George Garland senior was twice mayor of Poole and also M.P. for Poole 1801-6. He invested some of his money in property such as 'Stone Park' near Wimborne and Leeson House (in Langton Matravers), now a Field Studies Centre maintained by Dorset County Council. He was a great benefactor to the borough and among his bequests was a group of 12 almshouses at Hunger Hall and an endowment to provide there for widows, widowers and impoverished couples. The Garland Almshouses remained there until 1965, when they were in need of substantial improvement. They were demolished in the course of the re-development of the Old Town. George Garland was a progressive Whig in politics, standing for a reform of the Parliamentary electoral system and more openness and efficiency in local government. He died as the result of a tragic accident when the four-wheeled gig in which he was travelling from Stone to Wimborne crashed into a post by the side of the road. 'Mr. Garland was thrown under the gig . . . His feet and lower part of one leg was so badly injured and crushed that an amputation was necessary'. He died soon afterwards.

George Garland's eldest son, Benjamin Lester-Lester (1779-1838), mayor in 1815, was repeatedly elected as M.P. for Poole, serving from 1809 to 1835. Like his father, he was a Whig and a champion of Parliamentary Reform. Another son, Joseph Gulston Garland, became a Rear-Admiral and was the last member of the family to be mayor of Poole – in 1830. One of the other sons, John Bingley Garland (1791-1875), became the first Speaker of the Newfoundland House of Assembly in 1833. Later he returned to Poole and settled down to the life of a country gentleman at Leeson House. He had been mayor of Poole in 1824 and 30 years later made a gift of land to provide Poole with a new cemetery, where he himself is buried.

Another family involved in the Newfoundland trade, the Kemps, came from Christchurch and became prominent in the early 18th century, when a sea-captain named James Kemp had a trading base at Carbonear. A relative named Martin Kemp took over his business there and back in Poole led a group of Nonconformists who found themselves expelled from the old Independent chapel in Hill Street, when it was taken over by Unitarians. Martin Kemp and his Congregational friends set up a chapel in Lag Lane (Lagland Street). A new imposing chapel was built in 1777 in Skinner Street and the two sons of Martin Kemp (who died relatively young in 1772), George and James Kemp, became leading figures in this Congregational chapel and also in local politics, though George was an ardent supporter of the Whig party which normally championed the Nonconformists, whilst James was a staunch Tory. As Nonconformists they did not try to secure municipal office, but they used their votes in elections, usually cancelling out each other's vote! While the two brothers were under age after their father's death, the firm of G. & J. Kemp, as it was styled, was maintained on a sound basis by a wealthy uncle, the banker, George Welch. In 1788 George Kemp was prosperous enough to buy and to move into Sir Peter Thompson's old house, the Poole Mansion, when he married. Typical of the sudden upsurge in fortune which could occur to a firm engaged in the Newfoundland trade – to offset the losses due to storms and privateers – was a voyage by two vessels belonging to G. & J. Kemp in 1810, when in the Peninsular War the Royal Navy was blockading all the ports of Spain, then occupied by French troops, in retaliation for Napoleon's Continental System banning British ships and goods from Europe. The two ships managed to evade the blockade and were able to land their cargoes of cod and to sell it at exhorbitant prices to the deprived Spaniards and to take on board a return cargo of wine, purchased at very low prices and later to be sold in London at enormous profit. So G. & J. Kemp seemed to be moving from strength to strength; George Kemp was soon said to be worth £250,000 and to own half Poole. Then personal tragedy struck the family. The eldest son of James, Edward Kemp, the firm's agent at Brigus, was drowned in 1817 when an open boat in which he was cruising to the firm's other base at Carbonear was overturned in a squall. The Newfoundland trade declined rapidly after the end of the wars with France and suddenly in 1824 the great firm of G. & J. Kemp sold out to another Poole firm – Fryer, Gosse & Pack.

Another of the Newfoundland trading firms was that run by the Slade family, one branch of which occupied the fine Georgian mansion, Poole House, No. 13 Thames Street facing St James's church. The Slades established their headquarters at the most northerly port in Newfoundland linked with Poole – Twillingate. They were often feuding with Isaac Lester, their next-door neighbour in Thames Street, who maintained that 'John Slade . . . is mean enough to ship our people after they have agreed with us and conceals them. He or his son is at ye door all day and watches to see who goes in or out of our house and nabbes them and gets them into his house'. The Slades may have been very hard-working or lucky, or skilful exponents of sharp practice, but it was later to be stated that 'John Slade, of Poole,

89. 'Poole House', No. 13 Thames Street. At this doorway John Slade and his son waylaid Isaac Lester's best employees.

who carried on business in Twillingate . . . died in 1792, leaving a fortune computed at £70,000 sterling all made out of the Newfoundland trade'. In 1824 various members of the Slade family owned 39 ships trading out of Poole with Newfoundland and Canada. A younger member of the family, Robert Slade, was mayor in 1832, but died of a stroke just after taking office and was succeeded by his cousin, another Robert Slade, for the next three years, who in turn was followed by Robert Slade junior in 1835 and 1836, and by Thomas Slade in 1838. In 1845 when gas-lighting was introduced in St James's church, John Slade purchased the discarded chandeliers and wall sconces and presented them to St Peter's church at his base at Twillingate. Yet in 1861 the old firm of Slades was declared insolvent.

Another Poole firm prospering from the Newfoundland trade throughout the 18th century was that belonging to the Spurrier family. The Spurriers started as seamen in the fishing vessels crossing the Atlantic, worked their way up to be sea-captains and eventually set themselves up as merchants. When the Treaty of Utrecht (1713) conceded that the whole of Newfoundland was British, the Spurriers enterprisingly established themselves in the southern, formerly French, part of Newfoundland, especially at St Mary's Bay on the south of the Avalon peninsula. There they could catch cod earlier in the season because the seas were less troubled by ice than the more northerly areas such as Trinity Bay. Particularly outstanding was Timothy Spurrier, mayor in 1722, 1725 and 1730-1 – especially energetic at promoting fire precautions and improving the environment in Old Poole. It was said of him, when he died in 1756, that 'he was so remarkably temperate in his drinking that . . . he was never intoxicated with liquor, although he arrived at the age of 84 years'. Perhaps that was why he was so long-lived!

His grandson, William Spurrier (1734-1809), prospered and later took over the Poole firm of Waldren and Young, also operating in south Newfoundland and at Burin and Fortune Bay. He was mayor of Poole three times, but ruined his reputation by his efforts in 1809 to try to secure the election of his young son, Christopher, as M.P. for Poole. Happening to be in London when a writ for an election in Poole was being prepared, he undertook to deliver it to the sheriff direct, but then deliberately withheld it for a fortnight, hoping thereby to give his son an advantage. The deception was discovered and he was summoned to the Bar of the House of Commons and sternly rebuked. He might have been sent to prison but for the fact that he pleaded that he was 'now of the age of 73 . . . and – very lame, deaf and otherwise infirm'. He died two years later.

The son, Christopher Spurrier, left the management of the Newfoundland business to two relatives and concentrated on social and political ambitions. In 1814 he married Amy, daughter of George Garland, who brought with her a dowry of £4,000, and hoped that this link with the powerful Garland family would help him to become one of Poole's M.P.s, but he spoilt his chances by double-crossing his father-in-law, coming forward as a candidate in 1817 contrary to a previous promise. He did become M.P. for Bridport in 1820, but his expenditure on the election undermined his financial stability. He had purchased a 900-acre estate just outside Poole and in 1816 had Upton House built on it, hoping that this would outshine all the other Georgian mansions of Poole's Newfoundland merchants. Meanwhile he resorted to gambling and extravagant holidays in Europe and, partly in consequence, his marriage broke up. At last in 1828 his debts caught up with him and he had to sell Upton House to a Catholic gentleman, Edward Doughty. Two years later, after a particularly bad fishing season, Spurrier's Newfoundland firm went bankrupt. He had lost everything, his mansion, the family firm, his public position and his marriage. This ruined 'merchant prince' lived on in obscurity until 1876.

Edward Doughty sponsored the building of Poole's first modern Roman Catholic church, St Mary's (1839) in West Quay Road, where it was fully visible from Upton House. Meanwhile the new owner of Spurrier's mansion, Upton House, had become the 9th Baron Tichborne. His nephew and heir, Roger Tichborne, an irreligious, alcoholic adventurer, went off to South America and was eventually reported to have been drowned at sea. However in 1866 the 'Tichborne Claimant' turned up – a burly, bearded butcher from Australia, who had managed to convince a negro servant, Andrew Bogle, that he was the long-lost son of Roger Tichborne, heir to the title and the estate. A protracted and sensational trial (1871-2) resulted in his claims being rejected. He was then tried for perjury and sentenced to 14 years' imprisonment. Eventually Upton House was purchased in 1901 by William Llewellin, whose younger son was Minister of Food, 1943-5, and was created Baron Llewellin of Upton in 1945. He was Governor-General of the ill-fated Federation of Rhodesia and Nyasaland from 1953 until his death in 1957. His sister, Mary Llewellin, gave distinguished service on the Poole Borough Council from 1937 to 1954 and was elected mayor in 1951, the first woman to hold that office. Her elder brother, W. W. Llewellin, had a distinguished career in the prison service and in 1961 gave Upton House and its grounds to the Poole Corporation. There followed an unhappy period when the Corporation leased the house and estate to 'Prince Carol of Rumania', son of the morganatic marriage between King Carol II of Rumania and Zizi Lambrino. When that tenancy was terminated at the end of 1969, the Corporation then set to work to make the mansion and the grounds available to the people of Poole. Helped by the efforts of the Friends of Upton House, Upton House has been refurbished, though much still remains to be done, and the grounds have been remodelled and beautified and provided with a nature trail. It is particularly fitting that this mansion, built from the proceeds of the wealth of the Newfoundland trade, should, with its 'Country Park', now be available for the enjoyment of the ordinary people

90. Upton House (south front), built by Christopher Spurrier in 1816. From the drawing room here Mrs. Doughty could see St Mary's Roman Catholic church in West Quay Road – the first permanent Catholic church in Poole since the Reformation which Mr. Doughty helped to build in 1839.

of Poole, whose 18th-century Poole forerunners – apart from the 'merchant princes' – had little opportunity during the voyages across the Atlantic, or the hard, smelly work in Newfoundland or the winter months spent in Poole dodging the press-gangs, to enjoy the wealth which their hard labour generated.

Whilst the Poole merchants were making their fortunes in the Newfoundland trade and were building mansions, the gentry of the surrounding district were also busy extending and embellishing their country houses or building new ones, beautifying their estates, engaging in politics, and often adopting the new agricultural methods with enthusiasm and launching schemes to promote the welfare of the local population. In 1725 Sir William Hanham rebuilt Dean's Court as a symmetrical red-brick structure with stone dressings, and Denis Bond, Recorder (chief judge) of Poole, 1719-46, and also M.P. for Poole, 1727-32, lengthened and classicised the south wing of Creech Grange in the current Palladian style (1738-41). Nearby in the Purbecks George Clavell, who had been M.P. for Dorchester, added a new north-west front to Smedmore House – a masterpiece of symmetry in white Portland ashlar with pleasing semi-circular bays at either end. In 1790 Edward Drax built in the grounds of Charborough Park

91. Horton Tower.

an observatory tower, which was struck by lightning in 1838 and then rebuilt to a much greater height of over one hundred feet. It thus rivalled the 120-foot Horton Tower, the red-brick folly of six storeys built in the mid-18th century by Humphrey Sturt, M.P. for Dorset (1754-86). The film-makers chose it as the location for the cock-fight in the film version of Hardy's *Far From the Madding Crowd*. When he inherited the More Crichel estate from his cousin, Sir Gerard Napier, Humphrey Sturt added (1770-75) the pleasingly symmetrical south and east facades and the magnificent library, and remodelled the grand oak staircase. Hutchins commented that the building had been 'so immensely enlarged that it has the appearance of a mansion of a prince more than that of a country gentleman'. The most prized part of Sturt's inheritance was Brownsea Island, upon which he lavished some £50,000 and unlimited enthusiasm. He took over 'a ruined house and a little green round' and built 'a very excellent castle' by raising the blockhouse to four storeys and by adding lower wings on three sides, and also gave the island its present wooded character. Arthur Young, the agricultural pioneer, wrote that Sturt had taken over there 'nine hundred acres, quite wild and overrun with fern, furze and much ling . . . so very poor that . . . the only

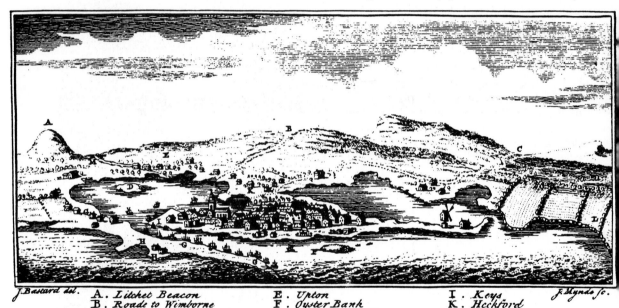

J. Bastard del.

A . *Litchet Beacon*	E . *Upton*	I . *Keys*
B . *Roade to Wimborne*	F . *Oyster Bank*	K . *Heckford*
C . *Roade to Christchurch*	G . *Ham.& Ham.Key*	L . *Parkson*
D . *Periams Island*	H . *Roap Walk*	M . *Road to Sturminster.*

J. Mynde Sc.

92. 'A Prospect of the Town of Poole from the West End of Bruncksey Island.'

use . . . made of it was to turn on a few lean sheep now and then'. He added that Mr. Sturt had 'planted, to the quantity of a million trees of various sorts, chiefly firs; so that the hills will be wooded and the vales lawns . . . and when the woods get up, the whole will be a glorious scene' – an accurate prediction which visitors to what is now, 200 years later, National Trust property will readily endorse. Sturt was a leading pioneer of the Agricultural Revolution, applying the new ideas of fertilisation and the rotation of crops. He imported large loads of manure and also of ash from soap factories to improve the poor soil, experimented with planting clover and grew turnips to provide winter fodder. Rhododendrons were introduced later. When in 1818 the Prince Regent was taken across to visit

Brownsea Island, he exclaimed that he 'had no idea there had been such a delightful spot in the Kingdom'. Humphrey Sturt's son, Charles Sturt, inherited both Crichel and Brownsea and was awarded a medal by the Royal Humane Society for leading a rescue operation in 1799, when a small cutter called the *Bee* was wrecked in a gale on some sandbanks in Poole Harbour and its crew seemed certain to drown. Charles Sturt and some of his men put out in a boat and, though they were thrown out of it and 'he was for a considerable time nearly up to his neck in water, buffeting the waves with an ardour that seemed to increase with danger', Sturt rescued the crew of the *Bee* and brought them safely to Brownsea Castle. His nephew, also named Charles Sturt (1795-1869), in his boyhood enjoyed exploring the wild places on Brownsea Island during his holidays. Later in life, by his discovery of the Darling River and his exploration of the course of the Murray River, he was to open up vast areas of the Australian hinterland.

Another improving landowner, like Humphrey Sturt, was William Morton Pitt, M.P. for Poole, 1780-90, whose father, John Pitt, an accomplished amateur architect, on taking over Encombe House south of Corfe Castle largely demolished it and designed a new house about 1735 with a wide, low two-storeyed front facing southwards over an artificial lake. The son, William Morton Pitt, presented to the Borough of Poole two fine maces to be carried in procession before the mayor, and set up a factory at Kingston, making cordage, sacking and sailcloth to provide employment for 200 local people and to win them away from dependence upon smuggling. He also appealed to landowners to provide more housing and fuel for the poor and set up a network of Sunday schools. Within the boundaries of the borough of Poole and now open to the public is one of the finest Georgian mansions of the area – Merley House. It was built between 1751 and 1760 by Ralph Willett, a wealthy and scholarly sugar planter from St Kitts in the West Indies. Later he built two additional wings, one containing a magnificent library. Sadly these two wings were demolished in the early 19th century and the

93. Charles Sturt (1795-1869) portrayed on a British stamp.

large collection of books and paintings was dispersed. A print in the Grey Room shows the house as it was in its full glory in the 1770s. The house contains many treasures, including a fine staircase with a handrail veneered in the exceptionally hard wood, lignum vitae. Merley House contains some of the finest Georgian plaster ceilings in the county – depicting Orpheus playing his lute. Bacchus receiving wine from Ceres and the Judgement of Paris. In the mid-19th century Merley House was owned and occupied by William Charles Wentworth (1790-1872), the pioneer of the freedom of the Press and of home rule for

94. Merley House (north front), built 1751-60.

95. The Judgement of Paris ceiling, Merley House.

Australia, who drafted the constitution which gave New South Wales full responsible self-government in 1856. Mr. and Mrs. John Hammick, owners of Merley House since 1967, have tastefully refurbished it and have installed in it a unique collection of miniature model cars and lorries as well as a model railway lay-out.

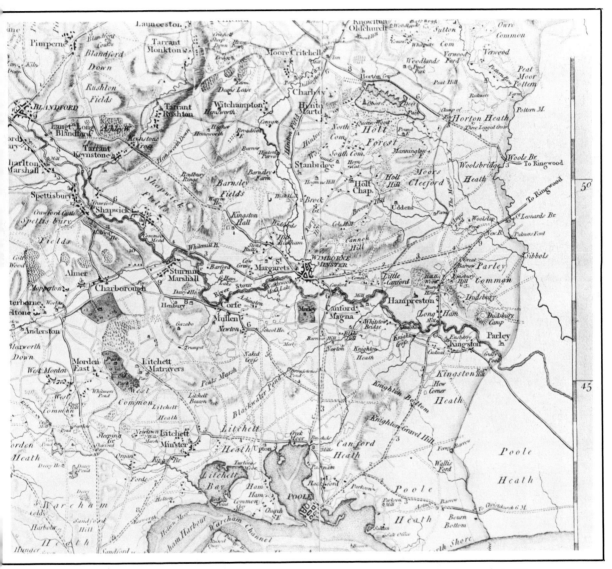

96. Part of Isaac Taylor's map, 1765. Note the spelling of Broadstone*s*, Parkson (for Parkstone), Kingston (for Kinson) and Patnam (an error for *Tatnam*).

The Poole merchants and the neighbouring gentry had co-operated in the mid-18th century to bring about the improvement of the conditions of the roads in the locality. For the past two centuries the parish authorities had been obliged to provide labour to maintain the roads in good condition, but in fact they usually failed dismally to do so. The solution was to construct turnpike roads for the use of which tolls would be charged. Thus funds would become available for the upkeep and improvement of the roads. In 1756 in response to a petition from local merchants and gentry Parliament passed a Turnpike Act 'for repairing and widening the several Roads leading from a Gate called Poole Gate in the Town and County of Poole' and appointed as trustees of the Poole Turnpike Trust 110 persons including such leading Poole merchants as Sir Peter Thompson, David Durell, Aaron Durell, George Hyde, William Jolliffe, John Lester, George Tito, Joseph White and Richard Weston together with various country gentlemen – George Trenchard, of Lytchett Matravers, who seems to have been the prime mover of the scheme and who was to act as Chairman, John Bankes of Kingston Lacy, Sir William Hanham of Dean's Court, Thomas Erle Drax of Charborough Park, Sir Gerard Napier of Crichel, Humphrey Sturt of Horton, John Bond of Creech Grange, John Pitt of Encombe, George Clavell of Smedmore and Ralph Willett of Merley. They were authorised to improve, build and maintain roads from Poole: (1) through Wimborne and Cranborne to link up with the Great Western Turnpike at Coombe Bissett; (2) to Bere Regis via Lytchett Matravers; (3) to Wareham via Lytchett

97. Poole toll house, demolished about 1926.

Minster; (4) to Ringwood via Longham Bridge and (5) to Christchurch via 'Bourne Bottom'. The trustees initially borrowed £2,000 at an interest rate of four per cent. per annum and drew up a tariff of tolls for road users such as

For every coach – drawn by six horses	9d.
For every coach – drawn by four horses	6d.
For every waggon – drawn by four horses	9d.

Oxen, cows and meat cattle (travelling to and from market on foot) were charged at the rate of 8d. per score. A certain William Sabine was appointed Surveyor at 10s. 6d. per day and one Thomas Jones as foreman of the work force at 10s. 6d. per *week*. Jones was ordered to purchase 24 good wheelbarrows (at not more than 10s. 6d. each) and 12 pickaxes. The turnpike roads were, of course, surfaced with gravel laid on a foundation of larger stones. Adjacent parishes were enjoined to supply labour, e.g. Great Canford one day, Kin(g)son two days, Longfleet three days and 'Parkson' four days. Many parishes arranged to pay lump sums in lieu of labour. When the turnpikes (toll-gates) were installed, collection of the tolls was farmed out. Thus in 1794 a William Helliar, yeoman, paid £110 a year for the gate at Walford Bridge on the north side of Wimborne and in 1800 the same man was collecting tolls at the Poole Gate for £655 a year. Alongside the toll-gate was the toll-house with windows facing in all directions to enable the toll-gate keeper to see the approach of all travellers and to spot any who might try to take off into adjacent fields to avoid payment of the toll. The Poole toll-house was standing at the junction of Wimborne and Longfleet roads until it was pulled down (about 1926) to make way for the *George Hotel*. Despite increasing competition from railways the Trust continued until 1883, and from 1888 the construction and repairing of major roads became the responsibility of the newly-formed Dorset County Council.

(*Left to right*): Arms of the Lesters; Arms of the Garlands; The Rolles Arms, as shown above Beech Hurst; Arms of the Spurriers.

Chapter Ten

Smuggling in the Poole Area

A major activity in and around Poole to which most of the inhabitants had an ambivalent attitude was *smuggling*. It provided employment for the smugglers and all their associates and dependents, and employment likewise for the forces of the government, trying to suppress the 'free traders' – the coastguards and riding officers – and for people at all levels of society it provided a wide range of goods such as spirits, wine, tea, coffee, tobacco, silk and lace at cut prices. Legitimate merchants stood to lose and were obliged mainly to concentrate on the handling of bulky, heavy goods, such as fish, grain and timber, leaving the smugglers to specialise in bringing into England less bulky but more costly merchandise upon which the government imposed such high duties that it was worth the risk of detection and punishment to bring in such goods duty-free, sell them at bargain prices but still make a good profit.

For much of the 17th century the job of collecting customs duties in each port was farmed out to groups of financiers who paid the king an annual lump sum and kept everything else they collected at the ports. This system removed an incentive to accept bribes from smugglers though the tax-farmers might make a handsome profit. When in 1671 the Crown once more took over the collection of customs, corruption and bribery soon followed. Thus John Willie, a Collector of Customs at Poole and himself a magistrate, was sacked for conniving with smugglers. In 1681 William Culliford of Encombe, later to become M.P. for Corfe Castle and one of the most trusted officials of the Board of Customs set up ten years earlier, was asked to report on corruption involved in the collection of customs in western ports. Roger Guttridge has researched the contents of the Culliford Report and has incorporated its salient features in his excellent, definitive study, *Dorset Smugglers*. Just after his arrival in Poole Culliford seized a cargo of tobacco worth £77 recently brought in on the *David*, one of Poole's most active smuggling vessels. Culliford then discovered that the most powerful of the Poole smugglers was a merchant and magistrate named John Carter, who employed a gang whose members armed themselves with clubs and swords and disguised their identity with masks. One favourite landing place, used by Carter and his partner, Moses Durell, was near a windmill, a quarter of a mile from the town, where the contraband was stored in a stable nearby and then spirited away in waggons to inland destinations.

Carter's shop was well adapted for concealing smuggled goods. A secret door was hidden by shelves of cloth, whilst in his yard a Purbeck stone slab could be lifted up to give access to a useful storage cellar beneath. Both Carter and Durell attained high office in the borough. Moses Durell was mayor in 1666 and 1678 and his son, Moses Durell junior, mayor in 1692. John Carter was mayor in 1676, 1699 and 1705. Another leading Poole smuggler at this time was Robert Bennett, who lived at the *George Inn* and stored in his cellar the large consignments of Virginia tobacco he brought in, rarely paying any duty. Culliford also found that Bennett had brought in some 7,600 pounds of tobacco, paying only a substantially reduced duty on the grounds that the cargo had been spoilt by sea-water during the voyage, although Culliford judged his vessel to be 'a tight ship', which 'came home well conditioned'. The commander of the Poole Customs smack, Dudley Hopper, was described as 'a very careless, negligent man ... seldom sober, when he is anywhere that he can come at drink'. Hopper regularly turned a blind eye to smuggling activities and was sacked for a series of frauds. Thomas Barney, the Customs surveyor, was observed to have three gold coins slipped into his hand by the master of the *William and Elizabeth* after which Barney ordered his searchers (tidewaiters) to leave the ship, yet later in the day 60 casks of wine were brought ashore without payment of duty. Both Hopper and Barney were sacked. Yet despite Culliford's determined efforts to eliminate bribery and corruption among customs officials, it is likely that within a few years the old dodges and frauds had crept back. In 1720 the mayor and burgesses of Poole petitioned the House of Commons to clamp down on smuggling because it was seriously undermining the legitimate trade and impoverishing the town. The government did in fact take vigorous steps to check smuggling but before long Poole and other towns were complaining that they were impoverished 'by reason of several of the unhappy inhabitants, who, through ignorance or inadvertancy either . . . imported or bought goods, which had not paid the duties, are now confined to prisons'.

War with France (1689-97 and again 1702-13) gave smugglers once more a free hand, but some increase in the effectiveness of the Customs services in the ports after the return of peace caused the smugglers to operate in well-organised gangs and increasingly to use desolate, sparsely inhabited stretches of the coast for landing the contraband. Among the areas most favoured by the smugglers were the Isle of Purbeck, Poole Harbour – 'the second largest natural harbour in the world', with its innumerable inlets and deserted beaches – and particularly the shores of Poole and Christchurch Bays behind which was a large area of gorse-covered heathland to which access was provided by one or another of the wooded chines between Sandbanks and Bourne Mouth. Up these chines on horseback or on wagons the smuggled goods could be taken to storage areas such as Kinson, four or five miles inland, from which the contraband could be taken farther afield to willing customers like the Somerset clergyman, the Rev. James Woodforde, who recorded in his *Diary of a Country Parson* for 29 March 1777 that 'Andrews the Smuggler brought me this night about eleven o'clock a bag of Hysson tea [green tea from China], six pounds in weight. He frightened us a little by whistling under the parlour window, just as we were going to bed. I gave him some Geneva [i.e. gin] . . . and paid him for the tea at ten and six per pound . . . £3 3s. 0d.' Maybe the vicar of Kinson turned a blind eye to the fact that kegs of brandy were being stored at the top of the church tower and was suitably rewarded by the smugglers for the use of church property.

During the course of the 18th century ever higher duties were imposed on an ever-increasing number of articles (over two thousand by the early 19th century) so that it became increasingly attractive to bring goods in without payment of duty and risk clashes with the forces of the Law, since a handsome profit was assured. Dr. Samuel Johnson might define a smuggler in his dictionary as 'a wretch, who in defiance of the law, imports or exports goods without payment of the customs', but doubtless he knew only too well that much of the tea which he himself consumed in such large quantities had paid no duty. At one stage a keg of the best French brandy purchased at Roscoff, or in the Channel Islands for 16 shillings (80 pence), if smuggled into England, could be sold for say, 22 shillings (£1.10 pence) and still leave the 'Gentlemen of the Night' a good profit, instead of being sold for 32 shillings (£1.60 pence), if duty were paid. The economist, Adam Smith, who held that the imposition of protective duties by a government hampered individual freedom and the creation of wealth, was of the opinion that 'a smuggler is a person who, although no doubt blameable for violating the laws of the country, is frequently incapable of violating those of natural justice, and would have been, in every respect, an excellent citizen had not the laws of the country made that a crime which Nature never meant to be so'. In other words smuggling was a by-product of unnatural barriers to trade. But in 1776, the very year in which Adam Smith wrote *The Wealth of Nations*, the vicar of Christchurch, the Rev. William Jackson, pressed by his clerk to say whether smuggling was a sin, declared emphatically that whoever defrauded the king of his dues by engaging in smuggling did indeed commit a grievous sin. To this the clerk retorted, 'Then may the Lord have mercy on the poor town of Christchurch, your Reverence, for who is there here who has not had a tub?'.

Most people in fact – not only in Christchurch – were ready enough to co-operate with the smugglers. The Venturer who organised and financed a run was usually a man of substance, perhaps a local landowner, whose identity would be secret. He secured the services of a bold and experienced captain to bring the smuggling vessel to the appointed place off-shore. The third key man in the gang was the Lander, responsible for getting the contraband ashore and transported inland. He recruited local men of physical strength who knew the district well, and at a time of low wages it was not difficult to find labourers, craftsmen or former soldiers or sailors willing to earn ten shillings – more than a normal weekly wage – for a hard night's work. Horses and waggons would have been organised, and most farmers would willingly respond to a note requiring a stable door to be left open so that horses could be borrowed – in confident expectation of a keg of brandy or a few dollops (waterproof bags) of tea as a reward. To protect smugglers' convoys there were 'batmen', armed preferably with large clubs, since using a firearm against a preventive officer carried the death penalty. If, however, a confrontation arose, then swords, knives or guns might be used.

In 1733 Sir Robert Walpole, George II's chief minister, proposed an Excise Bill to check smuggling by collecting excise duties on tobacco and wine from retail dealers instead of levying customs duties on them at the ports. Fears that the new scheme would mean government officials searching shops and warehouses and that this amounted to a violation of basic human rights caused such hysterical opposition that Walpole dropped the proposal. Three years later he tried again to check smuggling – this time by the Indemnity Act, offering a free pardon for past smuggling offences to any person who would provide the names of smuggling associates, but smugglers who did not avail themselves of this opportunity would in future run the risk of the gallows for wounding or using arms against a revenue officer and also hard labour, flogging, transportation or impressment in the Royal Navy for unarmed resistance. The following year it was reported that in Dorset evasion of customs duties by smugglers continued 'without any regard to the late Act, as much or more than before'. Very few smugglers took advantage of the chance of a free pardon as a reward for betraying their fellows.

In fact it was held that people who were themselves not involved in smuggling would, if they had any sense, look the other way and keep their mouths shut, if they saw or heard anything suspicious. The 3rd Earl of Malmesbury in his *Memoirs of an Ex-Minister* related how in his youth, when he was bird-nesting in the park of Hurn (Heron) Court, he was seized by a smuggler hiding kegs of brandy in the wood and made to swear not to tell anyone about what he had seen. After an hour he was given a nip of brandy and released – and duly kept his mouth shut. The Earl also recorded the story of an incident concerning Hurn Court, when in about 1780 it was owned by Squire Edward Hooper, a J.P. and Commissioner in His Majesty's Customs. The squire was entertaining to dinner the 5th Earl of Shaftesbury when 'Suddenly an immense clatter of waggons and horses disturbed their meal, and six or seven of these, heavily laden with kegs, rushed past at full gallop. Lord Shaftesbury jumped up to look at the sight, but the old squire sat still, refusing to turn round and eating his dinner complacently'. Soon afterwards a squadron of dragoons arrived and their officer was shown into the dining room and asked whether the squire and his guest had seen a convoy of wagons going by. The squire rightly confessed that he had seen nothing and Lord Shaftesbury likewise said that he had witnessed nothing unusual that evening. Apparently 'The smugglers had dashed through two deep fords in the Stour close by, which the soldiers had refused and so lost their prey'.

An informer was regarded with particular hatred by the smuggling fraternity and in 1762 the following was reported in the *Salisbury and Winchester Journal*: 'In September a gang of supposed smugglers consisting of eight men, . . . broke into the house of William Manuel at Iford, near Christchurch, seized his son Joseph, dragged him by force out of the house across Bourne Heath towards Poole and forced him to a lonely house near Decoy Pond, notorious as a house frequented by smugglers'. The kidnapped young Joseph Manuel was taken across to the Channel Islands, where later he managed to escape, though he incurred severe injuries. 'This outrage was prompted', said the *Journal*, 'by the suspicion that the victim had given information to the Excise officers and the men who committed the crime were, it was said, hired or instigated to do it by some of the smugglers in that part of the coast.'

Whereas most Dorset smugglers seem not to have resorted to violence, Poole had become involved in 1747 in the activities of the most ruthless, violent gang of smugglers in England – the Hawkhurst Gang, who from their base in the village of Hawkhurst, Kent, had long terrorised the customs officers and general public of Kent and Sussex. The 1747 case, involving a successful raid on Poole Custom House and subsequently two particularly vicious murders, was probably the most fully documented case in English smuggling history, since a very full, well-researched account was written and published two years later by 'A Gentleman of Chichester', generally believed to be the Duke of Richmond who was waging a campaign to stamp out smuggling. On 22 September 1747 the Poole revenue cutter, *Swift*, commanded by Captain William Johnson, intercepted in Poole Bay a smuggling vessel the *Three Brothers*. 'After firing several shots at her', reported Johnson, 'I brought her to. I went myself on board, and found she was loaded with tea, brandy and rum. The tea was in canvas, and oilskin over that, the usual packing for tea intended to be run'. Johnson towed the vessel to Poole Quay and duly handed over the contraband to the Collector of Customs who placed it in the Custom House. Unfortunately, the seven smugglers on board the *Three Brothers*, including John Diamond who had been born and brought up in Dorset (at Nether and Over Compton near Sherborne), escaped capture and made their way to Sussex, where it had been intended to land the tea. Members of the Hawkhurst Gang, led by two ruthless men, Thomas Kingsmill and William Fairall, decided that they were going to recover what they regarded as their property. In October 1747 some thirty smugglers arrived in the Poole area. Exactly what happened was related by one of them who turned King's evidence: 'When we came near the town of Poole, we sent two men to see if all things were clear for us to go to work in breaking in the warehouse'. They reported thus:

> There is a large sloop lying up against the Quay; she will plant her guns to the Custom House door and tear us in pieces, so it cannot be done. We were turning our horses to go back, when Kingsmill and Fairall and the rest of their countrymen [i.e. the Hawkhurst Gang] said 'If you will not do it, we will go and do it ourselves'. Then it was reported that as the tide had turned and was then low, it would be impossible for the guns of the sloop to be turned on the Custom House. Accordingly, the gang moved in under the leadership of Kingsmill and, encountering no customs officials, smashed open the door of the Custom House with hatchets and crow-bars. They then removed 38 cwts of tea, which they said was theirs as well as 40 barrels of brandy and rum and a large bag of coffee, which had been taken from the *Three Brothers*, but did not take anything beyond what had been taken from their smuggling vessel, as they informed the terrified warehouse watchman. Loading their contraband on the backs of their horses, they then made good their escape and had breakfast at Fordingbridge.

There the Dorset born smuggler, John Diamond, spotted in the crowd a middle-aged

The Smuglers Breaking open the Kings Custom House at Poole Oct.r 7. 1747.

98.   Etching of the 1747 raid on the Poole Custom House.

shoemaker, Daniel Chater, who had once worked with him on a farm. Greeting him, Diamond threw him a bag of tea for old times' sake. The gang then moved on with their tea and spirits to Sussex, but Diamond was caught and lodged in Chichester gaol. Chater in Fordingbridge talked about his windfall – the bag of tea – and word of this reached the Customs authorities who called on Chater to make a statement concerning Diamond's involvement in the Poole raid. Accompanied by William Galley, an elderly Customs official from Southampton, Chater set out to report to a Sussex magistrate. Doubtless Chater had no desire to betray his old acquaintance, Diamond, who had tossed him the bag of tea but, if he did not do as required, he could well find himself being charged with receiving smuggled goods and wilfully withholding information. On their journey Chater and Galley stopped at an inn, where Chater let slip the nature of their mission. News of this reached some smugglers, who were friends of Diamond, and they came to the inn, plied Chater and Galley with rum and trussed both of them up, seated them together on one horse and drove off with them, repeatedly whipping them. At one point, the saddle-girth snapped and the two men slipped under the horse and their faces and heads were horribly injured as they were dragged along over rough ground at high speed. After further mutilation and torture, old Galley, the customs officer, collapsed and the smugglers dug a shallow grave and dumped him in it. The account by 'The Gentleman of Chichester' commented, 'It must be presumed that he was buried alive, because when he was found, his hands covered his face as if to keep the dirt out of his eyes'. Chater was then taken on to the home of Richard Mills, whose two sons had taken part in the raid on Poole. Chater was kept chained up in a yard for two days and subjected to further attacks and abuse. Several of his teeth were knocked out and both his eyes were terribly injured. The smugglers then decided to kill him as an example to 'informing rogues'. As he was saying his prayers for the last time, he was slashed two or three times across his mutilated face with a knife. Chater was then taken off to a well, where a cord was tied round his throat, and the other was wound round the guard rail and Chater was left to dangle their half-strangled for a quarter of an hour. Finally the old cobbler's battered body was pushed over and plunged to the dry bottom of the well, and since one of the smugglers thought he heard groans coming from beneath, they threw several large stones on top of the mangled body. Information about the murders filtered through to the authorities and the murderers were tracked down, tried at Chichester, found guilty and hanged. One of them, Henry Sheerman, before he died gave a revealing account of the methods used by smugglers for getting contraband landed and then distributed. The two leaders of the Hawkhurst Gang, Kingsmill and Fairall, as well as Richard Perrin, were tried at the Old Bailey, found guilty and hanged. The Dorset-born John Diamond, who had involved poor Chater by tossing him the bag of tea at Fordingbridge, turned King's evidence and escaped the gallows.

The Preventive Service – the government organisation to combat smuggling – had been, in effect, established in 1698, when the Crown appointed 299 Riding Officers initially to stop 'owlers' (smugglers by night) *exporting* wool without payment of the duty introduced as long ago as 1275. Almost at once the Riding Officers were mainly concerned with stopping goods being imported without payment of customs duties. A Riding Officer had to provide his own horse though he received a standard issue of a sword and pistol; his salary was low, and his duties, if conscientiously carried out, were extremely heavy, involving endless patrolling along the stretch of coast assigned to him, theoretically a mere four miles but often four times that distance. At the end of each day, too, the Riding Officer had to compile a report. Probably because a Riding Officer was entitled to prize money in the event of a seizure, there seems to have been no shortage of applicants for the post. Inevitably some Riding Officers, faced with an increasingly difficult task, just gave up – or else succumbed to the lucrative temptation of making private arrangements with the smugglers. By 1713 Riding Officers received some help from the army in the shape of troops of Dragoons, mounted infantry, stationed at various points along the south coast. Dragoons were held to be particularly useful, since they were trained to ride hard to the point where the smugglers were landing their contraband, and there dismount and deal on foot with the smugglers. After 1759 the Preventive Officers on this part of the coast had the help of the Royal Navy cutters and their crews and an account by the Poole Collector of Customs related how in March 1765 Lieutenant Down, Commander of the cutter *Folkestone*, landed on the north shore between Poole and Bournemouth with 14 of his men and found 20 smugglers loading a consignment of tea on to the backs of their horses. A scuffle occurred in which the smugglers beat several of the *Folkestone*'s men with the solid ends of their horsewhips, discharged two pistols at them (one able seaman Eneas Atkins being shot through the leg), and dumped one of the R.N. men, Edward Morrice, in the breakers (though he managed to crawl out before he was drowned). Lieutenant Down threatened to fire at the smugglers if they attempted to carry away any of the tea. The smugglers 'then made use of the means in their power to defend themselves and secure the goods. And one Robert Trotman, of a village near Devizes, the head of a desperate gang of smugglers was killed. But as it was dark, neither Mr. Down nor any of his men can be certain who shot him, whether they or the smugglers . . . As soon as Mr. Down came up to Poole with the goods the next morning, the collector went with him to an attorney for his opinion how it would be proper to act in regard to the man killed'. The attorney advised them to report to the Parkstone parish officer that 'a man lay dead on the shore that was killed in an engagement the night before between the commander and the men of the *Folkestone* cutter and a gang of smugglers, and advised him to acquaint the coroner thereof' and to offer to give evidence when required. Before Lieutenant Down could follow this advice the smugglers had contacted the coroner and an inquest held at North Haven House, Sandbanks, at 2 p.m. the next day resulted in a jury (possibly composed of smugglers) returning a verdict that Trotman died as a result of 'wilful murder by persons unknown'. The epitaph on Trotman's tombstone in Kinson churchyard indicated the contemporary attitude towards smuggling – or at any rate the attitude of those who had the gravestone inscribed (perhaps friends of the smuggling fraternity)

> To the Memory of ROBERT TROTMAN Late of Rond [it should be ROWDE,
> lettering incorrectly restored in 1960]
> in the County of Wilts who was barbarously Murder'd
> on the Shore near Poole the 24 March 1765.
> A little Tea one leaf I did not steal.
> For Guiltless Blood shed, I to GOD appeal.
> Put Tea in one scale human Blood in tother
> And think what tis to slay thy harmless Brother.

The smuggler was clearly thought of as a harmless brother – even as a Freedom Fighter – who had purchased his goods to sell at bargain prices to the public. He had stolen nothing and he was guiltless, since his evasion of the payment of duty demanded by the government was viewed not as a crime but a public service.

It is interesting that, seven years earlier when Customs Officers found in Bitman's Chine several casks of liquor and bags of tea and a clash occurred between them and the smugglers, it was reported that the smugglers were Wiltshiremen, that they had 'gone off with the tea towards Kingston [Kinson]' and that two of those involved were named Mark Chamberlain and Isaac Gulliver.

Isaac Gulliver (1745-1822), the celebrated smuggler of the Wimborne area, was born in Semington, Wiltshire and is described in the parish register as 'son of Isaac and Elizabeth Gulliver'. Maybe the man involved in the 1758 scuffle was the elder Isaac Gulliver and either he or the son may have been with Trotman on the shore near Poole in 1765. Possibly even the elder or younger Isaac Gulliver may have paid to have Trotman's tombstone erected and inscribed. Isaac Gulliver (the younger) seems to have married in 1768 Elizabeth Beale, daughter of William Beale, who kept the *Blacksmith's Arms* at Thorney Down on the Blandford-Salisbury road, one of the main routes for the transport of smuggled goods. The Poole collector of customs reported in 1774, 'We find that Isaac Gulliver, William Beale and Roger Ridout run great quantities of goods on our North Shore between Poole and Christchurch . . .'. Thereafter Gulliver lived at various times at Longham, Kinson, West Moors, Corfe Mullen and Long Crichel – all places with strong smuggling traditions. For example, grooves worn in the sandstone parapets of Kinson church tower are said to have been caused by the ropes used for hauling contraband up to the roof of the tower for storage, and a chest tomb near the church door has a conveniently pivoted side facilitating the hiding of smuggled goods within. There are many local stories of underground tunnels in Kinson and certainly on the demolition in 1958 of Howe Lodge, Kinson, which Gulliver owned for some time, it was found that there was a secret room accessible only through a door 10 feet up a chimney, and there was also a bricked-up tunnel leading from a basement which was entered through a trap door in the dining room.

Isaac Gulliver was clearly a highly intelligent man with great organising ability. He kept forty or fifty men constantly employed and these wore a kind of livery, powdered hair and smock frocks, from which they attained the name of 'White Wigs'. Despite the vast

99. Tombstone of Robert Trotman,
Kinson churchyard.

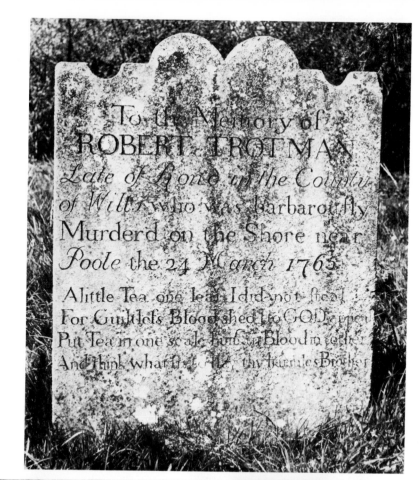

To the Memory of
ROBERT TROTMAN
Late of Rond in the County
of Wilts who was Barbarously
Murderd on the Shore near
Poole the 24 March 1765

A little Tea one leaf I did not steal
For Guiltless Blood shed I to GOD appeal
Put Tea in one scale human Blood in tother
And think what tis to slay thy harmless Brother

100. Table tomb in Kinson
churchyard, used by smugglers.

101. Isaac Gulliver.

scale of his smuggling activities, Gulliver proudly boasted that the men under his command had never inflicted physical harm on any revenue officer. Masterly organisation, quick-wittedness and amazing daring enabled him to pull off one coup after another and to prevent the customs men from being able to arrest him or to collect sufficient evidence to convict him. Numerous stories of his escapades have been passed down. One day the Revenue Officer called at his house in Kinson with a search warrant, only to be told that he had just died and was lying in his coffin upstairs. The Revenue Officer asked to be allowed to see him and was duly led to the open coffin in which Gulliver indeed was lying, his face deathly pale – as a result of the skilful application of hair-powder. The officer was convinced that Gulliver was dead and apologetically withdrew. Gulliver is even said to have organised his own mock funeral with the Vicar, completely bamboozled, conducting a service over a coffin filled with stones. After that Gulliver disappeared for a time and then surfaced once more to continue his profitable trade.

On another occasion he is said to have spent a whole day walking round Wimborne Market disguised as a shepherd wearing a smock to avoid being questioned by the authorities. At another time Gulliver evaded the 'Philistines' (i.e. the Customs men), when he was spotted in Poole, by dodging into an inn where the friendly landlord hid him inside a large cask, loaded it on to a wagon, which was then driven out along Poole High Street under the noses of the revenue officers.

In 1782 the government offered a free pardon to all smugglers who would either serve in the Navy or provide two substitutes. Gulliver then surprisingly applied for the pardon. He was easily able to pay for two substitutes to join the Navy. After 1782 he gave up smuggling tea and spirits and concentrated on his business as a wine merchant, but a report of the Collector of Customs at Poole added that 'We are well informed that he constantly sold wines considerably under the fair dealers' price, from which circumstances there is no doubt that he illicitly imported that article, but which trade we are informed he dropped some time since'. The Collector concluded this report (in 1798): 'He is a person of great speculative genius, and besides this he has carried on a variety of other businesses, but we find that he is not known at present to be concerned in any sort of merchandise, and lives retired at a farm in the neighbourhood having acquired, as it is reported, a very considerable property'. (This farm may have been Lilliput House, on the shore of Poole Harbour.) Among his many properties at one time was the farm at Eggardon Hill in West Dorset, where he planted a small plantation of trees to act as a landmark for his smuggling ships. Although he was said by the Poole Collector in 1798 to have retired from smuggling, another account in the *Gentleman's Magazine* says that it was around 1800 when three of his luggers, loaded with silk, brandy and tobacco, appeared off Bourne Bottom and a two-mile long procession of his wagons and horsemen 'at the head of which rode the Old Chief, mounted on a spotted charger transported all the contraband inland'. A tradition handed down by his descendants is that he exposed a French plot to murder George III and that the king supplemented the free pardon with an injunction that Gulliver should be allowed 'to smuggle as much as he likes'.

In 1815 he moved back to Howe Lodge in Kinson and later bought a large T-shaped house in West Borough, Wimborne (today called Gulliver's House). He regularly attended the Minster church, and was elected a churchwarden. On his death in 1822 he was buried in the vault of the minster. A plain tomb slab inscribed 'Isaac Gulliver Esquire' was later moved to the centre aisle under the West Tower. He had attained a considerable social status. One of his daughters, Ann, married a Blandford doctor; another, Elizabeth, married William Fryer of Lytchett Minster, a banker with his own bank (Fryer, Andrews, Woolfrey and Co., later the Wimborne, Poole and Blandford Bank, finally absorbed into the National Provincial). A grand-daughter, Ann Fryer, married another banker, whose premises were where Lloyd's Bank now stands in Wimborne Square. Among the other descendants of that notorious smuggler were solicitors, soldiers and colonial administrators; two of whom were knighted and one the first Lieutenant-Governor of Burma.

It was not just the ingenuity of smugglers like Gulliver which made their capture so difficult. In 1759 Thomas Ireland, Poole Supervisor of Excise, whilst 'very drunk' and 'in public company in Wimborne', announced he would make radical improvements in the Poole Customs House, where, he declared, the customs officers were themselves smugglers 'and very considerable ones'. The Poole Customs men demanded a public apology from him for blackening their lily-white characters.

Riding officers based at Christchurch occasionally had their successes, but more often their failures. The Rev. Richard Warner in his *Literary Recollections* recalled how in the late 1770s from an elevated position in his schoolroom above the chancel of Christchurch Priory he had 'more than once seen a procession of twenty or thirty wagons loaded with kegs of spirits, an armed man sitting at the front and tail of each and surrounded by a troop of two or three hundred horsemen, each carrying on his enormous saddle from two to four tubs of spirits, winding deliberately and with the most picturesque and imposing effect along the skirts of Hengistbury Head on their way towards the wild country to the north-east of Christchurch, the point of separation'. The future clergyman commented on the fact that the Customs men seldom tried to interfere. Indeed, as he said, 'What could the opposition of a handful of Revenue officers have availed against bands of raw-boned ruffians, hardened, determined, desperate and half-maddened by liquor, consisting of one to three hundred in number?'. Sometimes in fact the customs officers would engage in friendly banter and exchange 'a flood of homely jokes' with the smugglers who showed their appreciation by giving them a few kegs and samples of other contraband. The Rev. Richard Warner, however, related the story of the fate of the father of one of his school friends, an over-conscientious riding officer named Bursey, who had made a nuisance of himself to the smugglers. He wrote, 'It was a dark winter night, after the worthy man had . . . retired with his family to bed that a loud rapping on the outer door roused him from his slumbers'. On looking out of the window Bursey saw two men who said that they had found a large quantity of contraband and that for a suitable reward they would lead him to the goods. Bursey 'the unsuspicious officer hastily clothed himself, descended unarmed into the passage, opened the door, and in one minute his brains were dashed out upon the threshold'.

In the circumstances one can understand why in mid-July 1784 Joshua Jeans, Supervisor of Riding Officers at Christchurch, had actively discouraged his riding officers from taking any action when some of them had reported seeing a convoy of wagons being driven through Christchurch and out towards Mudeford, obviously in readiness for the arrival of some large assignment of contraband. Jeans told them to go home to bed, since that was what he himself proposed to do. Captain Ellis, R.N., commanding the sloop-of-war H.M.S. *Orestes*, through his telescope clearly saw swarms of people bringing ashore from two smuggling luggers large quantities of contraband – actually kegs of brandy and bags of tea – and loading them on to a long line of wagons. Captain Ellis immediately decided to intervene and sent in six ship's boats with fully armed crews under the command of 24-year-old William Allen. Then began the famous Battle of Mudeford. As the six boats approached the beached smuggling luggers, Mr. Allen stood up and in the name of the king called upon the smugglers to surrender. He was met with a volley of small-arms fire and mortally wounded as he stepped ashore. The battle, however, is supposed to have continued from 6 a.m. until 9 p.m. The smugglers fought with great ferocity after retreating to the *Haven House Inn*. Many of both sides were wounded, but the smugglers successfully carried off huge quantities of contraband. One of the smugglers, George Coombes, was eventually caught and found guilty of the murder of young Mr. Allen. After Coombes' execution his body was hung in an iron cage from a gibbet on Haven Point, but later it was carried off by some of his associates and secretly given Christian burial by a sympathetic clergyman.

One of the Christchurch smugglers involved in the Battle of Mudeford, John Streeter, had earlier come alongside Christchurch Quay with a cargo of grain in his 90-ton lugger *Phoenix*, only to have it thoroughly searched by a Revenue 'rummage crew'. Streeter professed himself to be utterly astonished when several barrels of gin, rum and brandy were found concealed under the grain. After his vessel was seized, Streeter set up a tobacco and snuff manufactory at Stanpit near Christchurch and, though he bought some of his tobacco from legitimate suppliers in London, much of his stock was undoubtedly smuggled in from the Channel Islands. After being sent to prison for his part in the Battle of Mudeford, he escaped to Guernsey, there organising supplies of tobacco for his factory at Sanpit, which his wife continued to run. Later he returned to Christchurch and lived there quietly, undisturbed by the authorities until his death at the age of 74 in 1824.

A journal kept by Abraham Pike, Supervisor of Customs of Christchurch, covering the years 1803-4 is of special interest. It survived when other records were destroyed in 1817. Pike had to patrol the whole 16-mile coastline from Poole to Hurst Castle beyond Christchurch. On a right-hand page of the journal under the heading 'Transactions and Observations' he recorded on 13 October 1803: 'Set out with Mr. Wise and a party of the Twentieth Regiment of the Light Dragoons to Bourne, where I found and seized sixty-three casks of foreign spirits and one of tobacco'. However a more typical entry in February of 1804 was: 'Surveyed the coast to Bourne. Informed by Mr. Newman that he had seized a wagon and about seventy casks of spirits on a common near Shirley, and that he was afterward attacked by several persons unknown, and the wagon and goods rescued . . . I set out with my Riding Officers and a party of the Royal Horse Artillery in pursuit of it to Shirley, Sandford, Kingston [Kinson] and Avon. Searched several suspected places. *No success*'.

Among the army officers engaged in helping in the struggle against the smugglers was Lewis Tregonwell, from Cranborne Lodge, who as captain in the Dorset Volunteer Rangers was put in charge of protecting the shore between Poole and Christchurch against invasion by Napoleon's troops in 1804-5. Abraham Pike probably met him. After retiring from the army Tregonwell built a seaside resort at the mouth of the Bourne which became known as the Mansion. It has been suggested that Tregonwell may have developed a friendly understanding with the smuggling fraternity. For his butler, Symes, Tregonwell built a thatched cottage later known as Portman Lodge – on the site of the later Hants and Dorset bus station. When Portman Lodge was demolished in 1930 the workmen discovered three feet below ground level an underground chamber 10 feet long, seven feet wide with ample headroom and access only through a trap door. Symes seems to have been in residence throughout each year and one is tempted to conclude that his cellar served the purpose of storing contraband with or without the knowledge of Lewis Tregonwell. Perhaps there was even a working arrangement between Tregonwell, Symes and old Gulliver, when the latter retired from the open smuggling business.

Just at the time when Tregonwell was building his own mansion and butler Symes' cottage, the Poole Customs officers (1813) in a report, brought to light by Roger Guttridge's research, said that:

The manner in which the contraband trade is at present carried on . . . is for the importing craft to sink their goods according to a previous arrangement at different places on the coast . . . the smuggler, proceeding by land, acquaints the owners of the marks by which they may find their respective goods . . . The means by which the landing is effected is small open boats, usually employed during the day in fishing, which at night are hauled upon the beach, frequently immediately contiguous to the spot where contraband goods are sunk. . . . The number of casks usually landed in this manner is from twenty to forty and are with inconceivable promptitude, . . . concealed in caves . . . situated in the vicinity of the spot where the landing takes place. These caves or cellars are formed with so much secrecy or ingenuity that their detection amounts almost to a matter of impossibility.

Was Symes' underground chamber one of these caves?

Other useful devices for landing contraband were drains or underground passages linking the cellars of one or two inns, with openings in the stonework of the quay at Poole, so that kegs could be attached to ropes when the tide was low and then hauled up the passages into the inn. One Poole innkeeper, who also ran a funeral service, used his enormous hearse or Shillibier for the conveyance of contraband.

In a report to Lord Shelborne, Home Secretary in 1782, a Captain Lisle alleged that, of the two revenue cutters guarding the coast from the Isle of Wight to St Alban's Head, 'that from Southampton makes some good seizures, the other from Poole very few . . . owing to the Master, Mate and crews being corrupted, and on certain signals . . . the latter withdraws to another part of the Coast to give opportunitys to the Smugglers to land, and carry off their Cargoes without interruption, tho' sometimes they are bribed with a few Casks, to save appearances'.

In 1807 the Controller at Poole reported that 'Mr. John Wise, Riding Officer, has been concerned in one seizure only, viz. 16 pounds of tobacco since December 1804 notwithstanding large quantities of smuggled goods are very frequently landed in this district and sometimes within two miles of his house and from thence conveyed past his door into the interior of the country . . . As we have strong reason to suspect that he is either extremely inattentive to his duty or that too good an understanding subsists between him and the smugglers, we . . . propose that he may be removed to Wareham'.

The return of peace in 1815 after the long Napoleonic wars with France meant that more naval resources were available for use against smugglers. The year 1822 saw the establishment of the Coastguard Service and with it an efficient central administration for the prevention of smuggling. The coastguard was mainly a land-based force which patrolled beaches and cliff-tops, armed with spy-glass, musket and 'donkey stool' (a one-legged resting-device like a shooting-stick, which, however, would dump the coastguard on the ground if he failed to remain vigilant). Helping them were the Revenue cutters manned by experienced seamen, under orders to cruise up and down their designated stretch of coast at night-time and in bad weather, when smugglers were often more active.

In 1830 the Poole Collector, quoted by Roger Guttridge, reported that 'a notorious gang of smugglers . . . who have infested this neighbourhood during the last two years, and who, we believe, have been more or less concerned in every illicit transaction which has taken place, have dispersed and . . . for the most part removed themselves ostensibly in pursuit of legal occupation'. A major blow, in fact, had been dealt by the seizure of their smuggling vessel the *Integrity*. Richard Charles, the gang leader's son and a very active member, was sentenced to serve in the Royal Navy and, although his father had protested that he was suffering from 'a consumptive habit of body and decaying constitution', the medical examinations at Poole and Portsmouth concluded that 'never was an individual sent to the navy under similar circumstances so fit and able'.

After 1830 coastguards were better trained and magistrates imposed more severe sentences

102. The Quay, showing the Harbour Office and Custom House about 1822.

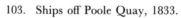

103. Ships off Poole Quay, 1833.

more consistently. Reports from Poole in the 1840s showed that smuggling continued only on a very limited scale and without violence. Drastic reductions in duties by Peel's Conservative government in the 1840s made smuggling less profitable anyway. Thus by 1850 smuggling in the Poole area had declined to a trickle.

Immediately after the Second World War there was a brief revival of smuggling in Poole Harbour when an ex-naval officer and his accomplices brought ashore at Shipstal near Arne from a war-surplus landing craft large quantities of liquor and then transported the contraband in a lorry up to London for distribution on the black market to various clubs. The police, learning from local inhabitants of the suspicious movements of the truck, caught the smugglers near Wareham and at the trial fines amounting to over £18,000 and terms of imprisonment were imposed.

In more recent years the Customs officers have been concerned with stopping two Wimborne businessmen from exporting electronic equipment destined for Communist Eastern Europe and also with preventing the smuggling of cannabis, cocaine and heroin into the country though the numerous yachts that frequent Poole Harbour. The current work of the Customs service was vividly portrayed in the B.B.C. Television series, *The Collectors*.

Chapter Eleven

Decline, Reform and Revival

In July 1814, after the abdication of Napoleon and his banishment to Elba, a great feast for 5,000 people at 70 tables was laid on in the Market Place and adjoining streets in Poole to celebrate what was believed to be the end of over twenty years of almost uninterrupted war. In the event Napoleon escaped from Elba the following spring and it required one final effort by Britain and her allies to defeat him at Waterloo in 1815. The victor at Waterloo, the Duke of Wellington, had in his boyhood at Eton been a friend of the Rev. Peter William Jolliffe, who said prayers at this festival and who was a member of the family long engaged in the Newfoundland trade. He was Rector of Poole for the unprecedented period of 70 years (1791-1861).

It was generally assumed that peace meant plenty, but there was soon to be disillusionment since a severe trade depression set in and there followed numerous bankruptcies and widespread unemployment. Britain as a whole, and Poole in particular, had benefited from the fact that, during the war when Britain had complete naval supremacy, Britain had a monopoly of world trade. This ended with the advent of peace and in particular there was a catastrophic collapse in Poole's trade with Newfoundland. As George Garland explained in evidence he gave on the Newfoundland trade in 1817 to a committee of the House of Commons, the actual catching and curing of the cod had long been taken over by the Newfoundland settlers (Planters) whilst the Poole merchants supplied them with implements, provisions and clothing and received in payment the cod and oil, which they then transported to southern Europe. However the peace treaty had allowed not only the Americans but also the French to fish off southern Newfoundland and there was far less cod and oil available for the Poole merchants. Moreover, the Yankee traders began to sell provisions and clothing to the settlers at lower prices than the men of Poole demanded. The market for the dried fish in south Europe was reduced as meat and other food became more plentiful in peace-time, whilst the Norwegians began to supply *klippfisk* from the Lofoten Islands. Furthermore, Spain, Portugal and Naples suddenly imposed much heavier duties on Newfoundland fish. As a result of all these developments, Poole merchants found that instead of receiving 40s. (at the high point during the wars) per quintal (or hundredweight) they had to be content with a mere 12s. In Newfoundland the settlers had to resort to rationing and there were riots and some looting of the Poole merchants' stores. Soon the Poole merchants faced severe financial difficulties. G. & J. Kemp sold out in 1824 to another firm. By 1820 George Garland was closing down some of his bases in Newfoundland and investing his money in land, whilst George Ledgard, a shipowner and rope-maker involved in the Newfoundland trade, also diversified, and in 1821 in partnership with Martin Kemp-Welch founded the Poole Town and County Bank. Christopher Spurrier, as we have seen, ignored all the warning signs and adopted an extravagant life-style to further his social and political ambitions as though the huge profits were still flowing in, until, after a particularly disastrous cod-fishing season, and despite the sale of Upton House in 1828 the firm of Messrs. Spurrier & Co. went bankrupt. In 1828 only 10 British ships were fishing in Newfoundland waters. The 'northern' branch of the Slade family at Twillingate concentrated increasingly on sealing as far north as Labrador and carried on for another generation. However the Slade and Kelson Diaries reveal that in the 'Year of Losses' (1846) 17 ships were lost in storms off Newfoundland in the space of two months. 1861 saw the

104. Rev. Peter William Jolliffe, Rector of Poole (1791-1861).

105. Old St James's church, demolished in 1819.

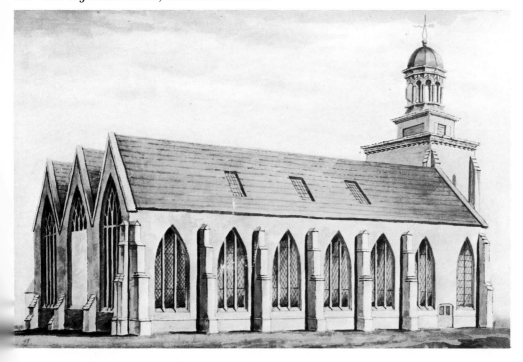

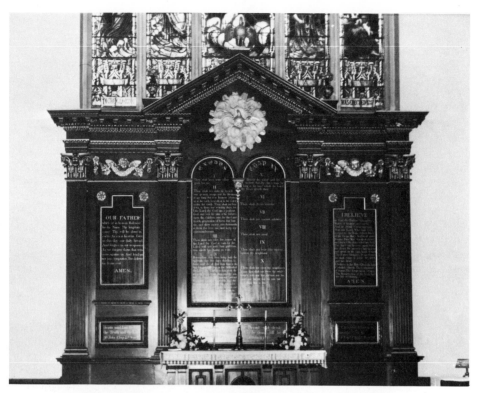

106. The 1736 reredos transferred to the new church in 1820.

107. Newfoundland pine pillars in the new St James's church.

bankruptcy of this old Poole firm, too. This decline was reflected in the size of Poole's merchant fleet in 1844 which was only one-fifth of what it had been at the end of the Napoleonic wars.

Just when the slump in the Newfoundland trade was particularly acute, it was decided in 1819 that the fabric of the parish church was so dilapidated that it must be completely rebuilt. The new St James's church, opened in 1820, incorporated a unique and appropriate feature – the use of magnificent pillars fashioned from pine brought across the Atlantic from Newfoundland. Fortunately the memorials in honour of many of the great personalities of 18th-century Poole were carefully replaced in the new building as too was the fine 1736 reredos on which are inscribed in gold on black the Lord's Prayer, the Ten Commandments and the Creed. The Royal Arms, the gift of George Welch Ledgard, mayor at the time, are those of the not very worthy Supreme Head of the Church in 1821, George IV, and incorporate the arms of Hanover, but do not include the French fleur-de-lys, since in 1800 the British king had abandoned the unrealistic claim to be king of France. The problem of paying for the rebuilding aroused some controversy. Nonconformists did not welcome the resulting increase in the rates and the Poole merchants in straightened circumstances did not eagerly respond to the mayor's appeals for donations. The Rector, the Rev. P. W. Jolliffe, in his sermon at the inauguration of the new church, appropriately chose as his text, 'Finally, be ye all of one mind having compassion one for another. Love as brethren, be pitiful, be courteous, not rendering evil for evil or railing for railing'. In actual practice the next 30 years constituted a period of deep dissension and bitter recrimination.

After 1815 there was also distress and discontent in the countryside round Poole. The collapse of the Newfoundland trade meant reduced employment for many people from surrounding villages, but the danger of an influx of cheap corn from Europe also threatened with bankruptcy many Dorset farmers who had ploughed up marginal land during the war when wheat fetched a very high price. To help them Parliament passed the Corn Laws of 1815 which forbade the import of foreign wheat unless the price of home-grown wheat had reached the famine price of 80 shillings per quarter. This ban kept up the price of corn for the producer, but increased the cost of living for the consumer. In 1815 husbandmen at Kingston Lacy were paid 10s. 6d. a week and 2s. 6d. a day at harvest time. A sheep at that time cost 35 shillings. Indeed labourers, whose hard work helped to produce the wheat, might not be able to afford to buy bread regularly; 1816 saw some severe Bread Riots in Bridport. It was naturally a temptation for a labourer to go poaching on the squire's game preserves, despite the severity of the Game Laws of 1816. Thus William Leaf was sentenced to two years' imprisonment for being caught by a gamekeeper on Mr. Sturt's estate at Long Crichel 'armed with a gun and having in his possession one cock pheasant and three hen pheasants'. Riots in London and demonstrations in the industrial north convinced the Tory government headed by Lord Liverpool (1812-27) that firm measures must be taken to prevent any uprisings. Consequently freedom of meeting and freedom of the Press were restricted and magistrates were authorised to search for weapons and to suppress any private drilling under the Six Acts (1819), one of the chief advocates of which was the Lord Chancellor – for 20 years (1807-27) Lord Eldon, who in 1807 purchased the Encombe estate from that great champion of the poor, William Morton Pitt. Remembering the excesses of the Paris and rural mobs in the French Revolution, Lord Eldon gave priority to the maintenance of law and order and feared that any drastic reform such as an overhaul of the antiquated system of electing M.P.s could spark off mob rule and anarchy. However, after 1822 when good harvests diminished the unrest, the Tories did accept several reforms such as Peel's abolition of the death penalties for many minor offences – in response to the agitation of Sir Samuel Romilly, former M.P. for Wareham – and also the legalisation of trade unions. They also accepted in 1828 a Whig proposal that Protestant Nonconformists

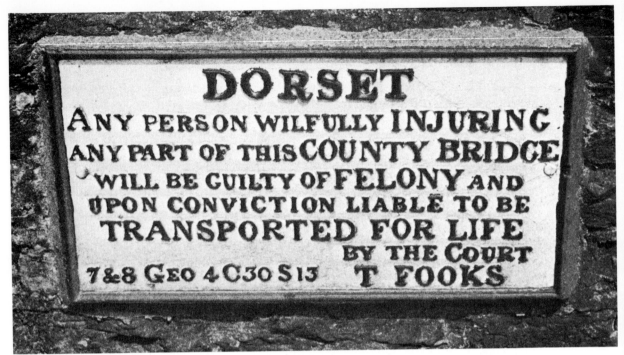

108. Transportation notice on Sturminster Marshall and Canford bridges.

109. An apology in lieu of punishment.

I, the undersigned, THOMAS WILLIAMS, do hereby express my sorrow and contrition, for having, in a state of intoxication, and without any provocation, on the Fourth day of June, instant, Assaulted and Abused, MR. CHARLES SATCHELL, the Bourne Postman, whilst in the discharge of his duty; and I am very thankful to MR. SATCHELL, for accepting this Apology, instead of Prosecuting me.

THOMAS WILLIAMS.

Dated this 12th day of June, 1841.

J. R. JUSTICAN, PRINTER, HIGH STREET, POOLE.

should be allowed to hold state or municipal office without having to take the sacrament according to the rites of the Church of England at least once a year. William Jolliffe had in 1821 declined to accept election as Sheriff of Poole on the grounds that he had never taken the Anglican sacrament in the course of his whole life and had no intention of doing so. Thanks to this change in the law in 1828 (the Repeal of the Test and Corporation Acts as far as Dissenters were concerned), he was able to serve as Mayor of Poole both in 1828 and 1829.

However, discontent flared up in the countryside especially because farm labourers feared that the new threshing machines, which had just been invented, would put them out of work. Some outbreaks of rural sabotage led Parliament to pass laws in 1827 prescribing the death penalty for setting fire to a rick, transportation for life for damaging a bridge and seven years' transportation for destroying a threshing machine. A disastrous harvest in 1829 greatly intensified the hardships of the poor, and, despite a good harvest in 1830, Mary Frampton, sister of Squire James Frampton of Moreton, wrote in her Journal in November 1830 of

> riotous mobs, breaking and destroying machinery used in husbandry, paper-mills, etc., and also surrounding gentlemen's houses, extorting money and demanding an increase in wages.
>
> On the 22nd of November the first rising took place in the county. Mr. Portman [Whig M.P. for Dorset] immediately promised to raise the wages of his labourers . . . [but] . . . my brother Frampton harangued the people at Bere Regis . . . refusing to concede to their demands whilst asked with menaces. This spirited conduct caused him to be very unpopular . . .

William Mate recorded that 'During the night of November 25, 1830 a threshing machine lying in a field at Parkstone was broken and the same week two machines, which were in a field at Lytchett were destroyed'. Mr. Castleman, agent and steward of the Bankes estate who had built Allendale House, Wimborne, in 1823, received this threatening note: 'Mr. Castleman, Sir – Sunday night your House shall come down to the Ground for you are an inhuman monster and we will dash out your brains. Banks and your sett ought to be sent to Hell. The Hanley Torches [a local gang] have not forgot you'.

In fact nothing happened either to Mr. Castleman or to his Allen-dale House and the riots died down after several ringleaders had been arrested. However, many local squires feared that some gigantic conspiracy to assault landowners and burn down or loot their houses was afoot. Thus in 1834 Squire Frampton was to get the six Tolpuddle labourers transported in 1834 for requiring members of their little trade union to swear oaths of loyalty and secrecy to the society.

Throughout the 1820s the Whig party had maintained the demand for a reform of the antiquated electoral system. Such parliamentary reform was consistently opposed by most of the Tories, especially Lord Eldon, and also by King George IV. George IV was deeply unpopular, especially when in 1820 he asked his ministers to secure for him a divorce from his wife, Queen Caroline. He had discarded her a few weeks after the marriage ceremony and she had travelled

110. Lord Eldon of Encombe House.

abroad for several years in the company of various disreputable companions. Most people felt that in view of George's numerous infidelities it was hypocritical of him to pose as the injured party. The government abandoned the divorce proceedings in the House of Lords and Lord Eldon received much of the odium for this whole undignified business of washing dirty royal linen in public. On his way back to Encombe, when he stopped to change horses, a crowd put their heads into his coach calling out 'Queen Caroline for ever'. In Poole there was much sympathy for Caroline and public meetings were held 'to congratulate her upon her Escape from the snares of her Enemies; and to express . . . esteem for her virtues'.

Caroline died in 1821 and when George IV himself died in June 1830, *The Times* wrote: 'There never was an individual less regretted by his fellow-creatures than this deceased King. . . . An inveterate voluptuary . . . is of all known beings the most selfish. Selfishness is the true repellant of human sympathy'. Yet the Poole archives show that £30 was paid out for 'hanging the Church in Black as a tribute of respect to George IV'. On the day of his funeral most of the shops closed for several hours and flags on ships in the harbour were at half-mast. There was a general belief that George IV's successor, his brother, William IV, was more favourable to parliamentary reform, and in Christchurch a handbill declared that now there was 'a King of the people' on the throne, 'Let our prayer be for Parliamentary Reform and election by ballot'.

One event that gave some stimulus to the reform movement in Britain was the 'July Revolution' in France. A month after the death of George IV, Charles X of France, who had aimed at making himself an absolute monarch and restoring the privileges of the aristocracy and Catholic Church and who had reduced the size of an already small electorate, had been overthrown in an almost bloodless revolution, to be succeeded by his cousin, Louis-Philippe, a model of middle-class respectability, who extended the franchise and who seemed to be inaugurating a movement of moderate sensible reform. To some people in England who had feared that reform must open the floodgates of revolution, anarchy and bloodshed as in the French Revolution, the events in France in 1830 seemed to suggest that perhaps after all moderate reform would not be disastrous.

The events in France were brought home to the people of Poole, when on 22 August 1830 the Royal Navy's steamboat *Meteor* arrived in Poole Harbour carrying the exiled King Charles X, his family, a huge retinue of courtiers and many members of his household ranging from his physician down to two under-cooks and four footmen. Charles X was apparently alarmed at the sight of the huge crowd awaiting him on shore, but was assured that he would receive a friendly welcome. Indeed he was received with courtesy, and landed incidentally on the Hamworthy peninsula opposite Poole Quay. Doubtless many Poole people regarded him as a bigoted tyrant, but also as a stupid, stubborn old man who had brought his overthrow upon himself. As one contemporary commented, 'They may have felt indignant at the conduct of Charles X as King of France, but they beheld only a wretched exile tottering to his grave and they did not hesitate to grant protection and pity'.

The leading Catholic in Dorset, Joseph Weld, had offered the king and his retinue hospitality at Lulworth castle, and the Tory mayor of Poole, G. W. Ledgard, offered the king the use of his coach as did the new Catholic owner of Upton House, Edward Doughty. And so the king and his family were taken staight off to Lulworth and on glimpsing its round towers he grimly commented *Voilà la Bastille*, the storming of which fortress in Paris in 1789 had been the first notable act of mob violence in the Revolution. Part of the royal party was accommodated overnight in Poole at the *Old Antelope Hotel* and the *London Tavern*. Incidentally, what was then called the *New Inn* in Thames Street was later renamed the *King Charles* after the French exile of 1830, not the 'Merrie Monarch' of England. At Lulworth castle Charles X attended Mass daily in the Catholic chapel there, went shooting on the Weld estate and met some of the local gentry, including James Frampton of Moreton, who was quite surprised that this upholder of Divine Right monarchy should condescend to say a few words in bad English to him and particularly to shake hands with a mere Dorset squire. In October another Admiralty steamship, the *Lightning*, came to Poole to transport Charles X and his court to Holyrood Palace in Scotland.

Throughout the 1820s there was a growing conviction in Poole as throughout Britain that, in the words of a petition to Parliament from the inhabitants of Poole in 1821, 'the only permanent security against a continuing mal-administration of the affairs of the nation is to be sought in an effectual Reform in the Representation of the People in Parliament'.

Nevertheless in November 1830 the Duke of Wellington, Tory prime minister (1828-30), made the extraordinary assertion that 'the system of representation possessed the full and entire confidence of the country'. He thus alienated moderate Tories who joined with the Whigs in voting against Wellington, who accordingly resigned and was replaced by Lord Grey, the Whig leader, who told King William IV that only 'an extensive measure of reform' could counteract the influence of revolutionary radicals.

Although the Tories argued that the existing Constitution had seen Britain safely through the long wars with the French, the defects of the old electoral system were plain to see. Each English county, regardless of size, had two M.P.s (apart from Yorkshire which since 1821 had four) elected by men owning freehold land valued at £2 a year. However five-sixths of the English M.P.s represented boroughs and these, usually electing two M.P.s each, varied immensely in population, from large ports like Bristol, Southampton and Liverpool down to small towns like Poole (with 6,459 people in 1831) and 'rotten boroughs' like Corfe Castle (1,712) and Old Sarum (with no human inhabitants at all). Yet some towns like Wimborne Minster (4,009) had no M.P.s of their own since they had never been invited to send separate representatives to Parliament, and huge new industrial towns, e.g. Manchester with 180,000 inhabitants, had no M.P.s. The franchise varied immensely from borough to borough. At Christchurch only the 24 members of the Corporation had the vote; the right to vote was given to all ratepayers in the 'scot and lot' boroughs of Corfe Castle (only 44 voters) and Wareham (only 150); in Poole only 'burgesses' or 'Corporators' (freemen of the borough), some of whom lived outside Poole, were entitled to vote. In 1830 each of the 48 burgesses living in Poole was allowed to nominate two further burgesses, but 37 of the newly-elected burgesses were minors and thus ineligible to vote until they were twenty-one. Thus there were only just over one hundred voters of whom 10 were Garlands and 11 Slades. Apart from the unfair, out-of-date distribution of seats and the haphazard variety of usually narrow voting qualifications, one other major defect was that all voting took place openly, so that a voter's landlord, employer or customer knew exactly for what person or party he had cast his vote. In the past this had been responsible for the creation of many 'pocket' boroughs, like Corfe Castle and Christchurch, where one or two powerful local landlords had the representation of the borough in their pockets. At Corfe Castle there were no contested elections throughout the 18th century, when the Bankes family of Kingston Lacy and the Bond family of Creech Grange each nominated one of the two M.P.s. Thus whenever there was an election at Corfe the result was never in doubt, but free beer was drunk and there was much cheering. In 1784 significant items in the election expenses of John Bond and Henry Bankes were 'To two persons to protect the beer, 2s. 6d.' and 'To 45 voters at 13s. each, £29 5s.' It was usual for the candidate to pledge himself to look after the interests of Corfe and to 'stick to the old place as long as one stone holds firm to another in the Old Castle'. Henry Bankes stuck to his seat for 46 years (1780-1826). At Christchurch until 1807 there had never been a contested election for over 150 years, since in turn the dominant local landowners such as the Hooper, Harris and Rose families had allocated the two seats as they pleased.

At Wareham from 1700 to 1760 the two seats were shared between the Pitt family of Encombe and the Erle (Erle-Drax) family of Charborough Park, but when there was a contested election as in 1747 the lack of a secret ballot facilitated intimidation. Thus the mayor, Henry Harbin, was accused of filling the streets with 'a great number of Persons armed with staves and other offensive weapons' to prevent the opponents of the Draxes from voting. In 1774 Thomas de Grey became M.P. for Wareham after his agent had spent £14 18s. 7d. on ribbons and £17 2s. 6d. on beer. Then the wealthy John Calcraft, of Rempstone Hall, bought up many properties in Wareham belonging to the Pitts and Draxes and became M.P. for Wareham in 1799. Thereafter until 1841 the Calcraft family controlled

Wareham. In Poole, where there were often contested elections, voters took it for granted that a candidate would wish to show his appreciation by a gift of money. Thus in 1768 the highly respectable William Knapp, the hymn-composer, had no qualms about receiving £40 from Joshua Mauger to 'plump for' (give both his votes to) him. In the same election an aged burgess in reduced circumstances, Joseph Wadham, gratefully accepted £200 from Mr. Mauger, and his daughter commented that 'Providence had been very kind in bringing such opportunities to provide for him'.

When the Whig government's Reform Bill was introduced in March 1831, it was supported by both the M.P.s for Poole – the greatly respected veteran merchant Benjamin Lester-Lester (M.P. since 1809) and the Hon. W. F. S. Ponsonby, a staunch Whig and Protestant, who had become lord of the manor of Canford by right of his wife, granddaughter of the last Catholic lord, Sir John Webb, and cousin of young Lord Ashley, Tory M.P. for Dorchester. The Reform Bill, which proposed to abolish many rotten boroughs like Corfe Castle, to transfer seats to the new factory towns and to enfranchise the urban middle classes, passed its first reading by just one vote. The man who tipped the scales in favour of reform was John H. Calcraft, hitherto Tory M.P. for Dorset who was so upset by the vicious attacks on him as a turncoat that he had a nervous breakdown and committed suicide. In the resulting by-election for this prestigious Dorset county seat the two candidates were Ponsonby (Whig), who resigned his Poole seat, and Lord Ashley (Tory), who gave up his Dorchester seat. Ashley opposed the Reform Bill arguing that it would cause 'the

POOLE ELECTION.

NOTICE IS HEREBY GIVEN, that the POLLING will commence To-morrow Morning at NINE o'clock precisely, at the Guildhall.

And in order to avoid partiality, and to prevent confusion and delay, the Sheriff has determined on taking the Votes for each Candidate alternately.

Voters in the interest of the Honorable G. BYNG are requested to present themselves on the *right hand side* of the Table; Voters in the interest of General Sir C. GRANT on the *left hand side* of the Table.

RICHARD LEDGARD.

POOLE,   *SHERIFF.*
19th May, 1835.

N. B. No Person will be admitted within the space below the Bench except the Poll Clerks, and the Agents for the Candidates.

J. SYDENHAM, PRINTER, POOLE.

111. Election notice, 1835, illustrating the lack of secret ballot.

aggrandisement of the towns at the expense of the agriculturalists'. Polling was spread over 15 days and Lord Ashley was declared to be the winner by 1,847 votes to 1,811 for Ponsonby. Bitter squabbles broke out; Ponsonby alleged bribery. A reformist mob wrecked the King William tavern in Parkstone and went on to use the torn-up signpost of the inn to batter in the oak doors of the house of Robert Parr (Lord Ashley's agent) in Fish Street, Poole. On 5 November the disappointed Whigs burnt effigies of Lord Ashley instead of Guy Fawkes. The anger and frustration of the reformers was all the more intense, because although another General Election had given the Whigs a large majority in the Commons, which then passed the Reform Bill, the Tory majority in the House of Lords rejected it (7 October). Lord Eldon was one of the Bill's leading opponents in this debate and Mary Frampton reported in her Journal that 'a mob from Poole were intending to attack Lord Eldon's place at Encombe', but 'all, however, passed off quietly'. Nevertheless, during the next few months revolution seemed near in view of the opposition of the Lords. However, the Whigs passed a modified Reform Bill through the Commons and King William IV promised if necessary to create enough Whig peers to deprive the Tories of their majority in the Lords. In the knowledge of this most of the Tory peers on Wellington's advice abstained and allowed the Reform Bill to pass, and the king gave his Assent on 7 June 1832.

The Great Reform Act provided for a substantial redistribution of seats. Any borough with less than 2,000 inhabitants, such as Corfe Castle with 1,712 people, lost both its M.P.s. Wareham was due to suffer the same fate, but it had its boundaries extended and was allowed to keep one M.P., although it still had only 443 voters, even though all male householders owning or renting houses valued at £10 a year now had the vote. Christchurch likewise was enlarged to include Holdenhurst and was allowed to retain one M.P. Under the Act any old borough like Poole with over 4,000 inhabitants was to keep both its M.P.s. Poole had 6,459 people and thus kept two M.P.s, but its boundaries were enlarged to include Hamworthy, Longfleet and Parkstone and so had an overall population of 8,216, but still only 412 voters. The Tories protested against this enlargement, believing that it would increase the influence of the Whig lord of the manor, who had many tenants in these areas, and arguing that the farming interests of the new areas would conflict with the maritime interests of the Old Town. The county of Dorset was allocated three instead of two M.P.s and in general well-to-do tenant farmers as well as the 40s. freeholders were given the franchise. However, since the secret ballot was not introduced, the influence of great landowners increased rather than diminished and some boroughs like Christchurch could be said still to be pocket boroughs. Christchurch had celebrated the passing of the Reform Act with a procession and a public dinner, but in only two out of the next nine elections was there more than one candidate. In 1837, when Sir George Henry Rose was opposed by a General Cameron, there was considerable evidence of intimidation, since the agent of Sir George Tapp-Gervis, lord of the manor, told his tenants they would lose their farms if they did not vote for Rose, and a lady closed her account with her draper because he had openly supported Cameron.

In the 1847 election Lady Charlotte Guest, wife of the new lord of the manor of Canford, Sir Josiah John Guest, owner of the Dowlais iron works in South Wales, commented that the Poole people were 'very corrupt and seem . . . to be looking for favour or some more direct bribe. They little know the man they have to deal with, if they think my husband will give way to anything so unworthy'. Sir J. J. Guest's nephew, the Liberal candidate Edward Hutchins, was defeated. When there was a by-election in Poole in 1850 Lady Charlotte Guest expressed a wish to witness an election meeting near the Town Hall and got more than she bargained for. She wrote that, provoked by a Liberal banner, the Tories 'tore it down and destroyed it . . . and our people, of course, retaliated upon their flags'. However, 'the flag fight being over', a Liberal speaker was

> interrupted with every imaginable noise, and presently a rotten egg was thrown at him, which took very full effect . . . it was followed by a regular volley mingled with apples, turnips and even stones and with these missiles the Tory mob continued pelting the gentlemen on our side of the hustings . . . The uproar was most tremendous . . . seeing the stones . . . I feared it must end badly and someone must be injured. But fortunately matters took another turn. Something put it into the head of the mob to carry on their pelting with balls of flour, which were very innocent, though their effect was very ludicrous, the flour sticking where the eggs had already taken.

The more politically conscious members of the working class had been disappointed at not receiving the vote in 1832, and the Chartist movement (1838-48) agitated for such objectives as Universal Manhood Suffrage and the Secret Ballot as a means of obtaining reforms to improve the lot of the poor. In 1838 a Chartist meeting, attended by 1,500 people including John Standfield, one of the Tolpuddle Martyrs, was held on Charlton Down, north of Spetisbury. It was not until 1867 that the Conservative Second Reform Act gave the vote to all male householders, regardless of the value of the houses they owned or rented, in the boroughs, and this meant that most town workers with a settled abode were enfranchised. However, the 1867 Act deprived two-member boroughs with a population of less than 10,000 of the second member. Thus Poole with just under 10,000 people was to have only one M.P. In the next election (1868), Poole elected Arthur Guest (Conservative), brother of the lord of Canford Manor, Sir Ivor Guest. The Liberal candidate and former M.P., Charles Waring, lost mainly because he had failed to keep his promises to bring the railway to Poole and to deepen the channel in the Harbour, despite the fact he backed Mr. Gladstone to the full and was in favour of the secret ballot. Gladstone passed the Ballot Act (1872) in his first ministry, whilst in his second he extended the vote to working men in the county constituencies (1884) and carried through a radical redistribution of seats (1885), by which boroughs with less than 15,000 inhabitants ceased to have their own M.P.s. The county of Dorset was given one more M.P., i.e. a total of four, one for each of four separate divisions. Thus Poole was merged in East Dorset and Wareham was incorporated in South Dorset. Christchurch on the other hand kept its own M.P., because of the rapid growth of Bournemouth, then in that constituency.

112.   William John Bankes (1786-1855).

When under the 1832 Reform Act the county of Dorset was allocated three M.P.s, three men of particular interest were elected to the first reformed parliament – William John Bankes, Anthony, Lord Ashley and the Hon. William F. S. Ponsonby – all with close links with the Poole area. William John Bankes (1785-1855), handsome, elegant, witty and charming had become a close friend of Lord Byron at Cambridge University and became a discriminating judge of poetry and art treasures. From 1812 to 1820 he was touring from one end of the Mediterranean to the other. At first he attached himself to Wellington's army – as a civilian observer – and succeeded in acquiring, sometimes by purchase and sometimes perhaps by more dubious means, a large number of exquisite paintings (by Zurburan, Velasquez and Murillo), now on display in the Spanish Room of Kingston Lacy House. One fragment portraying an angel was found in the knapsack of a dead French soldier. 'Gentlemen', said Wellington to his officers on one occasion, 'I will have no more looting; and remember, Bankes, this applies to you also.' Thereafter Bankes sent his latest acquisitions back to England addressed to the Duke of Wellington, c/o Kingston Lacy House.

Bankes then took off for the Middle East and, disguising himself in an Arab *djellabah* and pretending to be a half-witted beggar, contrived to enter the holy city of Mecca, forbidden to non-Moslems. Back in Egypt he was one of the first Europeans to enter the Great Pyramid and travelled up the Nile to Philae beyond the First Cataract. There he acquired a 22-foot tall obelisk of pink-mauve granite inscribed with hieroglyphics, and amazingly succeeded in getting it and a granite sarcophagus of the 14th century B.C. safely shipped back to England, where they are to be seen in the grounds of Kingston Lacy. The obelisk turned out to be a valuable clue to the decipherment of Egyptian hieroglyphics, since groups of them enclosed in oval surrounds or cartouches represented the names of Greco-Egyptian

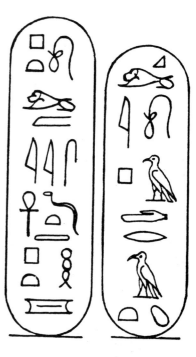

113. (*left*) Kingston Lacy House and the Egyptian obelisk.

114. (*above*) Cartouches of Ptolemy (left) and Cleopatra (right) on the Kingston Lacy obelisk.

115. (*below*) Egyptian sarcophagus, Kingston Lacy grounds.

royalty, Ptolemy and Cleopatra, and by linking these with hieroglyphics and Greek translations on the Rosetta stone it was possible to work out the phonetic value of the ancient Egyptian picture-signs. Thus Bankes' obelisk helped to unlock a vast store of knowledge concerning Ancient Egypt. On his father's death in 1834, William John inherited Kingston Lacy House and engaged Charles Barry to carry out major alterations, including the cladding of the brick walls with Chilmark stone. Then in 1841 disgrace effectively ended the career of W. J. Bankes. Prosecuted for a homosexual offence, he jumped bail, fled abroad and remained an exile for the rest of his life. He had been M.P. for Dorset for only three years, but his brother, George Bankes, was to represent Dorset for 15 years (1841-56).

116. Anthony Ashley-Cooper, Lord Ashley (seventh Earl of Shaftesbury).

Lord Ashley continued as M.P. for Dorset from 1831 to 1846 and, when he succeeded his father as 7th Earl of Shaftesbury in 1851, he continued to be a major force in British politics, primarily as the leading champion of social reform, until his death in 1885. The driving force throughout his career was his deep Evangelical Christian faith, which drove him on to strive against all forms of cruelty and actively to implement Christ's injunction, 'Love thy neighbour'. Although he was deeply suspicious of parliamentary reform and the secret ballot, Shaftesbury was said by Disraeli, the Conservative prime minister, to have done more than any other individual in his generation 'to elevate the conditions and raise the character of the working class'. Shaftesbury insisted that the upper- and middle-class Parliament must pass laws to 'protect those for whom neither wealth nor station nor age have raised a bulwark against tyranny'. Thus this 'friend of the friendless', who, as Gladstone put it, 'honoured God by serving his fellow men', spent his life exposing the awful conditions endured by the weak and the exploited – the child-workers in the factories and the coal-mines, the boy chimney-sweeps, the insane, the homeless and the slum-dwellers – and in securing effective legislation to eliminate or ameliorate the social abuses that sprang from the Industrial Revolution. He was in fact the embodiment of 'compassionate Conservatism'.

Factory-owners accused him of hypocrisy because poverty and squalor continued in the Dorset countryside, indeed on the family estates around Wimborne St Giles, Woodlands and Horton, but he had no control over these until the death of his father, who had little sympathy with his missionary zeal on behalf of the poor. As chairman at the dinner of the Sturminster Agricultural Society in 1843, he delivered a rousing appeal to the landowners and farmers present to take action against rural poverty. 'I ought not to be lynx-eyed to the misconduct of manufacturers and blind to the faults of landowners.' He urged his audience 'to mitigate the severity of the poor law . . . begin a more frequent and friendly discourse with the labouring man . . . respect his feelings; respect his rights; pay him in solid money'. He called upon farmers at harvest time to leave their fields open to gleaners – 'to the poor, the fatherless, and the widow'. Finally he spelt out his view of 'stewardship', and reminded his listeners that 'all wealth, talent, rank and power, are given by God for His own service, not for luxury; for the benefit of others, not for the pride of ourselves; and that we must render an account of privileges misused, of means perverted, of opportunities thrown away'. Ashley's viewpoint was at once denounced by his father, whilst George Bankes, who also spoke at the meeting, maintained that the accounts of poverty and squalor in Dorset were greatly exaggerated. Both Ashley and Bankes as Tories had been elected in 1841 pledged to uphold the Corn Laws, but bad harvests and the Irish potato famine caused Ashley, like his leader, the prime minister, Peel, to accept the view that the Corn Laws must be repealed so that imports of foreign wheat – in exchange for British manufactures – could help to keep the price of bread down to a reasonable level. The Whigs agreed with Peel's proposal to repeal the Corn Laws, but two-thirds of the Conservative M.P.s regarded this as a betrayal. J. J. Farquharson, of Langton House, 'the King of the Dorset farmers', was convinced that Repeal spelt ruin for the farmer and told Ashley bluntly that, if he voted for Repeal, he would be violating his election promises. Ashley held that Repeal would not injure the landowners 'if they did their duty by their estates and the people on them', but he lost the confidence of his constituents and resigned. It was only after 1851, when his father died and Ashley inherited the family estates and the title of Earl of Shaftesbury, that he was able to replace many of the tumbledown hovels with improved cottages, but even then he was handicapped by his own lack of money and experience, and embezzlement by his steward, R. S. Waters.

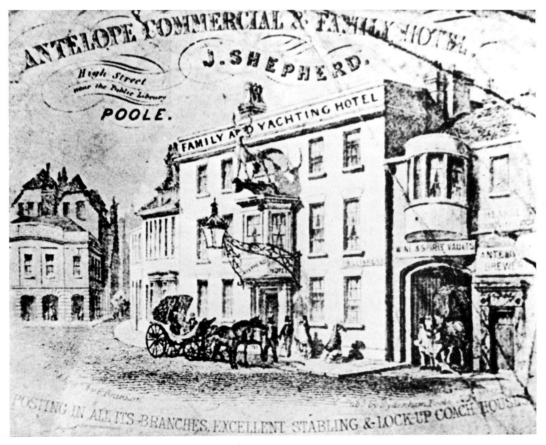

117. The first public library (1830) and the *Antelope Hotel*, Poole.

The third M.P. for Dorset elected in 1832 had been the Hon. William F. S. Ponsonby, who had been M.P. for Poole 1826-31, and was an ardent champion of Reform and Improvement. In 1830, jointly with Benjamin Lester-Lester, he gave Poole its first public library, located at the southern end of the High Street. This was a creditable first step, but only those who could pay a deposit of £10 and an annual subscription of a guinea could use it. Both Tories and Whigs on the Corporation agreed on a scheme to form a Poole Gasworks Company in order to provide the streets and quay with gas-lighting (1833), so that Poole became one of the first south-coast towns to be lit by gas. Ponsonby approved, but soon party strife broke out over whether a Tory or a Reformer contractor should provide the lamp standards. In the previous year the Tories had bitterly opposed the enlargement of the borough in the Reform Act to take in Longfleet, Parkstone and Hamworthy, being convinced that this had been brought about by the wicked Whig lord of the manor, intent on extending his control over Poole. Branksome was to be added in 1905, and Broadstone and Canford in 1933.

After the Corporation had passed a resolution in 1833 to the effect that 'a Bridge from Poole to Hamworthy would be of great public utility, more especially to the inhabitants of this town', Ponsonby gave the bridge scheme his enthusiastic support and asked whether the Corporation could contribute to the cost of building such a bridge. The Corporation replied that there were 'no funds to subscribe towards the proposed Bridge'. Ponsonby then promoted a Bill to authorise a private company to construct a bridge and to charge tolls for its use. It was now argued by many Tories that the building of a bridge would prevent the tidal waters from Holes Bay scouring out the channels from the Quay to Brownsea in order to preserve the depth of water at the Quay, an issue over which there was genuine concern. It was also feared that the already heavy burden of rates in the parish of St James would be increased if the building of a bridge were to encourage merchants living in old Poole to move their establishments across to Hamworthy outside the parish boundaries. When Ponsonby proposed that a turnpike road should be built from the Hamworthy end of the bridge to Upton, it was feared that road traffic to and from the west would be diverted down Poole's narrow streets and across the bridge because this route would involve a saving of two miles and that intolerable congestion would be caused in Poole. The opponents of the bridge accordingly managed to pass a resolution in a Vestry meeting saying 'That it is inexpedient to have a bridge from Poole to Hamworthy . . .' and that it would involve 'unnecessary expense'. The Corporation then authorised the town clerk, Mr. Parr, to oppose the Bill before a House of Commons Committee and he ran up a bill for over £1,260, which the Corporation then found could not be paid out of available funds. Ponsonby and the Poole M.P., Sir John Byng, were able to pass the Poole Bridge Bill in 1834. Ponsonby then went ahead with the erection of a wooden bridge with a steep gradient, which was to cause problems for the horses in years to come. It had a hand-operated centre span which could be swung open to let ships pass through. It cost some £9,600 and Ponsonby footed the bill. An alternative bridge with cast-iron arches on stone piers would have cost nearly three times as much. This first bridge was to be replaced in 1885 by a second bridge constructed of iron, but it continued to be operated by a private company charging tolls, until in 1926 Poole Council purchased it for nearly £16,000 and abolished the tolls. The present bridge was opened in 1927.

A leading Tory opponent of Ponsonby, the banker, George W. Ledgard, also made a bid to claim the gratitude of the townsfolk by sponsoring the building of an additional Anglican place of worship, St Paul's church in the High Street (1833). The Tories in the old Poole Corporation in 1834 deeply resented the victory of the lord of the manor over the Bridge Bill and the fact that his company would own the new bridge and be able to charge them to cross their own channel. They also resented the fact that Ponsonby was an influential member of the Whig establishment. His first cousin, Lord Althorp, had been Chancellor of the Exchequer (1830-34), whilst Ponsonby's brother-in-law, Lord Melbourne, was Home Secretary (1830-34) and then Prime Minister (1834; 1835-41). Melbourne's government in 1835 passed the Municipal Corporations Act replacing the old borough corporations, many

118.   The first Poole bridge.

119.   Poole's second bridge, opened 1885.

120. The third Poole bridge, opened 1927.

121. St Paul's church, Poole High Street, consecrated in 1833 and demolished in 1963.

of them extremely corrupt, by new councils elected by all male ratepayers and comprising councillors serving for three years, one-third of whom were to retire each year, and aldermen forming a quarter of the council, serving for six years, to be elected by the councillors. The old Poole Corporators had in fact looked after the interests of the community quite well, taking many sensible measures such as preserving oyster beds, protecting consumers, promoting good hygiene and widening some of the streets, but they were nevertheless a self-elective oligarchy. However, they sent a petition to the House of Lords against the proposed changes and argued that the vote should be confined to wealthier ratepayers, that annual elections would encourage party strife and that, if the Corporation's Admiralty jurisdiction were abolished, it would be impossible to protect the port and its fishermen. The petition failed.

There followed 16 years of bitter strife between the Liberals and the Tories, and prolonged and ruinous litigation. In 1835 the Whigs and the more radical Liberals with the encouragement of W. F. S. Ponsonby combined to form the Poole Reform Association with a sea-captain, G. L. Parrott, as president, whilst the Tories set up the Poole Conservative Association with the mayor, Robert Slade, as president. The first elections to the new Poole Borough Council were fought at the end of 1835 with great bitterness. In the 'North-West' Ward (half the old town together with Parkstone) nine Conservative councillors were elected and in the 'South-East' Ward (the other half of the old town plus Longfleet and Hamworthy), seven Reformers and two Conservatives were elected. The Conservative majority then elected six Conservatives as aldermen much to the disgust of the Reformers who held that at least two of their men would be selected. Thus the Conservatives had a majority of 15 to seven on the Council. The rancour continued as Reformers and Tories each accused the other side of bribery in the election. Costly lawsuits followed.

A further complication was that Robert H. Parr, the last town clerk of the old Corporation (1833-6), claimed £4,500 as compensation for the loss of this post and various other minor offices, and, perhaps because he was a staunch Tory and ally, the Tory majority on the council agreed to pay him and proposed to impose an enormous rate to raise the necessary money. The Reformers, who believed that Parr had fraudulently helped the Tories in the March 1835 election, protested that such a rate was illegal and Mr. Ponsonby himself served a High Court writ on the new council alleging that its agreement to pay compensation to Parr was illegal. Party strife was intensified when Russell, the Whig Home Secretary, appointed six new magistrates, all Reformers, who then refused to uphold summonses against the many Poole householders who refused to pay the new Tory rates to compensate the greedy ex-town clerk. In 1839 officers of the High Court seized all the property of the Corporation including the Guildhall, its fine furniture, the Borough's ancient seals, the two great maces of office and the silver oar of the water bailiff, and gave Mr. Parr possession of them. The council was virtually bankrupt and there was no money to feed the prisoners in the gaol or to make the usual grants to the poor. Likewise, since there was no money to pay for the gas used in the street lamps, the town was plunged into darkness in the winter evenings. Incidentally, while the Tories were in power on the council (1836-40), Poole's two M.P.s were Liberals – one of them from 1837 to 1847 being Charles F. A. S. Ponsonby, the son of the lord of the manor. Meanwhile W. F. S. Ponsonby himself had been raised to the peerage as Lord de Mauley (1838) but, when his wife died in 1844, it was necessary under her grandfather's will for him to sell the estates and pass them or the proceeds on to the children. Thus the Ponsonby connection with Poole came to an end in 1847, the Canford estate having been sold for £335,000 to an iron-master from South Wales, Sir Josiah John Guest. Eventually the Court of Chancery decided that the persistent R. H. Parr was entitled to compensation, amounting with costs to nearly £7,000, and to meet this bill the council sold the Rectory and the right to nominate the rector of St James's, and also raised a loan

122. The Old Fish Shambles, Poole Quay.

of £5,000 from the Economic Assurance Company, to be repaid in instalments down to 1865.

Just at this time in the 1840s when the prestige of the council and its financial resources were at their lowest ebb, Poole's economy was likewise in the doldrums. The Newfoundland trade had come to an end apart from the Northern Slades' sealing activities; the oyster beds had been over-dredged to extinction, and fewer and fewer people came to the market on the Fish Shambles. In 1847 the extension of the London and South Western Railway from Southampton to Dorchester by way of the winding 'Castleman's Corkscrew' via Ringwood, Broadstone and Hamworthy Junction was completed and on 21 May the first train arrived by a branch line from Hamworthy Junction at a station called Poole near the Hamworthy side of the bridge. One might have thought that the advent of the railway would have meant steady economic revival for Poole, but, in fact, it resulted in the collapse of the considerable coastal trade operating from Poole Quay and employing 64 ships in 1847. By 1852 there were no Poole ships thus employed. Several of the merchants moved out of their Georgian houses in the old town and many of these were divided into tenements and let out to the poorer members of the community and too often allowed to deteriorate. In the latter half of the 19th century Poole's Thursday market steadily declined. In 1851 the fish market was largely deserted and fish caught had increasingly been taken to other towns. More and more foodstuffs were sold in permanent shops, especially those established in the High Street. The May Fair seems to have died out by the opening of the 20th century, although the November Fair continued fitfully, but only as a 'fun-fair'.

Another local domestic industry which collapsed after 1850 was button-making. The Case family of Shaftesbury and Bere Regis had built up a flourishing business making decorative buttons. Originally these consisted of discs of sheep horn covered with embroidered linen. In the 18th century these horn discs were replaced by wire rings on which a wide variety of designs – eventually over 100 – were embroidered by women in their cottages who, if skilled, could earn much more than they could working in the fields. At Lytchett Minster there was a depot in a room in the St Peter's Finger inn where once a week the buttons were offered for sale and the women received their wages and new materials. Then in 1850 the newly-invented Ashton's patent machine began mass-producing wire rings covered with cloth and these could be sold at a price with which the Dorset women, making buttons by hand, were unable to compete. Some 1,000 workers were plunged into poverty, although some were helped by local gentry to emigrate to Canada and Australia. Buttoning lingered on at Lytchett Minster into the early 20th century, but button-making by hand had as a whole been destroyed.

It was precisely at this time of strife and stagnation at Poole that 'the marine village' at the mouth of the Bourne in the barren heathland between Poole and Christchurch began its explosive growth into a major seaside resort. Bournemouth in 1851 had a population of only 691, compared with Poole's 9,255; by 1881 Poole's population had increased to 12,301, thanks mainly to the growth of Longfleet and Parkstone, but Bournemouth had outstripped Poole with a population of 16,859 – a 24-fold increase in a generation. The Dorset squire, Captain Lewis Tregonwell of Cranborne Lodge, who had been stationed at the mouth of the Bourne at the time of the Napoleonic invasion scare of 1804-5, is commonly regarded as 'the founder of Bournemouth' since he was the 'first proprietor resident'. He bought eight and a half acres of land there from Sir George Ivison Tapps, lord of the manor of Christchurch, for £179 11s. and duly built what they called 'The Mansion' and took up residence there in the spring of 1812. Later, when it was let to the Marchioness of Exeter, it was known as Exeter House and it is now incorporated within the structure of the Royal Exeter Hotel. Tregonwell purchased more land and built on it more large houses in assorted styles set in extensive grounds and thus laid the foundations of Bournemouth's special charm.

Meanwhile Sir George Tapps, impressed by the elegance of Tregonwell's developments, had further beautified the area by planting large numbers of pines, and his son, Sir George Tapps-Gervis, employed a brilliant young architect, Benjamin Ferrey, to design a marine watering place, which he hoped would soon rival Weymouth and Brighton. Ferrey was responsible for the planning of Westover Gardens and the building of the Westover Villas and the (Royal) Bath Hotel, opened by Sir George Gervis on Queen Victoria's coronation day in 1838. Bournemouth's destiny was further affected by the enthusiastic praise it received from Dr. A. B. Granville in his celebrated book *The Spas of England* (1842), in which he declared that Bournemouth had the potential to become 'the very first invalid sea-watering place in England' and 'a winter residence for the delicate constitutions requiring a warm and sheltered locality' and 'ideal for patients in the most delicate state of health as to the lungs and for the wealthy afflicted with disease'. Dr. Granville insisted, 'You must not let in . . . brick-and-mortar contractors to build up whole streets of lodging houses or parades and terraces interminable, in straight lines facing the sea', but the aim must be to develop a unique resort 'for the upper and wealthier classes of society'. Dr. Aitken, of Poole, examined the waters of the Bourne and pronounced them to be quite free from any infiltration of dung. In 1856 the Bournemouth Improvement Act empowered 13 commissioners, including the Poole banker, George Ledgard, to levy rate of up to 3s. in the £ to facilitate improved paving, sewerage, draining, lighting and cleansing and to borrow up to £5,000 to build a new pier. Gas lighting came in 1864, piped water soon afterwards, and a cemetery in 1878. A London physician, Dr. Dobell, extolled the medical benefits of Bournemouth, especially the balmy, resinous aroma from the pine-trees, invaluable, he believed, in the cure of many chest complaints, and he built in 1881 the Mont Dore Hotel (now Bournemouth Town Hall) so that sufferers from a wide range of diseases could drink, gargle and bathe in some special mineral water which he had imported from France.

Sea-bathing was also becoming very popular, although strict by-laws were introduced to maintain propriety. Although there were a few limited areas where mixed bathing was permitted, elsewhere it was an offence to bathe within 20 yards of an area reserved for the opposite sex and ladies were specifically required to wear a tunic or blouse reaching from neck to knees with a belt and knickerbocker drawers. Bathing-huts, donkeys, rowing-boats, Punch-and-Judy shows were additional amenities and an iron pier was constructed in 1880. Paddle-steamers provided sea-trips to Swanage. Horse-buses were available for those without their own carriages. As the population grew, so Bournemouth needed and secured more self-government. In 1890 it became a municipal borough and in 1900 a County Borough, with an elected council having powers equal to those of the Dorset and Hampshire County Councils. In 1918 it was to obtain its own M.P.

Mr. Merton Russell-Cotes, mayor in 1894, became a great benefactor since he and his wife were to bequeath their home, East Cliff House, and a fine art collection to form the Russell-Cotes Museum and Art Gallery. In 1893 Dan Godfrey set up the Municipal Orchestra, the forerunner of the Bournemouth Symphony Orchestra. Estate agents like William Rebbeck and Anthony Stoddart Fox set up in business to deal with the booming market in houses, whilst solicitors like Henry Mooring Aldridge from Poole arrived to draw up the necessary deeds as well as the wills for the growing number of wealthy but ageing residents. More and more shops opened their doors and among them was a needlework shop started by a retired missionary, Frederick Bright, and the Fancy Fair launched by a Weymouth draper and lay preacher, John Elmes Beale, famous for his business skill and his absolute integrity. Later he was to become a popular and effective mayor. These small shops were soon to grow into multi-storey department stores.

All this development would have been impossible, of course, but for the advent of the railway. When the L.S.W.R. opened its line from Southampton to Dorchester in 1847, there was no reason why it should pass through Bournemouth with its 500 inhabitants. For many years therefore travellers from London would alight at Christchurch Road (now Holmsley) Station and complete the last 12 miles to Bournemouth by horse-drawn bus, which ran thrice daily to the Bath Hotel. In 1862 a very slow branch line was inaugurated from Ringwood to Christchurch and in 1870 this was extended to 'Bournemouth East' station in Holdenhurst Road. But the Commissioner insisted that the line should be kept well away from the select area of the town. The station was in fact sited in an area of brickworks. Soon railway links with the west and north were established. In 1872 a new branch line from Broadstone ('Poole Junction') was built to the east of Holes Bay and a station was opened at Poole on its present site. Then in 1874 the line was extended eastwards from Poole through Parkstone and Branksome to Bournemouth West, and this meant that both Bournemouth and Poole were linked by way of the Somerset and Dorset Railway to Bath and the west and north. Between 1871 and 1881 Bournemouth's population increased almost threefold. Later in 1888 a new branch line to Bournemouth from Brockenhurst – long opposed by the New Forest authorities on the grounds particularly of fire risks – was opened, whilst after 1893, when a causeway was built across Holes Bay, trains could run direct from Waterloo to Bournemouth and Poole and then on to Weymouth.

Incidentally, when in 1874 the line from Poole to Bournemouth was constructed, a causeway was built across part of the harbour thus creating what became the seawater Poole Park Lake. Many travellers arriving at Poole by rail have been impressed by the experience of gliding along this causeway with water below on both sides. Likewise the construction of the line only slightly above sea-level at the station made it necessary to cut across

123. Construction of the footbridge at the High Street level crossing, 1874.

124. The High Street level crossing.

Towngate Street and Poole High Street and to construct footbridges and crossing gates which had to be closed whenever a train was approaching. Waiting for the crossing gates to open has been a major feature of Poole life for more than a century. One pair of crossing gates has been eliminated with the building of the Towngate Flyover, but the other pair remains.

125. *Waterwitch*, the last square-rigged vessel to trade under the red ensign from a home port. She was built in 1871 by Thomas Medus of Poole and made her last trip in British waters, carrying coal, in 1936.

The rapid development of Bournemouth, although it meant that Bournemouth outstripped the ancient borough of Poole in population in the 1870s, nevertheless gave a new stimulus to Poole's economy. In order to meet the needs of the Bournemouth building boom, timber was imported from the Baltic and North America to Poole in great sailing ships, and there emerged such family firms of timber merchants as J. T. Sydenham & Co. and John J. Norton, which still flourish, and which had their own wharves along the West Quay. Roofing slates were also brought into Poole Quay from North Wales. There was abundant clay on both sides of the harbour to provide the raw material for bricks, floor and wall tiles, and pipes. In 1856 the South Western Pottery Company was established in Parkstone by George Jennings, a London businessman, and bricks, drainpipes and, later, sanitary fittings were manufactured to meet the needs not only of the expanding districts of Parkstone, Longfleet and Bournemouth, but also of many overseas markets. The South Western Pottery went on to specialise in the production of cream terracotta ware in the form of decorative chimneys, door and window surrounds and such special local features as the eagles on the gateways of Poole Park and the Poole coat-of-arms in the wall of the lodge at the western end of the park. Another pottery was set up to produce bricks and pipes at Bourne Valley by Sharp, Jones & Co. A small pottery producing red floor tiles was started on the East Quay by a certain James Walker. In 1873 he sold it to Jesse Carter, an ironmonger and builders' merchant from Weybridge, Surrey. Jesse Carter moved his young family to No. 20 Market Street and later was able to buy West End House, the fine Georgian mansion alongside St James's church. One son, William, ran a little brickyard at Foxholes, Parkstone, and married Eliza, eldest daughter of Councillor Alfred Balston, a Poole ship-owner and owner of a rope-works on the West Shore. His two younger brothers, Charles and Owen Carter, were to marry two other daughters of Councillor Balston. William Carter later purchased the so-called 'Kinson Pottery' at Newtown. Meanwhile Jesse Carter at his Poole Pottery was producing not only 'Carters Red' floor tiles but also glazed, modelled and painted wall tiles, and in 1895 he purchased the Architectural Pottery at Hamworthy specialising in architectural faience and floor tiles. Jesse Carter took two of his young sons, Charles and Owen, into partnership. Charles, who earlier had worked in the ironmongers (now W. E. Boone & Co.), became a borough councillor and later mayor, and made notable contributions to education, especially by campaigning for the establishment of Poole Grammar School. Owen Carter specialised in the artistic and chemical aspects of potting and was largely responsible for the pre-eminent position in artistic ceramics achieved by Poole Pottery in the 20th century on the rapidly expanding East Quay works. Clay from the south of Poole Harbour continued to be transported in barges across to Poole Quay to be sent by sea to the Staffordshire potteries and many foreign destinations. Between 1866 and 1956 a

126. Terracotta Poole coat of arms, Poole Park Lodge near Park Gates West.

127. Terracotta gate-post, Park Gates West, made by the South-Western Pottery.

tramway, constructed by Pike Bros., brought the clay to Ridge on the river Frome, whilst Fayle & Co. operated a tramway from Norden to Middlemere and Goathorn from 1806 onwards, one of the earliest such lines in southern England. However, by 1914 railways were seriously competing with ships in the transport of clay. Export of clay by ship virtually ceased in the 1950s, although a small but steady export trade in clay by sea has continued into the 1980s, but sadly almost entirely in foreign ships.

In 1884 Daniel Ballam purchased from Lord Wimborne a site at Foxholes in Newtown and there excavated the clay and made bricks. For five generations the Ballam family has been in charge of brick-making here and at Creekmoor and currently at Beacon Hill, Corfe Mullen. Sand lime (calcium silicate) bricks are produced at this last site. As many as 75 clay-working sites have been located in the Borough of Poole, operated over the past 135 years but usually only for very short periods. Before the First World War haulage dependent upon horses limited the area a brickyard could supply to a radius of five to ten miles. Many brickworks shut down in the winter because frost prevented manufacture and the men would then go to work for the Gas Company until spring.

In 1895 H. & H. Burden, ship chandlers and coal merchants, owned two small steamships in which they imported coal to Poole for the use of the growing conurbation. Likewise G. & T. Belben, corn merchants, owned three small vessels which imported grain, which was then milled to meet the flour requirements of the hinterland. By this time many ships were of deeper draught and a vast improvement was effected by the Poole Corporation in 1893-5 when the quay was extended in an easterly direction and also outwards so that a much greater depth of water alongside the quay was secured.

To meet the need for iron products an ironmonger named William Pearce had in 1841 established a foundry on a triangular site at Baiter Green between Green Road and South Road. Poole Foundry was later owned by Stephen Lewin and manufactured threshing machines and a patent folding stacker and elevator for the rural areas, besides a variety of steam launches and yachts, as well as colliery, tramway and railway locomotives. Widely respected as a benevolent employer, Lewin granted his workmen a nine-hour day in 1872 and 70 of them showed their appreciation by marching round the town carrying banners and flags and headed by a brass band until they reached Lewin's house where the band played and three hearty cheers were given. Sadly Lewin went bankrupt in 1883, after a serious fire had caused him heavy losses in 1876 and his works manager, William Tarrant, left and became the manager of the rival Dorset Iron Foundry in West Quay Road. The premises of the Poole Foundry later became Butler's Brush Factory until that too was brought to an end by a fire in 1956. The Dorset Foundry specialised in casting drain gratings, manhole covers and lamp posts, ornamented with the Poole Borough coat of arms.

Another growing industry in 19th-century Poole, despite the Temperance movement, was brewing. The Towngate and Poole Breweries, founded in 1795 by James and Joseph King, later merged and were taken over in the 1850s by Frederick Styring. He operated in impressive premises in Dean Hay Lane and had agencies in Bournemouth and Wimborne and as far afield as Sturminster Newton and Southampton. As the need for consumer goods increased with the growth of Longfleet, Parkstone and Bournemouth, so the number of shops increased in Poole High Street, where the lower portions of several grand Georgian houses were converted into shops. Two particularly impressive shop fronts were those of J. A. Hawkes, boot and shoe manufacturer and leather seller, founded in 1830 and close by W. E. Boone & Co., ironmongers. These two old-established firms flourish in the same premises today.

There was a steady demand for footwear in the 19th century, when so much more walking was essential. Some speeding-up of communications came with the advent of bicycles in the 1890s and the Osborne Cycle Co. sprang up in Poole to supply them. Moreover in 1900

128. Hawkes's boot and shoe shop, No. 99 High Street, Poole, in 1897. At the left-hand doorway is Joseph Alfred Hawkes who was Mayor of Poole in 1911.

129. The unchanging shop-front of W. E. Boone & Co.

Poole. Town Cellars.

130. The Town Cellars or 'Woolhouse': an early 20th-century scene.

131. Longfleet tram terminus and interchange, 1902.

the Poole and District Electric Traction Company spent £64,000 laying tramlines and overhead wires to link Poole Station via Park Gates East, North Road, Constitution Hill and Ashley Road to County Gates on the border with Bournemouth, and during the years 1901-5 it successfully operated a fleet of pale blue and white tram cars, the whole journey from Poole to Westbourne costing only 3d. The Poole Corporation then bought up the private company and made an arrangement with the Bournemouth Corporation by which the new trams ran from Poole right into Bournemouth, and continued to operate for the next 30 years.

COLE AND SIDBALL,
LINEN DRAPERS, SILK MERCERS,
Haberdashers, &c.,
120, HIGH STREET, POOLE.

Funerals completely Furnished with every article of Family Mourning.

Chapter Twelve

The Guests and their World

Poole's development was very closely linked with the Guest family for some 80 years after the Canford estate was purchased in 1846 by Sir J. J. Guest. Hearing that Lord de Mauley wished to sell, he and his young wife, Lady Charlotte, had visited Canford. She was enraptured. 'The gardens, the house, the village, the grounds and trees around it, and above all the clear blue river, conspire to make it a delightful place'. And so Sir John bought Canford manor for £335,000. He owned Britain's largest iron works – at Dowlais in South Wales – and in 1833 he had married Lady Charlotte Bertie, daughter of the 9th Earl of Lindsey, 27 years his junior, only three months after their first meeting. Because she had married 'into trade', it was some years before she again became socially acceptable in aristocratic circles, yet this remarkable lady was to earn an international reputation as a scholar and as an art expert. As a dutiful Victorian wife she gave birth to five sons and five daughters within the space of 13 years. During that time, having already learnt seven foreign languages, she embarked upon the challenging task of learning Welsh and then translating into English the great Welsh medieval epic, the *Mabinogion*. Lady Charlotte arranged for Sir Charles Barry to supervise extensive alterations to make Canford House an even grander building. Her husband was the Liberal M.P. for Merthyr and she herself was an ardent Liberal who strongly supported Peel's repeal of the Corn Laws as she put it, 'to give the people bread and abolish that wicked tax on corn', at a time when Protectionist Tories like George Bankes were accusing Peel of betraying the farmers and the landowners. She regarded the Chartist demand for full democracy as dangerously premature at a time when half the working men were illiterate, but she put her finger on the main cause of Chartist agitation when she declared 'Something *must* be done for our unemployed'. Meanwhile the Dowlais Ironworks flourished as a result of the boom in railway construction both here and abroad. When in 1851 the St Petersburg-Moscow railway was to be opened, her husband was disappointed not to be able to attend, since Dowlais had supplied most of the railway lines for it. The following year he died and for the next few years Lady Charlotte had to manage the ironworks and to bring up her large family.

She employed Charles Schreiber, a young Cambridge scholar, as tutor to her eldest son, Ivor, and fell in love with him when she nursed him back to health after he almost died of a fever. In 1855 Lady Charlotte, a 42-year-old widow married the 28-year-old tutor, in the face of opposition from most members of the family. The love-match produced a very happy marriage despite the fact that Schreiber was a Conservative because, as she said, 'Knowing we could not agree on it, we determined never to speak on politics to each other at all'. However, later when in 1878 Britain seemed on the verge of war with Russia after Russia had invaded Turkey to liberate the Bulgarians and proposed to set up a Russian satellite state extending to the Mediterranean, Lady Charlotte confessed that, 'I go with the Conservatives on their eastern and foreign policy, and I utterly abhor Gladstone and all his works politically speaking'. She and her husband went to Berlin, when the Congress was held in which Disraeli, the Conservative prime minister, put pressure on the Russians so that they accepted a compromise agreement, and there she renewed her acquaintance with Disraeli, who in her young days had sent her flowers and escorted her to a concert and an exhibition. At the time her cousin and son-in-law, Sir Henry Layard, who had won fame excavating carved sculptures in the ancient Assyrian town of Nimrud, which he mistakenly believed to be Nineveh, was British Ambassador to Turkey and played a leading part in the Berlin settlement. In the very heated General Election of 1880 her husband, Charles Schreiber, was elected as M.P. for Poole – as a Conservative, by just 6 votes – after he had been hit in the face by a stone and threatened by gangs of 'roughs' and after 'several small outrages' such as 'fires in the heaths and plantations' of the Canford estates. Two of her sons, standing as Conservatives, were defeated but a third, 'Monty', 'triumphed at Wareham of which I am most glad'. He was the Liberal candidate and defeated C. Drax (the Conservative). Charles Schreiber died in 1884, still only fifty-seven. During her many tours of Europe with her husband, Lady Charlotte had built up a unique collection of china which she donated to the Victoria and Albert Museum in memory of her husband. She had also amassed collections of fans and playing cards which she presented to the British Museum. Sadly she developed glaucoma and became completely blind and after 58 years had to give up writing her journal. She died in 1895 whilst visiting her beloved Canford House.

132. The kitchen staff in John of Gaunt's Kitchen, Canford House, about 1900.

Canford had acquired a new mistress in 1868 when Sir Ivor Guest married Lady Cornelia Churchill, daughter of the Duke of Marlborough – as charming and strong-willed as her mother-in-law, Lady Charlotte. Sir Ivor was raised to the peerage in 1880 as Baron Wimborne of Canford Magna. He was a kindly landlord and employer and a great

133. Foundation plaque of the Free Library, 1887.

134. Poole Free Public Library in Mount Street.

benefactor to the area. He was responsible for the erection of new churches in Upper and Lower Parkstone as well as Broadstone and for the establishment of new schools in Broadstone and Longfleet. It was he, too, who founded the Broadstone and Parkstone golf-courses. Lady Cornelia was actively involved in many of the schemes for the improvement of the area. In fact, one mayor of Poole, P. E. L. Budge, made the comment that 'she had an irresistible way of getting her own way which would cause any man who did not agree with her to fly to the uttermost ends of the earth'.

As the Golden Jubilee of Queen Victoria's accession approached, discussions took place as to the best way to mark the occasion in Poole. Lady Wimborne pressed for a hospital, but in fact it was the suggestion of the timber merchant, J. J. Norton, for a free public library that won the day. Lord Wimborne provided a suitable central site in Mount Street (now the northern end of Lagland Street) and J. J. Norton undertook to meet the whole cost of erecting the building (£2,500), which was duly opened in November 1887; he also gave a further £2,200 to provide a museum and gymnasium on the same site. Over in Bournemouth a hospital scheme to mark the Queen's jubilee was approved and, on land donated by William Clapcott Dean and his heir, James Cooper Dean, in 1887 the foundation stone was laid of what became the Royal Victoria Hospital, officially opened by the Prince of Wales in 1890. Lady Wimborne meanwhile started a small infirmary for the poor in a house in West Street and then in 1890 persuaded her husband to buy Sir Peter Thompson's mansion to provide larger premises to accommodate 30 beds. In 1906 Lord Wimborne donated two-and-a-half acres of land in Longfleet for a new hospital and this was opened in 1907 by his wife and was appropriately named the New Cornelia Hospital.

Yet another gift to the Corporation of Poole by Lord Wimborne was an area of 40 acres alongside Parkstone Bay for the creation of a 'People's Park'. Lord Wimborne's only condition was that the Corporation should lay out the site as a public park 'as soon as possible' and maintain it as such for the use of the inhabitants of Poole for ever. The work was well done and the park developed into a uniquely charming attraction for residents and visitors alike with its cricket field, salt-water boating lake, fresh-water lake with a fascinating variety of wild birds, tennis courts, bowling green, miniature railway, palm trees and flower beds. Poole Park was officially opened by the Prince of Wales (the future King Edward VII). He and several members of his family were due to stay at Canford with Lord and Lady Wimborne in January 1890, and it was arranged that the Prince should officially open the Royal Victoria Hospital at Westbourne and also Parkstone and Poole Parks. But on Saturday, 19 January the opening of Poole Park did not quite go according to plan, for an overnight gale flattened the large marquee in which the opening ceremony was to take place and the Bournemouth Silver Band was to play the National Anthem. In the event the official opening of the park took place in the booking office of Poole Railway Station just before the Prince took his departure by train. Appropriately in 1896 Lord Wimborne was chosen as mayor of Poole in recognition of his many benefactions to the borough, despite the fact that he had never served as an elected councillor.

The author's grandfather in his holiday journal recorded two visits he paid to Bournemouth and the area at Easter in 1891 and 1892. On each occasion the rail journey from Clapham Junction (South London) to Bournemouth East took 4 hours 25 minutes and the return excursion fare for himself and one child amounted to 15s. 0d., and three return tickets to Swanage cost 3s. 0d. The total cost of fares, accommodation, and refreshments for one adult and a child for eight days was £3 4s. 9d. Like Mr. Gladstone, whom he much admired, he was a great walker, and so he walked

> along the beach to Durley Chine and past Canford Chine (broken sea-wall, all in ruins) and had refreshment at the Flagstaff Cottage, kept by Miss Eliza Jane Ridout (bread, ham, cheese and 6 large glasses of milk – total cost 1s. 0d.) smugglers once lived here. Near the Haven Hotel picked

135. Skating on Poole Park lake, *c.*1910.

up a pipe-fish – numerous sand-hills, and razor fishes about 6 in. long. Walked to Parkstone-on-Sea, passed the Beehive Inn and Model Farm Dairy, which we thoroughly inspected. Thence by the new road, close to the Harbour, under the Railway Arch, thro' the People's Park (laid out by the Corporation – land given by Lord Wimborne). Visited the Free Library (1887) in Mount Street . . . Reached Bournemouth E. 10 p.m.

On 12 April 1892:

Started for Wimborne 11 a.m. walking (very cloudy, threatening weather), thro' Lansdowne Road . . . thro' Winton (oil lamps and pine posts) . . . thro' Moordown, Redhill, Kinson and Canford. At 1 o'clock very warm indeed and sunshine. Saw a great many butterflies (especially admirals) . . . Bees' nest over the bay window under the tiles at the Lodge at Lord Wimborne's (the woman residing there told me she sold the honey for 18/- and obtained 4 gallons of mead from the produce of the nest last season). Visited the Church and Manor. Splendid view of R. Stour from the road. . . . Walked over the railway bridge and saw a very large number of bee-hives in adjoining garden; the Coach 'Tally-Ho' passed on entering Wimborne. Crossed the bridge over R. Stour [he noted a Dorset

notice warning that any person wilfully damaging the bridge was liable to transportation for life].
Saw a man fishing who had caught several dace. Lovely walk by the side of the Stour.

He then thoroughly explored Wimborne Minster, inspecting the Beaufort tomb, the 'Man
in the Wall' and the Chained Library and

left Wimborne 7 p.m. by train for Bournemouth West (10d. single) thro' Broadstone Jn., Poole and
Parkstone, arriving 7.25. Stroll on West Cliff until 9.30. Needles Light (red revolving) clearly seen.

At the end of the 19th century educational advance was very much under discussion. In
previous centuries whether children secured any schooling largely depended on whether
any local benefactor had endowed a school. At Pamphill in 1698 a school for 40 boys and
almshouses for four poor men and four poor women over 55 years of age were built from a
bequest under the will of Roger Gillingham. The schoolmaster, who must be unmarried,
was paid the quite high salary of £20 a year and one of his duties was to read a chapter
from the New Testament each day at 11 a.m. and 5 p.m. to the assembled children and
almsfolk. The building and its commemorative tablet is still there. At Corfe Mullen a
school was endowed under the will of Richard Lockyer in 1706 and provided that, in return
for a weekly fee of 2d., 30 boys and girls were to be instructed in reading and needlework
by a discreet spinster. Each Whitsun Monday the mistress and pupils were to be examined
by the rector in the catechism and as a reward they were each to receive a penny loaf. The
trustees might also provide frocks for the girls and smocks for the boys. The scholars also
had to take it in turns to sweep out the school. The present Lockyer's School has been
enlarged and developed on the same site. At Sturminster Marshall in 1799 William
Mackrell left £1,200 to pay for the teaching of local children. At first the schoolmaster had
to teach them in his own house, but a local squire, William Churchill, donated some land
on which the school was built in 1832 with help from the National Society for the Education
of the Poor in the Principles of the Established Church, launched by the Rev. Andrew Bell,
rector of Swanage, one of the pioneers of the monitorial system under which much of the
teaching was done by older, brighter pupils, a device that did at any rate provide inexpensive
education.
    In Poole a day school had grown out of a Sunday School attached to St James's church
with over two hundred pupils by 1821. With the help of the National Society, the Corporation
and subscriptions organised by the Conservative Anglican banker, R. Ledgard, a new
National School was established in 1835 at Perry Gardens at the northern end of Lagland
Street. The subjects taught were reading, writing and arithmetic together with religious
instruction according to the particular beliefs of the Church of England. Nonconformists
had meanwhile established their own school attached to Skinner Street chapel which was
enlarged in 1833 to accommodate the Lancastrian Free School for Boys linked to the British
and Foreign School Society. This 'British School' taught the '3 Rs' and the study of the
Bible without the doctrines of any particular church being inculcated. In 1847 a British
School for Girls was set up with special emphasis on needlework and fees of 2d. per week
per pupil (with a special rate of 3d. for two sisters and 4d. for three sisters). The Education
Act of 1833 provided government grants to the two voluntary societies, the National and
the British, to be divided in proportion to their own individual contributions. In 1862 since
the National School had become overcrowded, a new National School for Girls and Infants
was built, near St James's church – what later became the church hall. The British Schools
were replaced in 1912 by a new South Road elementary school for children up to 14 under
the local authority. Primary education had been made compulsory in 1880 and free in 1891.
    The Conservative Balfour Education Act of 1902 set up Education Committees of local
councils to supervise schools financed out of public funds and gave additional financial aid

136. 1628 foundation stone of Thomas Robartes' Free Grammar School, Poole, now in Scaplen's Court.

out of the rates to National Schools. Some Nonconformist Liberals in Poole refused to pay their rates as a protest against public money being used to finance the teaching of the doctrines of the Church of England. The Balfour Act also empowered councils to establish, and to maintain out of the rates, secondary schools, offering foreign languages, science and other subjects beyond the '3 Rs' to pupils up to the age of 16 or 18, where no old-established grammar existed, as in Wimborne with its Queen Elizabeth's Grammar School. The free grammar school set up in Thames Street, Poole, by Thomas Robartes in 1628 had degenerated by the early 19th century into a school providing merely the '3 Rs' to a few poor children, and it was closed down in 1835. During the 18th century several dissenting academies specialising in mathematics and navigation had flourished in Poole and perhaps it was a teacher in such an academy whose burial was recorded in the parish register of St James's in these words: '1789 Feb. 27. George Strong, an old Experienc'd Navigator; he taught Navigation for upwards of 30 years and then Resigned his Soul to God'.

Thus throughout the 19th century Poole was without any secondary education. That deficiency was remedied by the energetic action of Councillor Charles Carter, director of Poole Pottery, who persuaded the Poole Borough Council to apply to the government for official sanction to set up a secondary school for boys and girls. It began in a very modest way in 1904, housed in the building which now accommodates the Poole Museum Service in Mount Street (now part of Lagland Street), close to the 1887 Free Library. In 1907 a new building for Poole Secondary School was erected in Kingland Road near the west gates of Poole Park on land donated by Lord Wimborne, and one of these first pupils, now aged over ninety, remembers seeing a farmer driving his cattle to what was then an essentially rural site. There were some free places for 'scholarship children', selected by examination, and after 1907 at least 25 per cent. of the places had to be free. However, fees were very modest and many shopkeepers and master craftsmen were ready to pay to obtain a more advanced education for their children. Soon to be known just as Poole School, it was renamed Poole Grammar School in 1927. Under two early headmasters, A. J. Mockridge (1908-27) and A. W. M. Greenfield (1927-50), Poole's grammar school strove successfully for academic excellence and by 1914 one old pupil, a girl, Gladys France, had obtained a university degree. Thus the new school provided a ladder of advancement for large numbers of Poole children with intelligence and an academic bent, although for most of the 'highfliers' at this period teaching was in the main the only profession open to them.

Bournemouth as a town of recent and rapid growth, of course, had no ancient endowed schools, but in 1886 a private grammar school for girls was opened as the Bournemouth High School, later renamed Talbot Heath School. In 1901 the Bournemouth Council opened a Secondary and Technical School for boys on the Portchester Road site and later this developed into 'Bournemouth School', a fully fledged grammar school. Not until 1918 was a similar municipal grammar school for girls established in its own premises, although Bournemouth Municipal College – with a technical bias – had been opened at Lansdowne in 1913.

Among the earliest residents in the Bournemouth area was Sir Percy Shelley. He lived in Boscombe Manor and was buried in the churchyard of St Peter's church and with him the heart of his father, the poet. Earlier Sir Percy had arranged for the reinterment of the remains of his mother, Mary Shelley, author of *Frankenstein* and of her parents, William Godwin, the militant anarchist and author of *Political Justice*, and Mary Wollstonecraft Godwin, the pioneer feminist who wrote *A Vindication of the Rights of Women* – a revolutionary trio indeed for conventional Bournemouth. Among the visitors attracted to Bournemouth were the philanthropist, Lord Shaftesbury, the Liberal prime minister, W. E. Gladstone, and his great Tory rival, Disraeli, who once held a cabinet meeting in the Royal Bath

137. The old Poole Grammar School building (1907-88).

Hotel. The Swedish queen, Sophia, was restored to good health here after many years of serious illness and when her grateful husband, King Oscar II, laid the foundation stone of the Mont Dore Hotel, he proposed the toast 'The Welfare of Bournemouth' saying that his wife had found there 'a quiet and comfortable home, mildness of climate and kindness from everyone'.

138. Lillie Langtry, portrayed on a Jersey stamp.

Lillie Langtry (née Emilie Charlotte le Breton), celebrated society beauty, lived for several years in the Red House, now the Langtry Manor Hotel in Derby Road, which was built for her by her royal lover, Edward, Prince of Wales. She scratched on a downstairs window with a diamond ring two hearts pierced by an arrow and the word 'Dora', Edward's pet name for her. There are many literary associations with Bournemouth. Robert Louis Stevenson lived in various houses in Bournemouth and Branksome in the hope of curing his tuberculosis, and whilst there he wrote *The Strange Case of Dr. Jekyll and Mr. Hyde* and *Kidnapped* (1886). John Galsworthy spent five years at a preparatory school in Bournemouth and Rupert Brooke paid many visits here to stay with his grandfather and aunts.

Lord and Lady Wimborne entertained lavishly at Canford and among the visitors was her nephew, the youthful Winston Churchill, who, whilst staying at their seaside house, Branksome Dene, spent three days unconscious after falling from a bridge in Alum Chine. When Joseph Chamberlain tried to persuade the Conservatives to adopt Tariff Reform, involving protective duties on foreign manufactures and also on food, which would raise the cost of living for the working class, Lady Wimborne persuaded her family and Winston Churchill to cross over to join the Liberal Party in order to uphold Free Trade. Thus the Guest family circle played a leading role in helping to lay the foundations of the Welfare State, notably by the introduction of old-age pensions, and fully supported Lloyd George's 'People's Budget' of 1909 in which he proposed to pay for these pensions and also more battleships with additional taxes on the rich, especially landowners. Lady Wimborne's second son, Henry Guest, was Liberal M.P. for East Dorset between the two fiercely contested elections in 1910 over the Budget and the reduction of the powers of the House of Lords, where the Conservative majority had rejected the Budget. 'Freddie' Guest, Lady Wimborne's third son, succeeded as Liberal M.P. for East Dorset from December 1910 until 1922, and helped to carry through further radical Liberal reforms such as the Parliament Act, the Payment of M.P.s and the National Insurance Act. Lady

139. & 140. Two levels of Edwardian society: (*left*) Cornelia, Lady Wimborne, hostess and benefactress of Poole and founder of Poole's Cornelia Hospital, and (*right*) 'Granny' Cousins, Poole's last 'knocker-up', who roused the Rope Walk workers in the early hours by tapping on their bedroom windows with her long pole.

Wimborne's eldest son, Ivor, having succeeded to his father's title in 1914, served as Viceroy of Ireland, 1915-18, during the critical upsurge of revolutionary republicanism. Just before the fateful Easter Rebellion (1916) he pressed for the arrest of the republican leaders, who were known to the police, but he could not get the necessary approval for such a precautionary measure from Birrell, the absentee Chief Secretary for Ireland. In 1918 he opposed Lloyd George's proposal to force conscription on the Irish people and was replaced by the hard-line Lord French. Had Lord Wimborne's advice been heeded, the course of Irish history might have been very different.

The Conservative rival of the Guests in Poole, Charles Van Raalte, Mayor of Poole in 1902, and his wife Florence, entertained lavishly on Brownsea Island, which he had purchased in 1901. Among the guests was the Queen of Rumania. A frequent visitor to the Poole area was the flamboyant German Kaiser, Wilhelm II. Whilst staying at Highcliffe Castle in 1908 at a time of growing Anglo-German tension over naval strength, he gave an

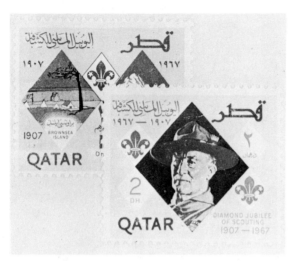

141. (*above*) Qatar stamps showing Brownsea Island and Baden-Powell, commemorating the first scout camp there in 1907.

142. (*below*) The grave of Alfred Russel Wallace in Broadstone cemetery, surmounted by a petrified tree.

interview to the *Daily Telegraph* in which he tactlessly chided the British people for not responding to his efforts to preserve peace, declaring that only a minority of his countrymen shared his love of England. The interview caused a storm of protest both in England and Germany – and certainly did nothing to avert the drift towards war.

The Poole-Bournemouth area was closely associated with certain major developments at the opening of the 20th century. Marconi, the Italian pioneer of wireless, set up his headquarters in the Haven Hotel, Sandbanks, Poole in 1898, as well as another base at Madeira House, west of Bournemouth Pier. He transmitted his first radio messages between the Isle of Wight and the Haven Hotel, where a plaque in one of the lounges commemorates his pioneering work.

The Hon. Charles S. Rolls, co-founder of Rolls-Royce, epitomised the new technological advances marked by the advent of the motor-car and the aeroplane. Sadly, Britain's first international aviation meeting, which formed part of Bournemouth's centenary celebrations in 1910, was the occasion of Britain's first fatal flying accident, when C. S. Rolls' biplane broke up 50 feet above the ground and, although he was thrown clear, he was fatally injured.

A happier pioneering occasion had been the first Boy Scout Camp, held in the summer of 1907 by Major-General Baden-Powell on Brownsea Island. This successful ten-day experiment involved 20 boys from widely differing backgrounds – from Poole and Bournemouth, the East End of London and from Eton and Harrow – who learned to live in the open, cook their own meals and go tracking, and who in the evenings were entertained by Baden-Powell's stories and bird-calls round the camp-fire. Baden-Powell had an instinctive feeling for what appealed to boys and, whilst aiming to build character and self-reliance, he succeeded in making the experience great fun. Criticised on the grounds that he was encouraging militarism, because of his emphasis upon obeying orders, Baden-Powell maintained that his aim was to promote social harmony. Baden-Powell founded the Boy Scout movement in 1908 and with his sister set up the Girl Guides in 1910. Baden-Powell's young wife, Olave, who was the daughter of Harold Soames, of Lilliput, Parkstone, became Chief Guide in 1918. After the First World War Baden-Powell concentrated upon spreading the Boy Scout Movement throughout the world as a means of promoting peace.

The Poole area has been associated with four distinguished biologists. One, Professor Thomas Bell, F.R.S. (1792-1880), was born in Market Street, Poole, and lectured in zoology at King's College, London. He became President of the Linnean Society and was an expert on the naturalist, Gilbert White. His cousin, Philip Henry Gosse, F.R.S., was brought up in Skinner Street, worked in Newfoundland for one of the Poole merchant firms and became an authority on marine zoology, especially on sea-anemones. The rector of Bloxworth, the Rev. Octavius Pickard-Cambridge (1828-1917), was also an eminent zoologist and the leading authority on spiders. By 1900 the theory of evolution was beginning to receive general acceptance and its co-exponent (with Charles Darwin) Alfred Russel Wallace spent the last 11 years of his life (1902-13) in Broadstone, where he built 'Old Orchard' and created a magnificent garden stocked with unusual shrubs and trees. Wallace was buried in Broadstone cemetery, where his grave is surmounted by a fossilised tree which he had brought back from South America.

During that 1914-18 War many young men from Poole suffered death and injury especially since the Dorsets were heavily involved in the slaughter at the Battle of the Somme (1916). One positive contribution was made by the New Cornelia Hospital when it handled nearly three thousand casualties from the Western Front, with the loss of only seven lives. At the outset of the War Winston Churchill, then First Lord of the Admiralty, insisted that the Royal Navy must have its own independent supply of cordite, a mixture of nitroglycerine and guncotton, and the site chosen for the new cordite factory was Holton Heath, four miles west of Poole. It opened early in 1916 and drew heavily upon Poole for its work force. It was then essential to produce adequate quantities of acetone, whose solvent action assisted the incorporation of the nitroglycerine with the guncotton. An acetone factory was built in 1917 at Holton Heath and the scientist in charge of the production was a research biochemist, Dr. Chaim Weizmann. Some 20,000 tons of acetone was produced by his fermentation process at Holton Heath and the prime minister, Lloyd George, was understandably very grateful for this contribution to the defeat of German U-boats. Weizmann was the leading advocate of Zionism, the Jewish national movement aiming at the creation of a Jewish state in Palestine. In gratitude Lloyd George looked favourably on Zionism, and the Balfour Declaration of 1917 announced that Britain favoured the creation of 'a national home for the Jewish people' in Palestine, provided that 'nothing shall be done which may prejudice the . . . rights of existing non-Jewish communities in Palestine'. Britain had already promised independence to the Arabs of this area and in return they had revolted against the Turks and helped to drive them from Palestine. Lawrence of Arabia, whose aim was to secure independence for the Arabs, was to be killed in a motor-cycle accident near Wool in Dorset and his effigy in Arab attire is in the Saxon-Norman St Martin's church at Wareham.

Chapter Thirteen

The Last Seventy Years, 1918-1988

Between the two World Wars the population of Poole and Bournemouth continued to grow steadily and this meant an increased demand for gas. Accordingly in 1925 new retort houses were constructed on reclaimed land at Pitwines and linked by a bridge transporter to the East Quay where, by 1935, 130,000 tons of coal were being unloaded every year. The gigantic gasholder, 181 feet in diameter and 107 feet in height, became a major feature of the Poole landscape. At this time the water supply, taken over by the Corporation from a private company in 1906, drew largely on new supplies from Corfe Mullen, and Hatch Pond formed one of the early reservoirs. Sewage was improved by the establishment of purification works at Fleetsbridge in 1922. Communications were transformed when the 30-year tramway lease drew to a close. Bournemouth switched over to trolley-buses with overhead wires in 1933, but Poole arranged for the sale of operating rights in the Borough of Poole to the Hants and Dorset Motor Services, which introduced motor buses. The last electric tram ran on the Upper Parkstone route for the last time in 1935. By that year the process of enlarging the borough boundaries had been completed. Branksome Urban District had been added to Poole in 1905 and then in 1935 the Canford Magna Rural District – home of the old lord of the manor – was incorporated in the Borough of Poole. Incidentally by that time Lord Wimborne had lost interest in Poole. He sold Canford Manor in 1923 and the fine building became the home of an independent boarding school, Canford School.

A major event was the opening of the new Hamworthy bridge in 1927 – a development which greatly assisted the free flow of traffic. The 1920s saw a considerable revival of interest in Poole's past and heritage. In 1921 the ceremony of Beating the

A GRAVE OUTLOOK.

PROFESSOR: "I don't know what things are coming to."
UNDERTAKER: "Times are bad, why I haven't buried a living soul this last month."

143. Two famous Poole characters between the wars, 'Professor' White and Councillor Cole.

144. Last tram car in Ashley Road, Upper Parkstone, 1935.

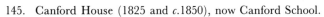

145. Canford House (1825 and *c*.1850), now Canford School.

Bounds in the harbour was revived and the activities of H. P. Smith, headmaster of South Road school, in excavating prehistoric and Roman remains and in revealing the unique nature of the old town house uncovered by a storm at Scaplen's Court aroused much public enthusiasm. The Society of Poole Men also embarked on their fine work of preserving this and many other buildings and in stimulating an interest in the borough's history.

The opening of the elegant new Municipal Buildings at Park Gates East in 1932 reflected a forward-looking mood, but also a growing awareness of Poole's distinguished past represented in the sculptured scenes from its history below the eaves. When the first council meeting in the new premises took place, there was one notable dissident, Alderman Harry Cole, the tall, bearded undertaker, resplendent in his long frock coat and top hat. He regarded the whole enterprise as unnecessary extravagance in the midst of the slump, even though the government had made Poole a large grant to help alleviate local unemployment by this building project. Harry Cole, who always had an effective way of making a point, as when he spoke over sixty times at one council meeting, particularly objected to the new, comfortably upholstered seats in the council chamber and himself sat down on a hard kitchen chair, which he had carried all the way from his home for the purpose.

Major employers during the 1920s and 1930s were the gas company, the shipbuilding yards which had benefited from the growth in trade at the beginning of the century and from the growing popularity of yachting, and finally the brickyards and the potteries. In 1921 the company known as Carter, Stabler and Adams (C.S.A.) was formed as a subsidiary of Carter & Co. Ltd. and took charge of Poole Pottery. John Adams, the new Managing Director, was a talented artist and played an active role on the design side. Soon Poole Pottery was producing the unique multi-coloured hand-painted tableware and ornamental plates and vases which were to carry the name and fame of Poole all over the world. At Poole Pottery there was a happy partnership between designers and craftsmen. Among the outstanding designers were Harold Stabler and his wife, Phoebe, remarkable for their sculptured pottery such as the Galleon, the famous Bull and the Lavender Woman. Arthur Bradbury designed the attractive ship plates. John Adams designed several intricate pierced trays, picotee ware and tableware, whilst his wife, Truda, designed the floral patterns on many vases and much of the tableware. Success of the final product, of course, depended on the skill of the paintresses like Ruth Pavely (Mrs. Thomson) and Anne Hatchard (Mrs. Milnthorpe).

Poole and its harbour acted as a magnet to many distinguished painters, especially during the years between the two World Wars. In 1911 Augustus John rented Alderney Manor from Lord Wimborne for £50 a year and led a bohemian life there for the next 16 years. He produced many of his most famous paintings there, such as 'Washing Day', depicting Dorelia hanging up the clothes on the garden line. Peter Davies in his *Art in Poole and Dorset* vividly describes and illustrates the work of such artists as Henry Lamb, specialising in street scenes such as 'Paradise Street', Bernard Gribble, with studies of the Guildhall, Arthur Bell and Leon Underwood, depicting buildings on or near the Quay, Leslie Ward, Arnold Knight and Arthur Bradbury, portraying scenes of the harbour and its shipping. The Poole Museum Service has been able to organise the works of many of these artists such as Frank Dodman's 'Market Street, Poole', reminiscent of Poole's crumbling Georgian glory.

Education continued to expand and both Poole and Parkstone Grammar Schools, equipped with Sixth Forms, sent a growing number of boys and girls on to university. In 1939 for no well argued educational reasons Parkstone Grammar School at Ashley Cross became a school for girls only and Poole Grammar School beside the Ladies' Walking Field had an intake only of boys. To provide secondary education for all, two secondary modern schools, named Henry Harbin and Kemp Welch after previous benefactors of education in Poole's past, were established, whilst a third in Hamworthy, not completed until after the war, was appropriately named after Herbert Carter (1880-1956), who had first become a borough councillor at the age of 25 and had served as mayor of Poole five times. A grandson of Jesse Carter, the pottery pioneer, he was a man of extraordinary talent, lively wit, liberal outlook and boundless enthusiasm for the welfare of the people of Poole. A great traveller, keen yachtsman and pioneer of the Sea Scout movement, his main concern was the advancement of education.

Poole and the surrounding area played an important role in the Second World War, although at first during the period of the 'Phoney War' Poole seemed to be remote from the front line. It was assumed that Poole was a relatively safe area, and so schoolchildren from Southampton and London were evacuated to Poole. School

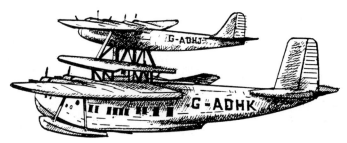

146. Flying boats in Poole harbour.

buildings were shared on a two-shift system over a six-day timetable culminating in a Saturday afternoon session ending at 5.15 p.m. The government had selected Poole as the southern base for the newly-established B.O.A.C. (British Overseas Airways Corporation) and Poole Harbour Yacht Club was commandeered as a 'Marine Terminal' from which passengers could be taken to and from the flying boats moored in the harbour. There were regular services to destinations as distant as India and Australia. Winston Churchill and many other war leaders frequently travelled on these flying boats through Poole to conferences and tours of inspection abroad. The War came much nearer when a motley assortment of craft arrived in mid-May 1940 from Holland, after the unprovoked German invasion of that country, transporting some three thousand Dutch refugees who were temporarily accommodated on Brownsea Island. The owner of Brownsea, Mrs. Bonham Christie, a recluse, had prohibited any unauthorised landings on the island with the aid of a Nordic Amazon, a female 'bouncer' named Bertha Olsen, but at the outbreak of war Mrs. Christie was obliged to move to the mainland and leave Brownsea to the military authorities. In response to an appeal for small boats to help in the rescue of the British and Allied troops trapped at Dunkirk, the Poole lifeboat and nine shallow-draught pleasure craft belonging to the Davis, Harvey and Bolson families rendered invaluable service evacuating the men of the B.E.F. Two of Poole's 'little boats' were sunk off Dunkirk. At the time of the Fall of France Poole boats also rescued more British troops from Normandy.

The threat of invasion was then very real. Indeed Poole was judged to be one of the four coastal areas most likely to be selected by the Germans for landing their troops. The beaches were placed under military control and obstructed with barbed wire. 'Dragon's Teeth' (anti-tank blocks of reinforced concrete) were installed across Poole Park and other vulnerable places, whilst inland pill-boxes were located at road junctions and anti-tank ditches were dug at Fleets Bridge and Sterte. During the 'Battle of Britain', though Poole was on the western fringe of the main combat, Spitfires from R.A.F. Warmwell played a vital role. During the subsequent mass raids by the Luftwaffe on industrial cities like Manchester and Coventry the people of Poole became accustomed to hearing the German bombers passing overhead just after dark and returning shortly before dawn, sometimes discarding any unused bombs. There was a theory that the glistening waters of Poole Harbour provided a useful marker for the bombers en route to the north, but in fact it was discovered by the scientists at the Telecommunications Research Establishment at Worth

147. 'Dragons' teeth' in Poole Park, 1945.

Matravers, where they pioneered the development of radar, that the German planes were following radio beams transmitted from the Cherbourg peninsula towards the industrial targets to be bombed. Poole was singularly fortunate throughout the war in that, despite its exposed coastal position, very little damage or casualties were inflicted by German bombers. The worst incident came on 27 March 1941 when a sneak raider dropped a bomb on the canteen of the Branksome Gas Works when 34 men having their lunch were killed. On the night of 24/25 May 1942 Poole and Bournemouth were saved from large-scale devastation and casualties by the successful operation of the 'Starfish' apparatus of the Major Strategic Night Decoy on Brownsea Island. When a force of 50 German bombers began to drop incendiaries and high explosives, the electrically detonated oil-fuelled system of fireworks featuring a device with a bath tub and two lavatory cisterns on Brownsea Island came into action and completely misled the German pilots, who dropped 150 tons of high explosives on the island, fully believing that they had virtually wiped out Poole. Ten days later a decoy system at Arne similarly saved the Cordite Factory at Holton Heath from destruction. Soon the military authorities were planning ahead for the time when an invasion of France could be launched. Accordingly H.M.S. *Turtle* was commissioned at Hamworthy as a base for combined operations training and indeed the 'Special Services Brigade' of Army Commandos and Royal Marines carried out many night landing exercises on Brownsea Island and Shell Bay.

Meanwhile over at Christchurch the Royal Engineers were testing and constructing the ingenious prefabricated 'Bailey Bridges', already used successfully in Tunisia and Italy and later to be so vital in the Normandy campaign. Bolson's shipyard and the Dorset Yacht Company were turning out specially designed 'L.C.T.' landing craft and 'Wolf in sheep's clothing' rocket launching craft. Likewise, the yards of Sydenham's, Newman's and Burt &

Vick were busy making the wooden decking for the prefabricated 'Mulberry Harbours' – concrete floating breakwaters. In order to test out the feasibility of PLUTO (Pipe Line Under The Ocean) to provide a steady flow of fuel, once the landings were effected, successful experiments were conducted in Poole Harbour and across to the Isle of Wight. As D-Day approached in 1944 the B.O.A.C. flying-boat base was moved to Pembrokeshire to leave room for the huge invasion fleet which had to be accommodated in Poole Harbour. The U.S. Navy established an Advanced Amphibious Base at Poole in May 1944 and soon vast quantities of vehicles and stores were being hidden away in the woods of the Poole area. Tarrant Rushton and Hurn aerodromes were to play a vital role as bases from which fleets of gliders transported troops, tanks, vehicles, guns and Bailey bridge pontoons. On D-Day H.M.S. *Poole* was one of the many mine-sweepers which, ahead of the assault convoys, cut and marked safe channels through the German minefields off the Normandy coast. The 1st Dorsets and the 1st Hampshires were among the first British troops to land in Normandy – on Gold beach. However, very heavy fighting lay ahead and a constant stream of supplies had to be maintained from Poole, and the boatyards were kept busy repairing vessels damaged in the assault on Europe. B.O.A.C. returned to Poole in September 1944. Not until VE-Day (8 May 1945) could Poole relax for a while to watch the victory parades of the armed and civilian services and to stage the many memorable street parties for the children.

Since the Second World War growth and change have characterised Poole and its neighbourhood – change so complete that some former residents, who have been absent for the past 20 years, find themselves utterly disorientated when they return, and frustrated by their inability to discern any of the remembered landmarks. During the war shipbuilding had received substantial stimulus and this flourished as Poole Harbour continued to attract more and more yachtsmen, and as the growing affluence of the nation made the ownership of a boat no longer the preserve of the rich. Shipbuilding in turn encouraged the growth of marine engineering. Some firms which began in a very small way, such as Hamworthy Engineering, expanded into many other branches of engineering, and with the advance of technology many firms in the Poole area developed in the field of electronics, some small and others quite gigantic like Plessey with its centres in Christchurch and in Sopers Lane between Poole and Broadstone. Some manufacturers, who had moved to Poole during the war, stayed on afterwards – notably British Drug Houses, Ryvita (Crispbread) and Loewy Robertson (now Davy McKee). As petrol became more abundant and motoring more prevalent, so there was a ready market for the caravans produced at the top of the hill alongside the Old Wareham Road. Other companies which established themselves in Poole were Max Factor (cosmetics), Metal Box (Wallis Tin Stamping) and De Vilbiss Co. (in the field of automatic paint spraying). The timber merchants held their own as a result especially of the constant demand for building materials, but most of the brickyards and the potteries specialising in drainpipes have closed down. As clay pits were worked out, so the South Western Pottery, the Victoria Brickworks at Foxholes, the Kinson Pottery in Newtown closed down and their sites have been redeveloped as housing or industrial estates. The Bourne Valley Pottery, though it had changed over to the manufacture of concrete pipes, also closed to be replaced by the Poole Commerce Centre. The old-established firm of Christopher Hill (corn merchants) has developed into Dalgety Agriculture Ltd. (animal feed manufacturers). Local breweries have disappeared, partly because of take-overs and relocation by big companies, but a small brewing company at Sterte, the Poole Brewery, is again producing 'real ale'. In the past few years local industry has been transformed by increasing computerisation and employment opportunities have been expanded by the arrival in the area of such institutions as Barclays International, the National Mutual Life Association of Australasia, the Chase Manhattan Bank and the Abbey Life Assurance Co.

Some industrial firms, as they have expanded, have moved out into new locations such as the Nuffield Estate, Mannings Heath, Fleet Lane and Ferndown. In view of Poole's ancient maritime associations it is particularly appropriate that the much respected Royal National Lifeboat Institution has established its national headquarters here in Poole – just south of Towngate flyover.

The Poole Harbour Commissioners are responsible for 'the conservancy, improvement and regulation' of the port and harbour of Poole. At present five of the 13 Commissioners are elected by the traders, five are appointed by the Local Authorities (one by the Dorset County Council, one by Purbeck District Council and three by Poole Borough Council), one represents fishermen, one yachting interests and one is appointed by the T.G.W.U. from the dock work force. The Chairman (before 1980 'the Mayor of Poole for the time being') is now appointed by the Secretary of State for Transport for a term of three years. Some 95% of the Commissioners' income is derived from the trade of the port (over 60% by the ferry services) and less than 5% by fishing, amenity and recreational services. It is the duty of the Poole Harbour Commissioners to preserve a balance between the various interests.

Technological changes have altered the local landscape. In 1949 a new power station with tall chimney stacks was built at Hamworthy and soon became a major oil-using electricity generating station in the region, but has declined in importance in competition with nuclear-powered stations. The advent of North Sea gas likewise led to the close down of the Gas Works in Poole and the disappearance of the coal tips and crane across the quay and of the gasholder that was such a prominent feature at Pitwines, to be replaced by the Quay Hotel at one end and the new Sainsbury's complex at the other. British Rail's hatchet-man, Dr. Beeching, wrought havoc in the area with his 1963 report and in consequence the Somerset and Dorset Joint line was closed down in 1966 and with it went the four-platform Broadstone Station, just at the time when housing development was making it in many senses the centre of gravity of the Borough of Poole. Councillor Cyril Tapper proposed a plan by which the line from London could cease at Parkstone, the two Poole level crossings could be eliminated, and the main line to Weymouth should run from Brockenhurst via Wimborne and Broadstone, whilst passengers for Poole could complete their journey along the southward line from Broadstone. His plan was not adopted. Later Poole's solid Victorian station with its protective waiting rooms and two entrances, so useful to the disabled, was swept away to be replaced by a shoddy little halt exposed to all the winds and gales. This is currently being replaced by an improved structure more in keeping with a town of 120,000 people. In 1971-2 the level crossing by the station was removed and the Towngate Bridge was constructed at a cost of nearly £1,000,000 to provide an unobstructed route from Hamworthy Bridge by way of West Quay Road, which became all the more necessary when the roll-on roll-off ferry service (at first only for freight, but recently extended to passengers) from the new terminal at the end of the Hamworthy peninsula was launched in the 1970s. The expansion of the population and of industrial traffic created an urgent need for an improved road system, to meet which the Fleets Bridge flyover was built to carry a greatly widened road from Lytchett Minster on the Old Wareham Road to Newtown, and more recently the Ferndown relief road. The Wimborne By-pass and Wessex Way in Bournemouth are among the many other developments to ease congestion.

The rapid growth of Poole's population placed increasing strain on the old Cornelia Hospital at Longfleet, even though it had taken over the old workhouse building in Longfleet and so from 1958 to 1962 a fine new building was built to house what was now called Poole General Hospital. Currently a new hospital for Bournemouth is nearing completion. Thanks to the pressure of public opinion Wimborne's friendly Victoria Hospital was saved from closure and, instead, enlarged and modernised. The increased proportion of elderly people in the population has created a need for special provision for those in need of continuous care and this has been mainly provided by St Leonard's Hospital, originally an American military hospital during the war. Poole Borough Council has also been particularly active in providing warden-supervised Elderly Persons Dwellings. In the private sector rest-houses and nursing homes have proliferated. In 1985 Poole Borough Council inaugurated its own crematorium – to reduce the waiting-lists at Bournemouth – and received a Civic Trust Award for its design.

In the sphere of politics the area has been predominantly Conservative, certainly since 1922-3, when the Liberal Guest family at Canford severed its close connections with Poole after the defeat of E. E. Guest, the Liberal M.P. since 1910, in the 1922 Election. The strong Liberal-Nonconformist traditions of the area helped to return a Liberal M.P., A. E. Glassey, from 1929 to 1931, but thereafter, as in Bournemouth, Conservative candidates have been returned. In 1918 Bournemouth had been allocated its own M.P. and in 1948 its growth in population earned it an additional M.P., so that there were two constituencies, Bournemouth West, and Bournemouth East and Christchurch. In 1948 Poole once more was allocated its own M.P. and the rural areas of East Dorset were divided between North Dorset and South Dorset. In the 1987 general election the percentage of votes obtained by each of the three parties in Poole were as follows: Conservative 57.5 (58.1); Liberal/S.D.P. Alliance 32.6 (30.7); Labour 9.9 (11.2). In brackets are the total percentages in Poole and the five other constituencies within 12 miles of Poole. On the Poole Borough Council the 1987 local elections gave the Conservatives 21, the Alliance 15 and Labour 0.

Foreign policy issues have involved M.P.s with local connections on two notable occasions, both concerned with the Palestine problem. Nigel Nicolson, M.P. for Bournemouth East in 1956, found himself unable with a clear conscience to support Eden's decision to send military forces into the Suez Canal zone. A vociferous group in the local Conservative party denounced his stand as disloyalty and, although he maintained that an M.P. should be free to act independently on issues of conscience and should not be the mere delegate of a majority of the party members in his constituency, Nicolson was ousted from his seat. In 1988 David Mellor, Foreign Office Minister, who was educated at Swanage Grammar School, was in the news when he voiced his sincere reaction to the dreadful conditions among the Palestinian Arabs in the Israeli-occupied territories of Gaza and the West Bank. All local M.P.s supported the government decision to liberate the Falkland Islands from Argentinian occupation and the Royal Marines, who played such a decisive role in the Falklands War, were sent to the South Atlantic from their base in Hamworthy and put into practice the skills learnt on manoeuvres in and around Poole Harbour. It was in 1954 that the Royal Marines took over the old landing craft base at Hamworthy and the former H.M.S. *Turtle* became the Amphibious School Royal Marines. In recognition of the vital part played by the Royal Marines, particularly the S.B.S., in the Falklands War, they were awarded the Freedom of the Borough of Poole and the pleasant venue in the extended Arndale Centre was named Falkland Square.

Shortly after the Second World War the continued expansion of the conurbation on either side of Bournemouth caused some empire-builders to suggest that Bournemouth, which had achieved County Borough status in 1900, should now be enlarged to incorporate Poole and Christchurch – a suggestion that was defeated by outraged objections from the two adjacent boroughs. Ironically in the 1974 Local Government reorganisation Bournemouth lost its county borough status and became a mere borough within an extended County of Dorset. In the sphere of education the County authorities were not averse to a changeover to comprehensive education and comprehensive schools duly came into being at Christchurch, at the relocated Queen Elizabeth's School at Pamphill and at Corfe Hills. However, within the boroughs of Poole and Bournemouth there was deep appreciation of the achievements of the four grammar schools, which had increasingly seen many of their pupils embark on careers in the teaching, legal, medical and nursing professions, the armed and civil services and the police force. Many had become distinguished scientists, engineers, television producers and leading members of the business world. Two former pupils of Poole Grammar School, for example, one a biochemist, the other a historian, became respectively vice-chancellor and president of universities in Australia and the United States. Thus Poole and Parkstone Grammar Schools, Bournemouth Grammar School for Boys and Bournemouth Grammar School for Girls have remained as grammar schools though full facilities have been evolved to enable pupils from the secondary modern schools to transfer at 16 into the sixth form. Parkstone and Poole Grammar Schools were given long overdue new premises at Sopers Lane and Gravel Hill in the 1960s. New schools were built to meet the needs of the growing outer housing estates, but the old premises of Poole Grammar School, occupied by Seldown School for Boys, are sadly to be demolished to facilitate the construction of a new road bridge. Seldown and Ashley Cross School for Girls are due to amalgamate as a co-educational secondary school on Canford Heath. Another local school, Lytchett Minster Comprehensive, occupies the Manor House which was the home of the Lees family. Madeline, Lady Lees (1895-1967) was one of the outstanding personalities of the area. Always enthusiastic and enlightened, she sponsored youth clubs, produced memorable nativity plays and religious films, staunchly supported the R.S.P.C.A., and championed the causes of education and international friendship, particularly the World Congress of Faiths, whose aim was to promote mutual respect and understanding between the religions of the world.

Transformations have occurred in the main traditional shopping centres. In Poole High Street, gone are the familiar names of 40 years ago – Miles (drapers), Bacon and Curtis (ironmongers), Burden's and Gifford's (family grocers) and Cole's furniture stores, whilst in Bournemouth takeovers have eliminated the well-known individual stores – Allen's, Bright's, Plummer's and Bobby's. There were once some 20 cinemas in and around Poole, but the advent of television has caused the demolition or conversion of most of these to make way for bingo-halls and supermarkets. St Paul's church in Poole High Street, with declining congregations, was also demolished to be replaced by a grocery store. Happily the old family firms of Hawkes (the shoe shop), W. E. Boone's (ironmongers) and Beale's in Bournemouth and the Poole Arndale Centre are still with us.

Poole had personal links with the growing role of broadcasting in national life. Stuart Hibberd, radio announcer, and Chris Chataway, broadcaster, athlete and M.P., both had family associations with Broadstone. Malcolm C. Brown, formerly a pupil of Poole Grammar School, B.B.C. television producer, has been responsible for several documentaries, particularly concerning 20th-century history. Television has also made even more popular the spy fiction of David John Cornwell (John le Carré), such as *Tinker, Tailor, Soldier, Spy* and *The Perfect Spy*. John le Carré was born in Poole and his grandfather, Alderman A. E. F. Cornwell, was Mayor of Poole, 1928-29. His uncle, Alec E. Glassey, was the local M.P. for East Dorset, 1929-31. Poole was chosen as the location for the fictional Wrelling in the popular B.B.C. Television series 'The Collectors', featuring the work of modern customs officers and portraying such familiar local features as the Custom House on the Quay, Upton House and Creech Grange.

Increasing post-war affluence has meant a great boom in tourism. Yachting and wind-surfing have attracted outdoor enthusiasts and the promenade has been extended from Sandbanks continuously to Southbourne and more and more hotels and restaurants have emerged. Beauty contests have taken place annually and it is notable that two Parkstone girls who won the title of 'Miss Poole' – Anne Sidney (1964) and Sarah-Jane Hutt (1983) – have gone on to win the coveted title of 'Miss World'. The advent of Hurn Airport has

148. The old thatched cottage and Miles (the drapers) in Poole High Street. The clock belonging to Cole's (the jewellers) is still working.

149. Amity Hall, High Street. This later became a cinema and Woolworth's now occupy the site.

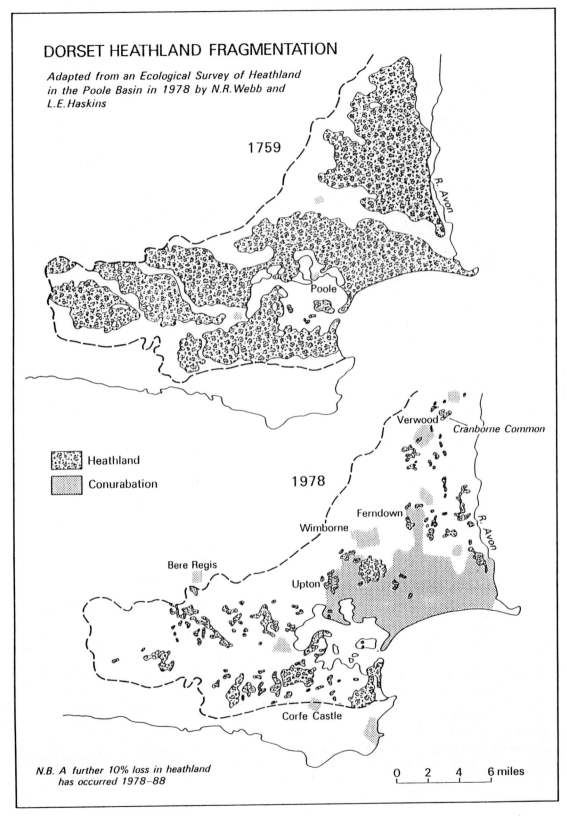

DORSET HEATHLAND FRAGMENTATION

Adapted from an Ecological Survey of Heathland in the Poole Basin in 1978 by N.R. Webb and L.E. Haskins

1759

R. Avon

Poole

Heathland
Conurbation

1978

Verwood
Cranborne Common

Ferndown

Wimborne

R. Avon

Bere Regis

Upton

Corfe Castle

N.B. A further 10% loss in heathland has occurred 1978–88

0   2   4   6 miles

150.   Heathland and Conurbation, 1759-1978.

enabled local residents seeking the sun in warmer climes to travel abroad with more convenience.

The need to provide housing, administrative facilities and recreational outlets for the growing population has led to much building and many transformations, notably a new Civic Centre block and law courts near Park Gates East, blocks of flats in the old town and more housing estates at Waterloo, Broadstone, Creekmoor, Canford Heath, Merley, Rossmore and beyond the borough of Poole boundaries, into Corfe Mullen. Similar expansion has occurred to the north of Bournemouth. In Poole in 1969 the pedestrianised Arndale Centre with its complex of shops as well as a sports centre and a fine new library was opened alongside a new bus station. Nearby in 1974 came the Dolphin Pool, whilst across the road in 1978 the fine Poole Arts Centre, complete with the Wessex Concert Hall, Towngate Theatre, Ashley Cinema, art gallery, restaurant and bars, was opened to the public. The High Street has also been pedestrianised (1987). In Bournemouth, after great controversy over the cost involved, the Bournemouth International Centre has been completed as a conference centre. Private business has also been responsible for many new building projects – several new blocks of offices in Poole, sometimes long unoccupied, and the dominant feature of the Poole skyline – the Barclays International Building. Opinion is divided as to whether this structure is a masterpiece of modernity or a monumental monstrosity.

Inevitably there have been clashes between developers and conservationists. Great concern was expressed about the effects of the development of Britain's largest onshore oilfield at Wytch Farm on the south side of Poole Harbour and at the extension of drilling activities to Furzey Island in the harbour. It is hoped that the reassurances of the developers prove to be valid and that life on land and in the sea will not suffer. Great anxiety, however, has been voiced by the Dorset Trust for Nature Conservation and other bodies about the encroachments upon the irreplaceable heathland and its unique flora and fauna as a result of the seemingly unrestricted growth in housing and industrial development under the South East Dorset Structure Plan. Despite protests by what would seem to be a majority of local residents and by Robert Adley, M.P. for Christchurch, who maintains that 'public pressure to protect the environment is stronger than pressure for affordable housing', the encroachments continue. Already the conurbation stretching from Creekmoor to Highcliffe has a population of some 420,000. Is it not time to call a halt, before the quality of life for the humans is undermined and no chance of life is left for many rare species of animals, birds, and insects – notably the sand lizard, the smooth snake, the nightjar, the Dartford warbler and the silver-studded blue butterfly?

Magnificent victories for the cause of conservation came in 1962, when Brownsea Island was acquired by the National Trust and in 1981 when Mr. H. J. Ralph Bankes also bequeathed his Kingston Lacy and Corfe Castle Estates, including a vast expanse of unspoilt heathland and natural coastline at Studland and Shell Bay, to the National Trust. Triumphs for the cause of conservation in Poole itself and a growing pride in Poole's heritage also came, thanks to the influence of enlightened citizens of Poole such as H. P. Smith, who master-minded the Pageant of Poole in 1952, and by the activities of the members of such organisations as the Society of Poole Men, the Poole Historical Trust, the Poole Museums Service, the Poole Maritime Trust, the Poole Museum Society, the Friends of Upton House, the Wessex Newfoundland Society, the Studland Bay Wreck Project and the Poole Industrial Archaeology Group. Some fine old Georgian houses had been allowed to decay beyond repair, but many old buildings have been saved and tastefully restored. The prize-winning St James's Close scheme, the development of Poole's three museums and the exciting new Waterfront complex due to be opened in 1989 deserve the admiration of all Poole's citizens and provide hope for the future.

Select Bibliography

* denotes primary or substantially primary sources.
† denotes publications of the Poole Historical Trust.

General
Bettey, J. H., *Wessex from A.D. 1000* (1986)
Cullingford, C. N., *A History of Dorset* (1980)
Fägersten, A., *The Place Names of Dorset* (1933, reprinted 1978)
Hutchins, J., *The History and Antiquities of Dorset* (1st edition 1774, 4 vol. reprint 1973)
Miller, A. J., *The Story of Poole* (1984)
Mills, A. D., *The Place Names of Dorset*, Part 1 (1977) and Part 2 (1980)
Newman, J. and Pevsner, N., *The Buildings of England: Dorset* (1972)
Oswald, A., *The Country Houses of Dorset* (1935, 1959)
Proceedings of the Dorset Natural History and Antiquarian Society (1877-1928)
Proceedings of the Dorset Natural History and Archaeological Society (P.D.N.H.A.S. – annually since 1929)
Royal Commission on Historical Monuments: Dorset, 5 vols. (1952-75)
Short, B. C., *Poole, the Romance of its Early History* (1932)
Short, B. C., *Poole, the Romance of its Later History* (1932)
Smith, H. P., *The History of Poole*, 2 vols. (1948 and 1951)
Sydenham, J., *The History of the Town and County of Poole* (1839, 1986 reprint)†
The Victoria History of the County of Dorset, vol. 2 (1908)

Studies of Particular Localities
Almack, T. F., *A Village Heritage: the Story of Blandford St Mary* (1961)
Bankes, V., *A Dorset Heritage: the Story of Kingston Lacy* (1953)
Bowring, N., *The History of Broadstone* (1972)
Davis, T., *Wareham: Gateway to Purbeck* (1984)
Dyson, T., *The History of Christchurch* (1954)
Edwards, E., *A History of Bournemouth* (1981)
Field, N. H., *Corfe Mullen: The Origins of a Dorset Village* (1988)
James, J., *Wimborne Minster: the History of a Country Town* (1982)
King, J., *Memories of a Dorset Parish: Bygone Lytchett Minster* (1988)
Lavender, R. A., *A Thousand Years of Christchurch* (1977)
Lavender, R. A., *From Pocket Borough to Parliamentary Democracy* – Christchurch (1976)
Lands, S. J., *Old Kinson* (1980)
Legg, R., *Brownsea, Dorset's Fantasy Island* (1986)
Mansel, J. C., *Kimmeridge and Smedmore* (1967)
Parsons, N., *The Manor of Canford Magna* (1974)
Percival, S., *A Dorset Village: Lytchett Matravers* (1982)
Popham, D. & R., *The Book of Bournemouth* (1985)

Chapter One
Cunliffe, B., *Hengistbury Head* (1978)

Drew, G. and Bugler, J., *Roman Dorset* (1974)
Haskins, L. E., 'The Vegetational History of South-East Dorset' (Ph.D. thesis, 1978)
Jarvis, K. S., *Excavations in Christchurch, 1969-1980* (1983)
Palmer, S., *The Mesolithic Cultures in Britain* (1977)
Putnam, W. G., *Roman Dorset* (1974)

Chapters Two, Three and Four
Garmonsway, G. N. (ed.), *The Anglo-Saxon Chronicle* (1972)*
*La Cronica de don Pero Niño**
Mills, A. D. (ed.), *The Dorset Lay Subsidy Roll of 1332* (1971)*
Morris, J. (ed.), *Nennius: British History and the Welsh Annals* (1980)*
Paris, Matthew, *Historia Anglorum* (1254)*
Rumble, A. R. (ed.), *The Dorset Lay Subsidy Roll of 1327* (1980)*
Talbot, C. H. (ed.), *The Anglo-Saxon Missionaries in Germany* (1954)
Thorn, C. and T. (ed.), *Domesday Book: Dorset* (1983)*
The Victoria History of the County of Dorset, vol. 3*

Chapters Five, Six and Seven
Bailey, A. R., *The Great Civil War in Dorset* (1910)
Bevan, B., *James, Duke of Monmouth* (1973)
Christie, W. D., *A Life of the First Earl of Shaftesbury* (1871)*
Glassey, A. E., *1662 and All That* (1960)
Gordon, G. N., *The Civil War in Hampshire* (1904)
Holinshed, R., *The Chronicles of England, Scotland and Ireland* (1577)
L'Estrange Ewen, C., 'The Pirates of Purbeck' (P.D.N.H.A.S., 1949)
Lloyd, R., *Dorset Elizabethans* (1967)
Nichols, J. G. (ed.), *Narratives of the days of the Reformation* (1859)*

Chapters Eight, Nine and Ten
Bankes, G. N. (ed.), *The Autobiography of Sergeant William Lawrence* (1886)*
Beamish, D., Dockerill, J., and Hillier, J., *The Pride of Poole, 1688-1850* (1974)†
Beamish, D., Hillier, J., Johnstone, H. F. V. and Smith, G., *Mansions and Merchants of Dorset*
    (1976)
Borough of Poole Archives*
Cockburn, E. O., *The Almshouses of Dorset* (1970)
Davies, G. J., 'Dorset in the Newfoundland Trade' (P.D.N.H.A.S., 1979)
Davies, G. J., 'Smuggling in Dorset in the 18th Century' (P.D.N.H.A.S., 1982)
Defoe, D., *A Tour through the Whole Island of Great Britain, 1722-26* (1971)*
Guttridge, R., *Dorset Smugglers* (1984)
Handcock, G., *The Poole Mercantile Community and the Growth of Trinity, 1700-1839*
Knapp, W., *New Church Melody, being a set of Anthems, Psalms, Hymns etc.* (1764)*
Mathews, E. F. J., *Gallant Neighbours* (1934)
Mathews, E. F. J., 'The Economic History of Poole, 1756-1815' (Ph.D. thesis)
Morley, G., *Smuggling in Hampshire and Dorset, 1700-1850* (1983)
Morris, C. (ed.), *The Journeys of Celia Fiennes* (1982)*
Parish records in the Dorset Record Office (from 1538)*
Smith, H. P., *William Knapp, the Dorset Composer* (1962)
Stagg, D. J. (ed.), *Christchurch Court Rolls* (1983)*

Chapters Eleven, Twelve and Thirteen

Battrick, J., *Brownsea Islander* (1978)†

Beamish, D., 'The Parliamentary and Municipal History of Poole, c. 1740-c.1840' (M.Phil. thesis)

Beamish, D., Dockerill, J., Hillier, J. and Smith, G., *An Album of Old Poole* (1975)†

Beamish, J., Bennett, H. and Hillier, J., *Poole and World War II* (1980)†

Bessborough, the Earl of (ed.), *The Diaries of Lady Charlotte Guest (1833-52) and of Lady Charlotte Schreiber (1853-91)**

Blake, G., *Poole Past and Present* (1985)

Bowditch, M. R., *Cordite – Poole: the Royal Naval Cordite Factory* (1982)

Bruce, G., *A Fortune and a Family* (1987)

Carter, H. S., *I Call to Mind* (1949)

Cullingford, C. N. (ed.), *The First Fifty Years: The Story of Poole Grammar School, 1904-1954* (1955)

Davies, P., *Art in Poole and Dorset* (1987)†

Hawkes, A., *Memories of Old Poole*, 9 vols. (1978-82)

Hawkins, J., *The Poole Potteries* (1980)

Hillier, J., *Ebb Tide at Poole, 1815-1851* (1985)†

Hillier, J., *A Portfolio of Old Poole* (1983)†

Knott, O., *Old Poole Town* (1975)

Lucking, J. H., *Dorset Railways* (1982)

Mate, W., *Then and Now or Fifty Years Ago* (1883)

McDonald, T. A., 'The Electoral History of Poole, 1832-1885' (M.Phil. thesis, 1981)

Mundy, H. G. (ed.), *The Journal of Mary Frampton* (1885)*

Wear, R. and Lees, E., *Stephen Lewin and the Poole Foundry* (1978)

Young, D. E. W., *Schools of Old Poole* (1983)

Index

A page number in bold type denotes an illustration

James I, 75-6, 77; James II, 89, 90, 92, 109, 112, 113
Jarvis, K. and Horsey, I., 7, 34, 61
Jeffrey, John, 127, 128
Jeffreys, Judge, 90
Jennings, George, 182
Jesty, Benjamin, **107**, 108
Joan, Queen of Scotland, 31
John, King, 30, 63
John of Gaunt, 48, 49, 53
John, Augustus, 202
Johnson, Dr. Samuel, 147
Jolliffe family, **93**, 112, **112**, 122, 128, 144, 160, **161**, 163, 165
Jolliffe, Peter, **93**, 112

Kemp and Kemp Welch family, 121, 123, 127, 136, 160, 202
Kimmeridge, 115
Kingsmill, Thomas, 149, 151
Kingston Lacy, 16, 19, 21, 33, 44, 46, 85, 163, 167, 170, **171**, 172, 211
Kinson, 16, 18, 28, 29, 30, 97, 110, 145, 147, 152, **153**, 154, 156, 192
Knapp, William, 109-12, **111**, 168
Knighton Heath, 3
Knowlton, 2, 15
Knut, 22

Labrador, 160
Lacy (de) family, 16, 33-4
Lake Gates, 7, **7**, 8, 10
Langtry, Lillie, 196, **196**
Lawrence, Captain, 81
Lawrence, T. E., 199
Lawrence, William, 117, **118**
Layard, Sir Henry, 188
Lay Subsidy Rolls, 43-5
Ledgard family, 160, 161, 166, 174, 179, 193
Lees, Lady Madeline, 208
Leigh, 15, 44
Leland, John, 56
Lely, Peter, 86
Lester family, 128, 131-2, **132**, **133**, **134**, 135, 144, **145**
Lester, Benjamin, 131-2, **132**, **133**, **134**, 135
Lester, Isaac, 131, 132
Lester-Lester (né Garland), Benjamin, 135, 136, 168, 173
Lewin, Stephen, 184
Lilliput, 154, 199
Lioba, St, 18
Llewellin family, 138
Lockyer, Richard, 193
Lollards, 52, 65, 67

Longespée, William I, 30-1; William II, 31-3, **33**, 35, **35**, 50; William III, 33
Longfleet, 15, 28, 98, 110, 121, 145, 169, 174, 179, 182, 184, 191
Longham, 15, 110, 114, 152
Louis IX, 32-3; Louis XIV, 109, 112, 113; 114
Lulworth, 112, 166
Lumley, Lord, 90
Lyme Regis, 81, 89, 127
Lytchett Matravers, 15, 16, 17, 26, 29, 42, 44, 45, 51, 86, 87, 90, 117, 144
Lytchett Minster, 15, 17, 44, 96, 97, 100, 107, 110, 123, 135, 144, 165, 179, 206, 208

Mackrell, William, 193
Malmesbury, 3rd Earl of, 148
Maltravers family, 12, 26, 29, 42, 44
Manuel, William and Joseph, 149
Marconi, G., 198
Margaret, Countess of Salisbury, 64
Markets, 35, 50, 178
Marshall, William, 16, 31
Mary I, 64, 68; Mary II, 90, 92, **93**, 109, 112
Masters, John, 127-8
Matilda, Empress, 30, 34
Mauger, Joshua, 131, 167
Mellor, David, 207
Merley, 80, 81, 115, 141, **142**, 144, 211
Minty, William, 88, **88**, 109
Missing, Thomas, 98
Miss World title, 208
Monasteries, 18-19, 24, 64, 65, 95
Monmouth, James, Duke of, 88-9, 90, **91**
Montacute family, 43, 46, 48, 52
Moortown, 2, 3
Morden, 15, 26, 45
Morton, John, 53, 54, 57
Mount Badon, 12-15
Mountjoy, Lord, 68
Mudeford, 155-6
Municipal Corporations Act, 174-7
Murders, 72, 94, 103, 150-1, 155, 156

Napier family, 93, 139, 144
Napoleon, 117, 160
Nennius, 12-13
Newfoundland, 56, 71, 73, 77, 103, 109, 112, 113, 114, 115, 116, 117, 118, 121-39, **126**, **132**, 160, 161, 178, 199, 211
Newton in Purbeck, 40
Nicolson, Nigel, 207
Niño, Pero, 47
Nonconformists, 87, 88, 89, 92, 109, 136, 163, 193, 194, 207
Norton, J. J., 51, 65
Nunneries, 18-19, 51, 65